T0285390

WHAT THINGS COST

WHAT THINGS COST

an anthology for the people

Edited by Rebecca Gayle Howell
& Ashley M. Jones

Emily Jalloul, Associate Editor

UNIVERSITY PRESS OF KENTUCKY

Scholarly publisher for the Commonwealth, serving Bellarmine University, Berea College, Centre College of Kentucky, Eastern Kentucky University, The Filson Historical Society, George-town College, Kentucky Historical Society, Kentucky State University, Morehead State University, Murray State University, Northern Kentucky University, Spalding University, Transylvania University, University of Kentucky, University of Louisville, University of Pikeville, and Western Kentucky University.

Editorial and Sales Offices: The University Press of Kentucky
663 South Limestone Street, Lexington, Kentucky 40508-4008
www.kentuckypress.com

Library of Congress Cataloging-in-Publication Data

Names: Howell, Rebecca Gayle, editor. | Jones, Ashley M., 1990– editor.
Title: What things cost : an anthology for the people / edited by Rebecca Gayle Howell &
    Ashley M. Jones ; Emily Jalloul, associate editor.
Description: Lexington, Kentucky : The University Press of Kentucky, [2023] | Includes
    index.
Identifiers: LCCN 2022034834 | ISBN 9780813182438 (hardcover) | ISBN 9780813195292
    (pdf) | ISBN 9780813195285 (epub)
Subjects: LCSH: Working class writings, American. | American literature—21st century. |
    Labor—Literary collections. | Work—Literary collections. | Working class—Literary
    collections.
Classification: LCC PS508.W73 W48 2023 | DDC 810.8/03553—dc23/eng/20221004
LC record available at https://lccn.loc.gov/2022034834

Member of the Association
of University Presses

To those who do the work

Contents

II | Just Don't Never Give up on Love

VII | Something Necessary to Give

Introduction

What Things Cost sings of the labor of the immigrant, the labor of women, the labor of industry, the labor of land. It sings of generations of work stolen and extracted, the work of hands that built this country but never had the right to it. It sings out from grid states, flyover states, indigenous states, addicted states; it sings across the rural-urban breaks. This book sings of the particular soul's labor, pressed against the soulless powers that be—exploitative capitalism, systemic racism, systemic heteronormative patriarchy, systemic classism, corporate imperialism. Oppression is never abstract. It is in the detail of human living where we labor, be it joyful or tiring. Or both.

Ashley's grandmother worked in Alabama fields picking crops, but she also worked in her children's lives. Ashley's father worked at the Birmingham firehouse, but he also worked in the temple of his own heart, making way for love even when it was not modeled by the home, state, and country that wanted him to see only darkness. Rebecca Gayle's grandmother raised ten children by subsistence farming in East Kentucky, a woman who loved her place above herself. Rebecca Gayle's father was an officer in the United States Marine Corps, a man who came home to spend the rest of his days as a fry cook, believing justice could be served one affordable meal at a time. Ashley works—not in the hard and unrelenting way of her ancestors, but on the page, and she works in the classroom, and she works as a woman and a Black person who wants only the liberation of all people. Rebecca Gayle works—not in the hard and unrelenting way of her ancestors, but on the page, and she works in the classroom, and she works as a woman and an Appalachian person who wants only the liberation of all people. It is from these experiences, these inheritances, these hopes that we have built this book.

In 1968, in the last remaining months of his life, the Reverend Dr. Martin Luther King Jr. founded a new movement, the Poor People's Campaign. It would be a multi-racial coalition of the working poor, what King called a "massive, active, nonviolent resistance to the evils of modern corporate society." He and his team spent those final, fateful months galvanizing those who lived in such places as the Deep South, the inner cities, Appalachia, California's agricultural belt, and the lands to which indigenous nations were forcibly displaced. Organizing the ignored into a new "nonviolent army," he called for another march on Washington: "We ought to come in mule carts, in old trucks, any kind of transportation people can get their hands on. People ought to come to Washington, sit down if necessary in the middle of the street and say, 'We are here; we are poor; we don't have any money; you have made us this way . . . and we've come to stay until you do something about it.'" King told reporters he expected an annual federal expenditure of $30 billion, all going toward antipoverty measures. (In 2022 dollars, that would be something like $245 billion. For perspective, contemporary annual military spending in the United States is about $750 billion.)

King's "Economic Bill of Rights" called for the following:

1. A meaningful job at a living wage for every employable citizen.
2. A secure and adequate income for all who cannot find jobs or for whom employment is inappropriate.
3. Access to land as a means to income and livelihood.
4. Access to capital as a means of full participation in the economic life of America.

The vision gathered support from a diverse group of leaders, including Cesar Chavez, Robert F. Kennedy, and Miles Horton. It also gathered the devoted fury of the FBI, which planted both rumors and violence to discredit, disrupt, and disband the Poor People's Campaign. The movement's original march on Washington was scheduled for June of that year; by April, Dr. King was dead.

In 2018, at the half-century anniversary of the original Poor People's Campaign, the Reverend Dr. William J. Barber II and the Reverend Dr. Liz Theoharis joined to remember and remake that vision. Today, "from Alaska to Arkansas, the Bronx to the border," their revival of the Poor People's Campaign is building a voting bloc larger than hate, a united people's bloc that holds the power to lead us all toward a moral economy by insisting that we understand it is only to one another we belong. This work began by building a sustainable, activated network that was at once local and national, one that was sourced in partnerships with the Kairos Center for Religions, Rights, and Social Justice; the Popular Education Project; and Repairers of the Breach, the 501(c)(3) organization that is at the core of today's campaign. Together, they are calling us toward the "Third Reconstruction," in which economic rights will be understood as human rights, in which US poverty and low wages will finally be addressed from the bottom up—a vision that is, as of May 2021, also called House Resolution 438, sponsored by California representative Barbara Lee, with more than twenty cosponsors. This resolution openly states, among many other surprising clarities, "it is a moral abomination that there are more than 140 million people in this country who are poor, low-wealth, or one emergency away from economic ruin." It goes on to say that Congress must prioritize and center "the needs of the 140 million in laws and legislation, including in infrastructure development." Godspeed, Barbara Lee.

Perhaps you are reading this book soon after its publication, while we are fortunate to have Barber and Theoharis ringing the alarm bell. Or you might be reading it during the movement's next iteration, or the one after that. It is not short work to protect human rights—especially when such protections also threaten the endless accumulation of wealth. Repairers of the Breach took its name from Isaiah 58:12: "You shall raise up the foundations of many generations; you shall be called the repairer of the breach." *Many generations.* Or, as Barber said in 2018, "We have these mythologies about the civil rights movement, about what it took to bring about change in

America. But none of that happened overnight. You need to have a long-term vision. This right here, this is only our foundation." Or, as King said in 1967, "We have an ultimate goal of freedom, independence, self-determination . . . but we aren't going to get all of that now, and we aren't going to get all of that next year." Who knows when this job will be done.

What we do know is this: That it is terrifying to not make rent. To have no medical care, for fear of the bill. To not breathe, for fear of being shot. To know that your choice is to go to work and likely catch a deadly virus or lose any chance of feeding your kids. We who are joining voices in this book have come together to say: *You are not alone.* We honor and support the laying of the foundation, as Dr. Barber named it, as well as the intention to continue this work until economic disenfranchisement is no longer a force of subjugation in the United States. We hope that inside these pages you will find a story, an experience that values you. We hope that, as you read, you feel a little less afraid—less afraid to guard your own life and to guard a life that does not resemble your own. All royalties from this book, from now until the day it is no longer printed, will go to serve the Poor People's Campaign. But beyond that, our prayer is that this book pays dividends of courage to any struggling person who reads it. Wealth does not have to be generated by suffering. It does not have to be this way.

Here is our offering: May it oil any gear that needs it. May it work just like a balm.

—Ashley M. Jones & Rebecca Gayle Howell

Ruben Quesada

Poetry Is Bourgeois

On the way home from work
on the northbound train
I heard a young woman say
poetry is meant for the rich
poetry is for the privileged
poetry is for those who can spend
time to write words meant for change
it is a life carelessly spent
writing. This is a lie.

I
When Will You Learn My Name?

Sonia Guiñansaca

America Runs on Immigrants

My mother works on the 23rd floor of a glass building in the middle of Times Square as a server of a catering company / My father rides the train home from work; in his backpack he carries a pair of Timbs with blotches of oil / Neither of them have eaten / The thing about America is that migrant workers go days without properly eating so that America can function / My mother who goes by Maggy will stand for 8 hours straight bouncing on the balls of her feet to catch any demands by white professionals that for some reason know how to work a Google drive but have no idea how to make their own coffee / My father who goes by Segundo ironically is always first to cook, first to burn his hands, first to serve, first to deliver so that men in suits can get their rush lunch order / My mother & father never get days off or paid holidays or bonuses or a 401(k) or health care / My mother & father depend on the power of Vicks, hot tea, and prayers to la Virgen / Sometimes my father and mother do not feel like mine—they feel like they belong to this country / My mother does not see father / My father does not see his brother / My siblings don't see mom or dad / America sees them at all times / America sees our parents more often than we do at 4 a.m., at 7 p.m., at 11 p.m., and midnight / My 9-year-old brother clasps his tiny brown hands to pray *Diosito please take care of mom* / My father carries our old school photos in his wallet, folded gently not to crease our faces, this is how he looks after us, this is how he holds on to us / My mother carries a large purse with all our documents because *just in case* / They both accommodate America's routine by moving around birthdays and bautismos and weddings / America is a spoiled brat wanting more and more and more / America screams *Go Back To Your Country, Stop Stealing Our Jobs* and simultaneously whines *Where is my lunch?*

Ruth Awad

My Father Dreams of a New Country

America, I see through your glass—
I reach my hand and my fingerprints
are everywhere. Like leaves the gust blows in.

I don't have money to feed your fountains
or enough water that it's never a wish,

but America, I can't stop drinking you in.
Your trains, their freight like hours,
like the vowels cut from my name.

When will you learn my name?

I'm running to you but I can't get there
fast enough. I'm strung up on gridirons
and city lights. Aren't my arms tired of reaching?

Isn't my back tired of carrying this night around?
Be good to me like a summer rain, I swear I'm burning.

Kevin Goodan

Untitled

We give
Our lungs
To the fire,
Their frothy
Pink and
Trembling
Capacities.
The hinge-work
Of our knees
Also.
What's good
Of our backs
We give,
Disks in
The spine
flattened,
Springing
To the nerves.
Shoulders
Tendon-bright,
Straining
The sockets.
We give
Bruise, we
Give gash
Whatever
Bleeds, bleeds—
Shin-bones
Divoted
From tool-blows,
Armpits raw
From sweat-rimed
Nomex
Grating under

Line-gear straps,
Heels
Blister-jelled,
Popping,
Back of neck
Seared, glistered.
Give ankles
Hobbled,
Ligaments
Tattered
Sutured
Tattered.
Skin we give
To ember,
To aramids,
To the long
Memory
Cancer has.
Ears given
To squelch,
Break,
Rotor wash,
A far voice
Calling
Weakly
For water
For god
Who is
Water
Out there
In the
Brittle woods.
Give lips
Heat-crazed
Blubbering
Double time
Double time,
Water
Boiling
From eyes,
Lashes
Rancid nubs,
A beard,
Moustache

Smoldering,
Tobacco spit
Tobacco
Slobber.
Fingers
In gloves
In ash
Swollen,
Putty
To the bone,
Lactic surge
In arms
In calves
As we pause
Swiping back
The grime-slicked hair
Then bending
To our
Ash-dark art
Once more.

L. Lamar Wilson

Burden Hill Apothecary & Babalú-Ayé Prepare Stinging Nettle Tea

We don't die. We fruitful & multiply like
The Good Master say. Fields of okra, snap peas,
Collards, cabbage spring out the ground, so many
Bullets sagging on the vine, you can hear 'em holla
Pull me. Cut me. Watch me grin. We oblige. So much
Green 'tween our waists & toes, we can't see
The clay caked in the spurs cutting our heels
For the pines that shade us. We tramp
Them cones they shed that seed the soil
That keeps us alive, our loins spilling,
More mouths begging to be filled
Every day. Dem peckerwoods would turn
Every limb into a grave if our Maker let 'em.
You talk 'bout how they strung up Claude,
But you done forgot that high yella sot Cellos.
Smashed his skull twain under that magnolia
Over yonder, where he seasoned these here roots
I'll boil to break that fever you so 'fraid
Won't loose you, but every season, more squash,
Kale, peanuts, melon split open, so sweet, so sweet,
Every body beg to sink they teeth in deep. Like
Them weeds we yank from this here earth,
We won't die. We your worst nightmare.
Shoot one of us down, & our chirren's chirren's
Seeds'll take root & shoot up right here like
Our pappy's pappy's done. Mustards, limas,
Sweet potatoes, whites, too. Our roots too deep.
You can't kill us all. Think of all that cane
You so keen to suck on. Drag that stalk

Too long, that juice'll turn bitter as the laughter
In your throat & choke. Don't let them fool you
Into cuttin' your tongues out your own
Mouths. These here is the best of times, where
The sun don't stop shinin' till you can smell
The moonshine midnight riders crawlin'
Out they bed to climb in yours & rub
'gainst you till you sang like locusts
In heat, a low hum, a steady moan, till they
Kingdom come & morning light appear.

Erika Meitner

the bureau of reclamation

we the loyal companions
we who are hyped about everything
we who cross the thresholds of accountability
our songs of praise sound like gunshots
we the supermarket shoppers
we the leggings-as-pants wearers
we the shade throwers
the riven in nostalgia itinerants
who avoid our mail at all costs
who remember all our exes unequivocally
we the hypervigilant
we who collect regular explanations of benefits
we who worry about food security
we the invasive species
we who dwell (mostly) in the body
we who buried our long-suffering ancestors
what would you like to cup in your hands again?
water? a flame?
we the doom-scrollers
we who own wildlife patrol cameras
we the rendered who keep rendering
Louise Bourgeois once said I can express myself only in a desperate fighting position
we who want approval or adoration
we who see photographs as contraband
the neighbor captures a bear on film ambling through his yard
he warns the rest of us by posting the video on Facebook
we who see photographs as gestures
we the night texters
we who see photographs as certificates of presence
my grandmother received reparations from the German government
this was for performing slave labor during the war
we who believe god is (not) a consuming fire
blessed is the spectrum
i am paying attention

we the delicate or empty
we the toughened and leathery
we who are bound with floss to anything proximate
we the fruit skins stitched back together after they've been peeled down
we who know the difference between chemistry and alchemy
my children's expired passports
the dream about the boat
we who gather the exiles

Marwa Helal

write this instead

you are thinking about the last white person you had to cut out of your life. the one who took a picture of dylann roof to the hairdresser "coz she wanted a look with 'creeper vibes.'" you wonder if the hairdresser was a person of color and rage fills you. how clearly you see that murderer while the hairdresser . . . and you do what you always do when this happens in public, you disassociate switching to the fantasy of having a particular baldwin quote* printed on billions of small cards and dropping them via drone all over this country. you are fantasizing about how you are always fantasizing about this but the quote is always changing and the location is always changing then you are thinking on home and language and how in some ways they have come to mean the same thing. the train arrives. you get a seat. at the next stop a large white man finds the open space beside you and you resist the reflex to make yourself small, to make room for him. he shrinks into the allotted negative space and reveals a pack of index cards with your mother tongue scrawled on them. you remember god is a surrealist poet and has a funny way of revealing herself to those who will believe. but you wonder why this campy looking man has such an interest in your language. a slew of predictable acronyms rush to the forefront of your mind: CIA, FBI, NSA—based on his age, you dismiss the possibility of the foreign service exam. you are tempted to ask, "why such an interest in arabic?" then you notice a golden band on his ring finger. perhaps he is learning it for the love of a woman who loves this language as much as you do. this sole warm thought is fleeting, as he is: he stands directly in front of you as he prepares to exit the train. you scrutinize him. you sense he senses it. you want to make him uncomfortable. you want to know what he is going to do with your language. but you do not ask. you go home and write this instead.

* "Until the moment comes when we, the Americans, are able to accept the fact that my ancestors are both black and white, that on that continent we are trying to forge a new identity, that we need each other, that I am not a ward of America, I am not an object of missionary charity, I am one of the people who built the country—until this moment comes there is scarcely any hope for the American dream. If the people are denied participation in it, by their very presence they will wreck it."
—James Baldwin, "The American Dream and the American Negro," March 7, 1965

José Olivarez

poem where no one is deported

now i like to imagine la migra running
into the sock factory where my mom
& her friends worked. it was all women

who worked there. women who braided
each other's hair during breaks.
women who wore rosaries, & never

had a hair out of place. women who were ready
for cameras or for God, who ended all their sentences
with si dios quiere. as in: the day before

the immigration raid when the rumor
of a raid was passed around like bread
& the women made plans, si dios quiere.

so when the immigration officers arrived
they found boxes of socks & all the women absent.
safe at home. those officers thought

no one was working. they were wrong.
the women would say it was god working.
& it was god, but the god

my mom taught us to fear
was vengeful. he might have wet his thumb
& wiped la migra out of this world like a smudge

on a mirror. this god was the god that woke me up
at 7 a.m. every day for school to let me know
there was food in the fridge for me & my brothers.

i never asked my mom where the food came from,
but she told me anyway: gracias a dios.
gracias a dios del chisme, who heard all la migra's plans

& whispered them into the right ears
to keep our families safe.

Yaccaira Salvatierra

Hummingbirds

1.

América, do you remember
   the scattered Home Depots
   on the East Side of San José;
Mi Pueblo Shopping Center
   on the corner of Story and King;
   or the Osh Orchard's Supply Store
where we bought bougainvillea,
   how hummingbirds gathered
   five to fifteen at a time
like framed pictures,
   blood warm and rapid
   ready to work?

2.

To sleep, you devour handfuls
of lavender, valerian and chamomile:
You are in Atotonilco, México.
You are someone else's body sleeping on a bed,
   an infant next to you.
The house is made of brick and iron,
   windows are decorated iron and thick translucent glass.
The window opens,
   two human-sized wings like thieves enter.
You are lifted into a feathery embrace with your child in arms.
You soar above mountain ranges.
You see one of the mountain ranges fill
   with California poppies.
Your husband, Mariano—
   in the middle of blood orange petals—
waves and calls to you.
He is barely audible.
Before you make out what he is saying
   you wake up.

3.

América,

if you see my husband as he leaves
for work in construction with your husband,

ask him if he watches over me when he dreams.

4.

Not of corrugated tin, or concrete but sky,
      the ceiling descends
      as I lie in bed—weightless wings paralyzed.

Reflected in the night, my eyes, two black moonstones.

Past midnight, walls spit bricks that pile up on windowsills.

The bed of twigs I bought with Mariano's American money
      is a coffin I wake in, a nightmare I cannot control.

This hummingbird beak of mine is not long enough to reach
      through the window before it is sealed.

O, Darkness, let me sip from Mariano's tongue before it
      slips back into his mouth.

O, Sweet Nectar, when will I taste you again?

5.

      A hummingbird's chest
      gleams azurite and copper
full of nectar for working:
      it is its desire.
Its size defined:
      magnificent.
      It chirps and hums a corrido
full of memory: why it left home,
to build a house for its family,
to safeguard its history.
      It chirps and hums a ranchera,
strums its wings through the air,
so it won't forget the aromatic
lyrics of its native country

or its sweetheart's caves,
damp and warm.
Its movement,
its journey: long,
        unpredictable.
Will the nectar it carries be enough?

Annette Saunooke Clapsaddle

All in Conflict with This Act Are Hereby Repealed

We know the Redbird is the daughter of the Sun, and if the men had kept the box
closed, as the Little Men told them to do, they would have brought her home safely,
and we could bring back our other friends also from Ghost country.
—James Mooney's account of the Cherokee story "Daughter of the Sun"

I.

1943 General Assembly
of North Carolina declared
the Cardinal official State

Bird. Adopted.

"All in conflict with this Act are hereby repealed."

II.

1946 General Assembly
of North Carolina declared
the Cherokee
official

voters. Adopted.

"All in conflict with this Act are hereby repealed."

III.

Messenger,
whisperer, bleeding
across Smoky snowscapes—wearing
your mask,

clan paint,
ceremonial slick,

to sing in their family trees
for spring's promised
seed.

Left to forage in winter's
forgetfulness.

IV.

The Gadsden bite will poison
your flight
if your song

grows stronger
in the rummage.

"All in conflict with this Act are hereby repealed."

V.

The honest wind will knock
you off their branches
when they catch you passing

in and out of Ghost
Country.

"All in conflict with this Act are hereby repealed."

VI.

You will never again
bring your friends
home

from Ghost
Country.

"All in conflict with this Act are hereby repealed."

VII.

Do you feel honored?
To have been claimed?

Chris Green

Workshop

My daughter, almost
sixteen, halts on the threshold.
Fields of corn, soybeans.
My wife and her cousin stand
on the porch where once they swung.

Thirty-foot rafters
hewn from centuries-old trees
still serve the workshop;
beaten ten-gallon milk cans, from
the farm's past life, line the loft.

(1843,
my wife's father's people, who
hailed from central North
Carolina, raised this In-
diana county's first house.
What did these Quakers,
whose families fled from England,
want? To break new ground,
not confounded by slavery?
What vast white wave washed
into that Northwest Terri-
tory torn from Tecumseh?)

Elihu, my son,
named for his great-great-great grand-
father, pets a cat.

Come, there's work to do.

Curtis Bauer

Dispatch Out of a Language I Used to Speak

Day coming into the day. Thirty-two years ago
I would have been up and in a field, have worked already.

Sparrows and swallows. Maybe
a crow but not this cacophony.

Would have been corn and soybean rows.
Oats growing high and alfalfa near to be cut.

Cattle. I worked cattle, which means I fed them.
The herd knew me and didn't spook

when I climbed the fence and walked to the corncrib
where the feed was an eight-foot-high cone of ground

shelled corn mixed with protein pellets, sometimes
sorghum to give them a taste. Sometimes I could

nearly fill a bushel basket with one scoop. We had two:
one to fill and carry to the fence while the other—

if there were two of us—walked down the line of bunks,
to the end, and dumped the powdered feed to the waiting

mouths, their implants already clicked to work: they were
always hungry and their work to fatten, fill out, wear lean

meat across their shoulders and rumps. And when that pile
was almost diminished I would pull the grinder mixer

behind the IH 560 to a grain bin auger, move the parts,
change the sieves, put in gear the power takeoff and start

the machine to hum. Open the tractor throttle and toss
the grain bin auger switch—corn would gush the spout

  [Distraction: going inside the bin when the level
  lowered and the grain wouldn't fall center. I'd
  climb 50 feet up, open a metal hatch and then
  climb inside. I'd jump at first, 15 feet
  to plunge hip deep into dust and grain, and that
  would be enough to shift the corn cascading down.

    [Stories of kids and men if not drowning in grain
    being caught in the center auger and the one outside
    knowing something was wrong before the corn
    stopped coming, by the corn turned red and then
    turning the flywheel back quick to release the meat
    the foot or hand inside had become.

      [This never happened to me. I have all my appendages.
      Only my insides are stained and because I can't see it
      I'm fine. But my hands recall the scoop handle,
      the bushel basket heft on my shoulder. Sweat.
      Even in winter freeze sweat and ache. I ache
      so much I didn't know when it stopped,
      what a body felt like without it. I did what I was
      told. Worked until I was done.]
                                    ]
                                      ]

like something broken letting loose what it
held in. An announcement or agitation, a giving up.

Tomás Q. Morín

Table Talk

One of the first scents I ever loved was wet cement. Sometimes my father would mix it all up in a wheelbarrow. Sand, water, cement. If he was touching up a house he had just built or just starting a new one, he would dump it all inside his mixer and pull it to the construction site.

The mixer was open at the top and shaped like a deep rectangular bowl, unlike the round drums most bricklayers use nowadays. It had two arms along a horizontal shaft on the inside. They would rotate along an axis until all of the ingredients had mixed and the cement had gone from clumpy tan to a deep grey. It was the shade of grey you might see on a quilt of storm clouds just before they drop their rain. The cement was cool on the tip of my fingers. It groaned every time my father sliced it with his trowel and pulled away and up the exact amount he needed.

The smell was clean. Not subtle. It's strong in the way cake frosting is strong. As you get closer to it, it moves from itself to your nose quickly and once it's inside, its sharp, metallic fullness crowds everything else out.

He was an artist. There's no question about that. Stone and women were his medium. And we kids, what were we? Maybe we were the grey sludge that held his families together. We were strong and made each house of love he built stand straight and tall. We would have lasted forever if only he had remembered that nothing lasts forever. Least of all what we build.

This would be where some old-timers like my grandfather would say, El que no mantiene no detiene. I can hear those words crackle in his mouth. But he'd be wrong. It wasn't a lack of care that made the families my father built crumble, it was the roofs. Or rather, the ones that weren't there. I never did see my father build one. That was for a different crew. You'd think somewhere along the line, a person would've told him that a house with no roof is just a box to hold the light.

For all his talent, my father only built my family two things. The first was a short, four-post brick fence. Each post was thick and made from fire-engine-red brick. Green metal flares connected one post to another.

The other thing he built was a laundry room for my mom. He started to, rather. After he laid the concrete foundation and collected cinder blocks, that was it. After it sat in our backyard for years, my mom relented to my constant requests to use it as a basketball court. I watched my father, for the last time, mix a small batch of concrete and cement a black metal pole to the center of a large truck tire. When the concrete had dried, I attached my backboard and rim to the pole. With someone guiding the top so it wouldn't hit the ground, I could lean my goal over and roll it anywhere in the yard I wanted.

Decades later when my mom and I drove by the old house, we found only a pair of foundations on the lot. A second arson had finished off our old house when the first one didn't. The railroad worker who owned the house before us had built it with materials that were no doubt free and handy at his work. We discovered this when we busted the wall in front in order to move the bedroom door over and found railroad ties instead of 2×4s.

When hurricanes came over from the Gulf of Mexico, our house felt like the safest place in Mathis. But now everything was gone, except for the two foundations and the fence posts whose red bricks were cracked and crumbling. They sat in front like squat sentinels in the near empty lot.

I admired the houses my father built. I was in awe at how he could take a dull pile of brick and make it a home. Sometimes a family requested stone.

One night I dreamed I was at his work site. Piles of sand surrounded me. I sat cross-legged so when I looked around, the shifting points of these pyramids were taller than I was. For a long time I believed my dream was real until one day in yoga class I grimaced and remembered how uncomfortable it has always been to sit with my legs folded in front of me.

In the dream, I study the grains of sand. They start their run near the top. It always happens suddenly. You would think a breeze or a fly disturbing the wall of granules would be needed to make it move, but that's not true. The pyramid's contract with gravity has an expiration date, especially when the sand is not packed. Sometimes the grains only make it halfway down the pyramid, while other times a few will build enough speed that their momentum will take them all the way to the leaves of grass and the dirt under them. I stare and wonder how long it would take for every grain to make it to the grass. Would a year be long enough for them to all run away and leave a beige circle where a pyramid had once stood? A year still feels like such a long time. You can fit so much pain into twelve months.

When my father tosses a stone back into the pile, the knock when it hits the other stones startles me. I've never seen him chop a stone with his trowel the way he will a brick that's too long. A stone fits or it doesn't. When I ask how he knows which stone will be next, he talks about puzzles. In the case of a house, there was no box with a picture to look at. He would look at the space he needed to fill, as well as the ones that didn't exist yet, and stay two or three spaces ahead. I could see those spaces, too. I figured everyone could see their unlined shapes until someone told me most people don't see negative space first.

The stone in his hand is the color of moldy bread. He fits it snug in the wall. Unlike the sand, it won't run. If people live in this house a hundred years and then abandon it for another hundred, it will still sit there with its blue-green eye, unblinking, full of hope.

Seth Pennington

Armory

The boy got out of the Marines to give himself
to God, to his wife, to the bullet factory eleven miles
outside a town outgrowing its one stoplight. Cars
pile up at shift change, block the highway. The ambulance drives
the shoulder when there is one, wails like something tied up, hungry.
The boy makes more than his Pa ever has. His Pa raised
enough kids to become tax exempt, all the kids his wife could
bear. The boy was first-born, brought up the rest. Taught them to
fish, trap, hunt; then clean, cook, freeze what's left. In Walmart,
there would be this end-of-the-month chain of them: carts loaded
to the gills, three of them pushing along behind
like a locomotive, what they know as that dead relic, that monument
outside the town square, rusting—the caboose
made more of beer cans and marijuana smoke than any dream
of solid work it once was. At 16 the boy started
lifting. In shoes, he was 5' 6". His arms were tanks: biceps as big as
other men's thighs, big enough they hid his pawnshop
guitar he played at the Baptist church. He was so ripped, the explosion
didn't kill him, but shattered his arms, gave him a slight severance, no work,
a "disability" check in the mail after "not meeting the requirements"
three times. He listens for a time when his hands made
music, remembers skinning a buck clean into pelt and meat.
He's full of stories about other people's lives; he's a walking radio,
bored and tuned to the weather. Three months along, now, his wife is
the one carrying. The boy's a bundle of nerves and can't lift a bowl of soup beans.
He flicks his fingers like a lighter, like he wants to start something.
Outside, dogs bark at the storm rolling in off the soy.
He turns off the light to watch it.

Faisal Mohyuddin

The Holiness of Our Fathers

My father left us while I was elsewhere
because he'd been unemployed for nearly
15 months and knew, despite whatever
reassurances people reflexively offered,
his chances of finding decent work
as a 58-year-old who had never finished
college were much too slim to not look
beyond Chicago. The nearly 25 years
he'd spent in steel had left him without
options, and secretly depressed. So when
my uncle, my father's only brother,
who years before had relocated to a region
of Oklahoma summered by tourists
to try his hand at running a gas station—
a venture destined to fail by the second
winter—called to share his discovery
that a Nissan plant outside of Nashville
was hiring contractors to lay the electrical
wiring for a new wing, my wistful
father recognized the beckon of another
migration. The hours were 6 a.m. to 6:30 p.m.,
seven days a week, half hour for lunch,
two 15-minute breaks. The hourly wage
wasn't considerable, but with ample
overtime and a 30-dollar per diem,
the job was too good to pass up. Plus,
my uncle, who'd been down there a week
already, assured my parents everything
was safe and clean, the fellow workers
kind, or quiet enough to tolerate.
He'd already secured a spot for my father,
insisted he just come. It wasn't until
I returned jet-lagged from a week spent
with college friends in Belgium over

my winter break holiday that I heard
the story, learned from my four siblings
that my father barely packed before hitting
the road, determined to arrive in time
to start the next day. My mother couldn't
say when he'd be back. It was work,
she sighed, and all work was good,
especially now, so the longer he was there
the better. Upstairs, in my childhood
bedroom, I sat under the covers, a stack
of ungraded student essays on my lap,
unable to stop imagining my father
and uncle living small like newly arrived
immigrants, cramped together in the cheapest
double at a Howard Johnson in Smyrna,
Tennessee, eating tasteless meals out
of a microwave, reminiscing about
their fatherless boyhoods in Pakistan,
the looping chatter of *Headline News*
always burbling in the background,
even during those fleeting hours of sleep
when each descended into dreams
about their own long-forsaken dreams.
In the morning, the two cautiously
sipped scalding hot tea from Styrofoam
cups as they drove through the icy darkness
toward the Nissan plant—neither man
taking a single day to rest, not even
when their aging bodies ached so badly
they needed the other's still-mighty strength
to uproot them from their beds. Despite
how much they missed their wives
and children, pined for the heartening
commotion of their homes and the familiar
contours of their own shabby pillows,
they silently cherished this time together
after having endured for decades the quiet
misery of separate lives. They prayed
constantly for more work, and more
chances to mend the fraying silhouettes
of their lives' respective trajectories,
understanding that one day too soon
all the wiring would be in place—and so
their lives no longer needed, cut loose

once again. And there, as a bright Chicago
snow fell outside, I sat in the haunting
stillness that had taken hold at home,
with the sweet soot of handmade truffles
still on my fingertips, feeling suddenly
disgusted with myself, with a belief
that a person should do what he loves,
a luxury my parents unceremoniously
traded their futures for. What epic self-
centeredness and ingratitude, to have
become a teacher who felt entitled
to leisure and comfort, who squandered
hours of free time writing frivolous
poems about the joy-giving power of fresh
flowers or the tender charity of the stars
instead of pursuing law or medicine,
or whatever immigrant parents dream of
for their children—anything that could've
paid me well enough to call my father right
then, cry, Come home, Daddy, and bring
Chacha with you, because I'm back,
and I'll take care of everything.

Yusef Komunyakaa

My Father's Love Letters

On Friday's he'd open a can of Jax
After coming home from the mill,
& ask me to write a letter to my mother
Who sent postcards of desert flowers
Taller than men. He would beg,
Promising never to beat her
Again. Somehow I was happy
She had gone, & sometimes wanted
To slip in a reminder, how Mary Lou
Williams' "Polka Dots & Moonbeams"
Never made the swelling go down.
His carpenter's apron always bulged
With old nails, a claw hammer
Looped at his side & extension cords
Coiled around his feet.
Words rolled from under the pressure
Of my ballpoint: Love,
Baby, Honey, Please.
We sat in the quiet brutality
Of voltage meters & pipe threaders,
Lost between sentences . . .
The gleam of a five-pound wedge
On the concrete floor
Pulled a sunset
Through the doorway of his toolshed.
I wondered if she laughed
& held them over a gas burner.
My father could only sign
His name, but he'd look at the blueprints
& say how many bricks
Formed each wall. This man,
Who stole roses & hyacinth
For his yard, would stand there

With eyes closed & fists balled,
Laboring over a simple word, almost
Redeemed by what he tried to say.

Javier Zamora

Second Attempt Crossing

For Chino

In the middle of that desert that didn't look like sand
    and sand only,
in the middle of those acacias, whiptails, and coyotes, someone yelled
    "¡La Migra!" and everyone ran.
In that dried creek where 40 of us slept, we turned to each other
    and you flew from my side in the dirt.

Black-throated sparrows and dawn
    hitting the tops of mesquites,
beautifully. Against the herd of legs,

    you sprinted back toward me,
I jumped on your shoulders,
    and we ran from the white trucks. It was then the gun
ready to press its index.

    I said, "freeze, Chino, ¡pará por favor!"

So I wouldn't touch their legs that kicked you,
    you pushed me under your chest,
and I've never thanked you.

Beautiful *Chino*—

the only name I know to call you by—
    farewell your tattooed chest:
the M, the S, the 13. Farewell
    the phone number you gave me
when you went east to Virginia,
    and I went west to San Francisco.

You called twice a month,
> then your cousin said the gang you ran from
in San Salvador
> found you in Alexandria. Farewell
your brown arms that shielded me then,
> that shield me now, from La Migra.

upfromsumdirt

Fair Gabbro in the Orchard

—*after* Privilege *and* Romanticism

in adjacent droughts they laze the fields
like heifers with attentive palms out
for borrowed cud / spread eagle or prim / demure
afloat in ponds, among the fronds, dainty jowls
nestled in knightly palms / those wild, windrow
of a woman over there with windswept skirts
basking the lawns in allegories of sun intimately
begging for recognition if not salvation but
we here carry our own wheat / as raised
and there is so much water in our walk
everywhere we settle in earth leaves a softened
flora when we're gone / lithe gardens in a sable
grove / working twice as hard for half the adulation
bearing from our forbidden limbs the most
resplendent fruit / the gods of an Ancient Order
dangle in our branches and Heaven blooms
in our slender boughs / even in our undergrowth.

Kendra Allen

Elegy for the Bloodline

This ain't no brand-new story, no brand-new song; but Granny raised her kids and then she helped raise theirs. She birthed five of 'em to be exact, but one died a few days after being born. It's not like I knew its name because nobody talks about it. Everyone is scared to ask Granny about their sister because they know pain makes her shut down. This is family tradition too. The only reason I know it happened is because Mama said it did, that things like having a baby one minute and not having one the next is just something that happens—especially in those days, in the sixties. Mama say that baby would've been the oldest. In those days, it was also something prideful about all coming from the same daddy. I don't understand it, because I'm an only child, but Mama say all her siblings having the same Mama and Daddy made people look at them differently, constantly asking them to be sure; *y'all got the same daddy?* as if it mattered, because he wasn't even in the house long.

But here's a brand-new story: If I knew my Granddaddy well enough to remember more than small details of his face, I don't think I'd like him. Him and Granny met at a high school. They weren't sweethearts; she was a student and he was a janitor. It seems as if someone would infiltrate, the age gap predatory and doomed, but there's no consequence for snatching up the Black youth. He sweet-talked her right out of her mama's house and right into marriage—twenty years her senior. I say I wouldn't like him because I mean I wouldn't respect him. By the time Granddaddy started beating Granny, she was forever young. He was a Korean War vet who relied on lazy lays, lying, and liquor most importantly. He outdrank the fish. When Mama was three—the third-born child—she saw her daddy slap her mama in their kitchen. That same day she had her first Fig Newton when she went to their neighbor's house and confessed what had happened was . . . & the neighbor gave her the tart because she ain't know what to say. That's how it always is. Grown folk beg kids to tell them the things their bodies went through and never know what to do with the information except for pacify you with sugar and sweets and sometimes kisses. Granny was getting beat on all the time, but whenever she tried to go back home, her mother—my great-grandmother—would tell her to go back home to her husband. That she chose him. When me and Granny sit in front of the TV one day to catch up on her daily talk shows and a singer's mother is telling the world how her daughter was hit upside the head and punched and bruised, we're both adults, and Granny's lips tighten up so hard the few wrinkles she got straighten out. She shakes her head side to side like somebody farted and stunk up the spot as she states more than she asks, *what is wrong with the men.* As if her being able to get this answered could save us all. I laugh a lil nervously in agreement but when she say she could never figure out what it is *she* did wrong or what it was to make him snap, how she'd just get hit for being an alternate battlefield, all I can say is *they throwed off Granny.* I don't really know what to do being in the midst of a memory like that either. But that's what we do too. For some reason we equate suffering to perseverance and misinterpret the weight of shame, the duration of its presence. Granddaddy said he truly loved Granny, but told my Daddy over beers one day that the problem was she just kept on having all them kids.

Granny divorced him less than a year after the slap but before the slew of other hits, all her children earthbound. To feed them, she worked the same job all Grannies in the South worked, which is playing cleanup woman. She'd take the bus before the sunrise and sometimes ain't get back home until after the sun set, her kids learning to fend for themselves. Granddaddy continued to work on drinking round the clock, looking hud out, and finding joy in terrorizing women. He moved to Grand Prairie, about forty-five minutes away from his first family. So essentially Granny raised their four kids during the seventies with no daddy. I only mention it because people tend to think it matters. I used to too, but Granny raised four kids during the seventies with no money, and this is way worse than no daddy. She worked the same job until her kids had kids. They lived in Oak Cliff, a neighborhood in Dallas that extends through four generations of our women. She raised hers all high as the streetlights and when they came on around six-thirty every night, they had better been back in her house whether she was home or not. The streetlight, I'm told, was the indicator of tardiness in times where camera phones and watches weren't an option. The streetlight is a yell, a warning, and responsibility. The streetlight is a burning man.

The young men weren't no better. Granny married both. Her second husband moved in with her and the kids—fifteen years her junior; so young her kids couldn't care for him. When he finally decided to rummage up his drug-induced courage to swing on her too, my mama 'n' 'em—bout as old as they stepdaddy—jumped him. Granny grabbed a knife. As she brought it down, she missed, and instead inserted the blade into my mama's left hand, which was swinging for his face. The scar still glistens today, slick like renewed skin. Both of Granny's husbands—no matter the age or pedigree—couldn't keep they hands from around her neck no matter what she did, even if it was nothing. Even if all she did was clean they dirty drawls. All she did was clean somebody's dirty drawls, cleaning up after white folks' filth for over thirty years. She worked long hours but she would still send the kids to church every Sunday where they sat until the pastor announced what he would be preaching on, and then they would sneak out, scripture embedded somewhere between the four of them.

Eventually, cleaning up at home and cleaning up at work took a toll on her body. All that bending over backwards trying to keep food on the table feeding the kids beets and beans and beating them heads under mattresses, nobody's heads above water—broke her hip, literally. It happened well into her adult life, early fifties still looking like a brick house. She hadn't made a dent into any life past surviving still. Never learning how to drive, never allowed the time to think about what it was she was good at let alone being able to pursue it. She sung, but stopped, because who got time for dreaming when you ain't got no babysitter. This breaking sat her down flat, sending her straight into retirement, a well-deserved break. But even now, she still don't know stillness. Finding dishes to wash, beds to make, food to cook. Her kids were already grown. They had kids who had kids who had kids and all she got was a JC Penney's card, great-grandchildren, her god, and the gout by the age of fifty-five. They put the young one back on the block after that one fight though and out of their house. Only they daddy get first dibs at disrespecting they mama.

When my Daddy started cheating on Mama, they both worked at the VA and Grand-daddy was dying of everything—lung and liver cancer mostly, but all of the cancers lived and died in him too. It was 1999 and him and Granny hadn't really spoke. She'd send her son to him in the summers but that was the extent of their relationship. He had been hitting and living with another woman, had other children the same age as the others, but Granny was still by his side in his last days. Called him by his nickname—Pigalee. Said *Pig, you need to get right with God* even though he put both hands on her. She was already half raising her first grandchild for over a decade—a granddaughter whose mother was addicted to drugs. I had just turned five. Mama worked round the clock, spending the last months of her Daddy's life going to the doctors to get him diagnosed with not only his cancers, but PTSD; making sure he got disability in order to pay for his doctors' bills, and generally playing the unofficial role of power of attorney because nobody else would do it. I think maybe this was the start of our entire family looking to Mama to fix things, to fix them. My first memory of it was years later with Granny's hip. I remember her having to use a walker and a sitting stool in her small bathtub. It felt like everybody was on constant edge she'd fall again. She didn't take well to not working or being in the house for long periods of time. Mama would go over, make sure she bathed her, fed her, etc. I remember always asking Mama why nobody else could do it. She had three other siblings who weren't really making no moves to assist. It felt weird to ask her why was she helping her Mama, but between them and their kids—they called Mama for everything. Rides to the grocery store, gas money, to take in and raise their children for a year here and there, to use her car; just anything they knew they could get away with. I don't know the psychology of partnership but I don't see the point if it means it's still one-sided. Mama never say no, and Daddy noticed. He would never be a priority. If I was a writer then, the only true thing I'd be able to write on Granddaddy's obituary is that he lived around the way, about forty-five minutes west of his kids, drunk to death on a porch and got along with my father—who also took pride in not working. Who found his manhood through belittling women who loved him. Who followed in the traditions of a bloodline that wasn't even his, revering my Granddaddy and referring to my Granny as mean instead of exhausted; who felt stripped of his masculinity instead of offering his wife help.

The women in my family worked nonstop; knew how to build things, carry furniture alone, fight a man, make buttermilk biscuits from scratch, and still found time to serve the Lord; had jobs— sometimes multiple from the time they could and then worked some mo' when they got home; cooking recycled meals. Mama began to fear for my safety and stopped leaving me alone with Daddy after he started acting like it was a burden to watch me. He got careless with my whereabouts, having me in rooms while he played cards with his friends or cut their hair. Not because he ain't know how to care for me, but because he just ain't want to, all that responsibility. That thing men do, half-assing a task like dish washing or car detailing so nobody will ask them to do it again—that's how he treated me the more I grew and the more I needed because Mama wasn't giving him enough attention. There was always a sister, a niece, or a friend who needed something from her. It didn't take long for both of us to realize it was a cycle Mama had no real interest in breaking. At first I didn't understand what was wrong with my Daddy; I thought he hated us—but as I grew, I realized my Mama would never have a life that was hers because she didn't want it, she didn't know she could have it. She never learned to say no. Daddy knew she would never say no, so he left. Then I knew I wouldn't be next in line to say yes.

Carter Sickels

Women's Work

1.

My grandmother, Wilma Eileen Sickels, my father's mother, was born in 1922 and raised four children in southeastern Ohio, in the rolling foothills of the Appalachian Mountains, where the trains used to carry coal from West Virginia, and out of the green hills people carved small sustenance farms. This was where her family had been for generations and she would live all her life. She grew up one of four, including a twin brother. I don't know much about her childhood—she rarely reminisced, didn't share her memories or stories or truths. Like many rural people, her family raised chickens and grew food and owned very little. My aunt remembers a story Grandma told her: she and her siblings received two pairs of shoes per year, and one time, overjoyed by her new pair, my grandmother went to bed with the shoes clutched in her arms like a teddy bear. I learned that her father, a coal miner, sometimes threw away his paycheck on drink and could be a mean drunk. But he put food on the table, as they say; he provided.

Not long after my grandmother married my grandfather, he enlisted, and the United States entered World War II. In 1944, on his sixteenth mission, his plane was shot down and he was captured by the Germans. My grandmother, home with their two young sons in Ohio, waited with dread for news. But at the end of the war, he was liberated and returned home—a veteran and a POW who would wrestle with his demons by turning to that imaginary balm, alcohol.

In postwar America, even in the rural hills of Ohio, white men and married couples had access to a slice of the middle-class dream. A son of a sawmiller and farmer, my grandfather first worked as an auto mechanic, then found employment at Tennessee Gas, which had natural gas pipes running through Ohio. He worked there, on rotating shifts, until he retired in the 1980s. In his free time, he played fiddle for various bluegrass outfits and square dances and hung out at the VFW. My grandmother took care of their children and their home. She cleaned, cooked, scrubbed, ironed, all of that, which she'd been doing since she was a little girl. My grandfather, as expected, never lifted a finger around the house. Grandma was also a licensed beautician. Women in the neighborhood would come over to get Toni perms, the sharp fumes of the chemicals wafting through the house along with the sweet scent of cooling pies.

2.

In the 1960s, my grandparents left the speck of a town in Vinton County where they'd raised their children and moved out to the country on fifty acres, not far from where my grandfather grew up. This was surely his idea. He built a small ranch-style brick house and soon populated the pastures with a herd of beef cattle. He had a soft spot for his beloved cows. Though he sold them at the stockyard, he never butchered or ate them himself; he and Grandma bought packaged meat at the grocery store. Sometimes Grandma drove the flatbed pickup when Granddad and their sons bailed hay, and when she tired of Granddad's orders, she'd threaten to throw the truck into park and let it sit. She occasionally helped him herd the cows from one field to another, which she did with stoic anger—she had better things to do.

On holidays, Grandma delighted in the arrival of her children and grandchildren. We kids ran in the fields and played Wiffle ball while the women toiled in the kitchen. Everyone packed into the small dining room and kitchen, seated around several tables for a meal that my grandmother had cooked almost entirely single-handedly: noodles, country ham, green beans, mashed potatoes and gravy, rolls, and several fruit pies. She was always the last to sit and ate very little. As Granddad regaled us with stories about his childhood and wilder days, Grandma rarely spoke up except to occasionally shoot off a sarcastic, snappy rejoinder in response to whatever yarn he was spinning. We all laughed, even Granddad. Grandma was quiet but not meek and had a sly sense of humor. In the mornings she was the first to rise and presented us with plates stacked high with buttered toast, bacon, fried eggs. She packed my grandfather's lunch and included a slice of homemade pie.

3.

Sometime in the late '60s, my grandmother got a union job at Ohio University, only twelve miles away but another world. She started as a housekeeper and then worked in the cafeteria, in charge of the salad bar. My father wonders if she initially applied for the job because she wanted to buy new kitchen cabinets. Her husband controlled the money, and she wanted to earn her own. But my aunt remembers it differently: my father was stationed in Germany, and Grandma was terrified he'd be sent to Vietnam—working a full-time job helped distract her from her worries. Maybe too she wanted a life away from her husband. He accompanied her just about everywhere, invited or not, even when she went bowling with the girls. Work drew her out of the house and away from the isolation of country life. The kitchen and housekeeping staff were all women, and they cut up and gossiped on breaks. The work was demanding but familiar—an extension of the unseen and unrecognized labor she and the other women had been doing for most of their lives, except now they were earning a paycheck. At home, my grandfather expected meat and potatoes with every meal and did not tolerate anything strange or new. My grandmother liked food he wouldn't touch—Chinese or Mexican—cuisines that perhaps she was introduced to when she worked at the university. Nobody in the family remembers if she ever talked about working there during the Vietnam protests or the shootings at Kent State. From what I remember, my grandmother seemed to enjoy the college students, some who were hippies and others who were jocks, rolling into the cafeteria with their hair uncombed or smelling of cigarettes, talking about wild parties, burning ideas and dreams, these wild kids, these good kids, who she fed and cleaned up after.

4.

My grandmother was petite, about 5′ 3″, and had the tiniest feet. By the sixth grade, I was already taller than her—we used to stand back-to-back, measuring—and when I set my gigantic sneakers next to hers, we'd laugh. Her hair was always dyed jet-black, and every week she went to the beauty parlor for a wash and set. For special occasions, like going out to eat at a sit-down restaurant, she put on pink lipstick and clip-on earrings, a nice blouse and slacks. Rarely did she wear a dress. She never traveled overseas or flew in an airplane or expressed such a desire. She traveled to the places my grandfather wanted to go, a few road trips to Tennessee or Georgia. I wonder what else she had wanted—like those kitchen cabinets—but knew she'd never get. Or maybe I'm just making this up. Maybe she had everything she wanted.

She taught me how to play cards—war, solitaire—and we watched television together. She loved television. "It's my entertainment," she'd say. She was the first person I knew who owned a satellite dish. When Granddad fell asleep in his recliner, as he inevitably did, she'd snap her fingers and holler at him to stop snoring. She liked to stay up late, no one around to bother her, to watch Johnny Carson and Benny Hill. She enjoyed *Green Acres, Hee Haw, The Carol Burnett Show, Murder She Wrote, Dallas.* She also watched her stories—*As the World Turns, General Hospital,* and a mystery-crime soap opera called *The Edge of Night.* On grocery trips she shelled out money for tabloid papers, what she called the "scandal sheets," and tucked them under the loveseat where she sat to watch her programs. Whenever I visited, I pored over the pages of the *Star* and the *National Enquirer,* discovering tawdry secrets about Cher and Michael Jackson and the royal family. I don't remember Grandma talking about celebrities, but she read those papers religiously. She used to tell my aunt, "If it's in the scandal sheets, it must be true." She gobbled up Danielle Steel novels and occasionally read biographies of country singers—Reba McEntire was one of her favorites. She did not care for Dolly Parton or Loretta Lynn because she believed, my father told me, that they were showy women. They sang—flaunted, in her eyes—about growing up poor, which for her was a source of shame.

5.

In 1991, a few years after my grandmother retired from Ohio University (which she did at my grandfather's urging—she liked her job and didn't want to go), I enrolled. I don't think I ever spoke to the cooks or the women serving us food except to ask for another helping. I'm sure I thanked them, but did I ever have a conversation? I was too busy being a student—reading and studying, learning about feminism and discovering new ways of seeing the world. I wrote a few columns for the college newspaper—my opinions on why we needed more diverse classes, including LGBTQ offerings, or how the university, during the AIDS crisis, should be advocating safe sex and distributing condoms. I didn't dare show my parents what I'd published, but my grandmother picked up the paper on her trips to town. Although she never spoke about the uncomfortable subjects I wrote about, she let me know she'd read the columns and that I did a good job. One time I won a fiction contest and my story was published in the same paper. It was a strange, surreal story about a boy, most likely gay, who was also an angel and included an explicit reference to sex. I was mortified when she told me she'd read it. She raised her eyebrows, quiet for a second, then cracked a grin. "It was a pretty good story," she said. I did not know back then that I would one day make my living by writing and reading and teaching. As a college student, I was already living a life my grandmother perhaps had never imagined, or maybe she did—I don't know. I believe she wanted her children and grandchildren to have a different life. A few times during the semester, I would peel myself away from my college activities to visit her. She cooked for me and folded my laundry. She'd often slip me a ten-dollar bill and say, "Now you be careful." My grandmother, like me, voted Democrat, joyfully canceling out her husband's vote.

6.

My grandmother worked her entire life, taking care of people. What a shame that her last few years on earth were spent in a nursing home. Deteriorating from Parkinson's, she was trapped inside an institution and her own body. Eventually, she lost the ability to speak. There were stories inside her I would never know. She did not like to look back. She didn't speak of her own suffering, never wanted to burden anyone else. She once told my mother, "I never could cry."

I visited her in the nursing home. Her tiny princess feet no longer needed shoes for walking. They were wrapped in pink footies and stuck out from under the sheet. I held her hand—a frozen claw—in mine. I wish I'd asked her more. I wish I had come out to her. She never knew me as a man (I'm trying to be a good man, Grandma), but long before I transitioned, when I still identified as a Queer woman, when she could still speak, she looked at me and asked if I was going to get married.

"I don't know," I said. "Do you want me to get married?"

She was sick, she was old, she was dying. No longer interested in small talk, in conversation that glosses, silences, smooths, she said, "I want you to be happy."

After her funeral, my aunt handed me a stack of newspaper clippings. They were the columns I'd written for the college newspaper. My grandmother had cut them out and saved every single one.

I do not know what my grandmother dreamed about or longed for. I knew nothing of her interior life or if she was happy. But I think of her on those early mornings, the sun just beginning to rise, when she drove herself to work, without her husband hovering or her father telling her what to do. She left as the sun was rising. Down the gravel driveway past the herd of blank-eyed cattle, then onto the winding roads, flying by green hills and farms and empty pastures until she reached the Hocking River and the campus that rose behind it like a small, majestic city. Driving along these familiar roads, smelling of carefully applied perfume and hairspray, dressed in her neatly pressed work uniform, did she turn on the radio or did she drive in silence? Did she ever think of continuing onto the freeway and following some unspoken dream and never coming back?

Ocean Vuong

The Gift

a b c   a b c   a b c

She doesn't know what comes after.
So we begin again:

a b c   a b c   a b c

But I can see the fourth letter:
a strand of black hair—unraveled
from the alphabet
& written
on her cheek.

Even now the nail salon
will not leave her: isopropyl acetate,
ethyl acetate, chloride, sodium lauryl
sulfate & sweat fuming
through her pink
I ♥ NY T-shirt.

a b c   a b c   a—the pencil snaps.

The *b* bursting its belly
as dark dust blows
through a blue-lined sky.

Don't move, she says, as she picks
a wing bone of graphite
from the yellow carcass, slides it back
between my fingers.
Again. & again

I see it: the strand of hair lifting
from her face . . . how it fell
onto the page—& lived
with no sound. Like a word.
I still hear it.

II
Just Don't Never Give up on Love

Emily Jalloul

The Taking Apart

*

As a child in Indiana, my mother was often beaten by her mother, whose blue-black rage filled all corners of the house, her hands gripping the whip or paddle or belt, whatever was in reach. "You knew her mood by the pounding of her steps as she walked up the stairs," my mother tells me. She grew up in fear, afraid to tell her mother when she'd compound-fractured her elbow, worried she'd be told to get a switch off the front tree for the hassle and cost of a doctor's visit. She slept on the broken arm until her mother discovered the blood in her bed.

*

I was twelve when I began emptying my mother's vials of Stadol, a narcotic pain reliever, prescribed to her to treat migraines. Usually administered intravenously before surgery or during labor, the drug is also available as a nasal spray to treat chronic pain. Stadol, otherwise known as butorphanol, is not well known: there are no news reports about it, no books written about the effects of withdrawal from it. Though similar in chemical structure, each one like a photocopy of the other turned on its side, butorphanol is three times stronger than morphine. I'd search and find the small brown bottles scattered in her bathroom drawers, her nightstand, her purse, and I'd pour the golden liquid down the sink, refill the bottles with water so she wouldn't notice them empty. I didn't know this would cause withdrawal or that she had other bottles hidden.

*

My therapist tells me that our brains seek out and hold on to information we need. For years, knowledge can remain suppressed, submerged, a raft held underwater waiting to break the surface.

*

Researchers estimate that one in five to one in nine girls will be sexually abused. Of cases reported, 93 percent of victims under eighteen know their abuser. Almost 60 percent of these are acquaintances. Over 30 percent are members of the victim's own family. Victims of sexual assault often suffer psychologically for years, especially if the assault is unreported or repressed, and they are three to four times more likely to suffer drug addiction, PTSD, and major depressive episodes.

*

My mother sits up in the hospital bed, hands in her lap, and she's telling me stories I've heard before. There's a wood cross hanging in her room I glance at occasionally while she talks. I'm nodding along to her story, but really I'm thinking that it's late, B. is probably in bed by now, and I hope her results come back soon so we can go home. My mother's narratives wind and consistently miss key parts of information—an erasure or redaction. She begins to tell me about Leah Carr, her best friend growing up. I've heard about Leah my entire life, how she and my mother first smoked cigarettes together, coughing and choking on the menthol lights, how they snuck sips of whiskey. I met her once in a Value City in Louisville when I was a teenager, but I remember nothing about her.

*

My mother tells me that she was at Leah's house one day, a house smaller than my living room and kitchen combined. She loved Leah's family, how her mother smiled when she said "good morning" and gave my mom her warmest socks to sleep in. She was asking to spend the night there in Leah's pull-down bed set up in the kitchen. I'm checking my phone, replying to text messages. My mother continues her story.

*

After years of sleeplessness, I see a psychiatrist. She's a bit taller than I am, straight brown hair pulled into a low pony. She's soft around the edges and seems kind. She seems like the kind of woman who has never taken an illicit drug, never puffed or snorted a thing. I choose not to tell her I smoke weed. I'm hoping she'll give me a prescription for something that will knock me out at night and send me on my way. Instead, looking at the anxiety score from my diagnostic analysis, she asks, "When did your anxiety first start?" I've never been asked this. I pause. "It's always been there."

And then I remember: panic attacks, bawling breakdowns as I was dropped off at school or gymnastics. As a child, I never slept over at a friend's house, and now as an adult, I say it's because my mother was afraid of their fathers—what they might do in the middle of the night—and that's true, but I don't mention the consuming fear when I'd realize I was about to be separated from her. I say I quit gymnastics because I hated competition, but truthfully, I couldn't tolerate knowing she wasn't right there, waiting for me to finish. I've never told anyone about the moment in Blockbuster when I, so small for my age, lost her in the towering shelves of VHS tapes. The store felt like a hedge maze, purposely complicated to navigate. It felt huge, and I felt alone. The relief that hit me when I turned around, tears streaming, to see her blond hair, tan face looking at me surprised—I felt saved, like god had sent down a hurricane that took my entire town but spared my home.

*

My mother's addiction, like most addicts, I suspect, consisted of peaks and valleys, times when she'd be "clean," or at least using less, and times when she'd be belligerent for days on end, sometimes unable to speak, walk, or drive. These days bled into one another; an all-consuming gray covered everything. I would lock myself in my room, sneak out at night, walk to the beach, meet boys from the internet or mall. We had a dog at the time, a huge German shepherd, who I'd have to drag outside by the collar to potty, she was so unwilling to leave my mother's bedside.

*

Botanically, rhizomes are a part of the plant that exists under the soil, a hidden pathway connecting one stem to another, holding both roots and shoots. Rhizomes don't have clear beginnings or endings; they grow expansively from every direction, both into and out of the soil. Postmodern theorists Gilles Deleuze and Felix Guattari apply this to philosophy, describing a nonlinear way of looking at history. They use this metaphor to suggest there is no distinction between an individual and a collective; there is no center or origin point.

*

I read that the children of addicts grow up in denial, unable to accept that their parent is unwell. I read that children of addicts grow up to be self-reliant; they avoid needing people. Children of addicts learn to live in fear, learn to be guarded, skeptical, and anxious. They learn to contain and deny emotions, or they become severely codependent. These children are twice as likely to become addicts.

*

"Leah's father said, 'Come over here and sit on my lap, and maybe I'll let you spend the night.'" My mother was eight or nine. I stop looking at my phone. I stop glancing at the cross. I watch her face, her lips, so much like mine. Her hands sit in her lap still, left hand inside the right. She sits hunched over, a child in confession. "I sat on his lap, and he grabbed my breast, like this." She takes her right hand and gropes herself. "They were tiny, barely there, I don't know why he did it, but I ran home and told my mom, which was a big no-no because she'd just gotten there, already put on her muumuu, and now I was coming to bother her with this."

Jason Kyle Howard

Mourning Hillary and What Might Have Been

I was eleven when I first saw her—on television, trudging through the snows of New Hampshire, campaigning for her husband in the 1992 Democratic primary. Back then she had an unvarnished quality to her: she was someone who was used to speaking her mind, someone who would stand in the middle of a diner, flanked by a phalanx of cameras, and talk to patrons in depth about the lack of universal health care and her choice to pursue a career outside the home.

Everyone in my small eastern Kentucky hollow, it seemed, was talking about this potential First Lady with the three names: Hillary Rodham Clinton. My Reagan Republican father, a high school history teacher, was dismissive. "Typical liberal," he muttered. My swing-voter mother was intrigued and began including her own maiden name when she wrote checks. My yellow-dog Democrat great-uncle was impressed. "Smart as a whip, buddy," he said. "She's going to do great things."

I agreed. For a young boy with inherent Democratic dispositions—four years earlier, as a seven-year-old, I had insisted on placing a "Dukakis for President" sign in my bedroom window—I knew I had a candidate in 1992. But it wasn't Bill Clinton. Sure, I liked and supported him, but I was more interested in the woman at his side. To me, it seemed that she should have been the one running for office.

"Finally, a woman who is just not going to cut ribbons and open bazaars," former First Lady Jacqueline Kennedy Onassis confided to a friend as she observed Hillary commandeering an office of her own in the West Wing, leading the charge for health care reform, and testifying before Congress as a policymaker in her own right. These actions were, of course, unprecedented, and the Clintons' "two for the price of one" mantra made many traditional Americans across the country deeply uncomfortable, posing a threat to their conservative beliefs and perceptions about the proper role of a woman and a First Lady.

I was captivated. By the time I was a middle school student, I was scouring my father's issues of *Time* and *Newsweek* for articles about Hillary. I wrote essays about her as a revolutionary First Lady, one who was rebelling against the status quo in ways that I was only beginning to fathom. I was thirteen, closeted, unable to live openly in my small Appalachian town where fundamentalist churches speckled the landscape like a murder of crows and preachers railed against the abomination of deviant lifestyles.

But seeing Hillary Rodham Clinton more than hold her own in the patriarchal world of politics gave me hope. Watching her navigate the critics of her hair, headbands, fashion, physical appearance, legal career, financial dealings, personnel decisions, and policy prescriptions made me realize something about myself and people like me—the ones destined to be outsiders in our culture: I needed to locate in myself the deep reservoir of strength and sense of self that I saw in her.

When she finally became a candidate herself in 1999, I sent her $20 from the small amount of money I had saved interning for the summer on Capitol Hill after graduating high school. Later, when I was back in DC attending George Washington University and interning again in a congressional office, I sometimes saw Senator Clinton walking across the lawn of the Capitol or on C-SPAN, calling for increased federal aid to first responders after 9/11. She was humble and deferential, as all freshman senators should be, when she could so easily have eclipsed all her colleagues with her fame and intelligence.

I wasn't blind to her flaws, both human and political. But for me they made her more relatable, more ordinary, a mirror of my own human frailties. I cheered and volunteered for her in 2008 and again in 2016. When I voted that Tuesday, I carried with me a photograph of my maternal grandmother, a woman who cleaned homes for a living—just as Hillary's mother, Dorothy Rodham, had—and who knew all too well the effects of misogyny on her own life. I voted with my husband and daughter, and we watched the returns together, consoling one another as our optimism turned to despair.

The next morning, I did not change from my pajamas. I did not bathe or even wash my face. I might have brushed my teeth. I did not go to work. Instead, I sat with my anguish and anger, awaiting Hillary's concession. And when it came—when I heard her speak, when I saw glimmers of grief and grit and courage peer from underneath her stoic political mask—I broke. I began to keen. My husband, seated alongside me on the sofa, turned to me, his mouth agape at such an uncharacteristic display of unrestrained emotion, and he reached for my hand.

For months afterward, I cultivated a parallel inner realm in which this had not happened. Hillary had won. After a historic inauguration, a women's march was organized as a celebration—and as a promise to hold the new administration accountable on issues of gender, class, race, orientation, identity, and immigration reform. In her first hundred days, President Clinton managed to push through a significant chunk of her agenda, including an infrastructure bill and humane, open-hearted, comprehensive immigration reform. She signed executive orders creating tougher environmental standards and providing more protections to Dreamers. Elizabeth Warren was confirmed by the Senate as labor secretary. Merrick Garland finally took his rightful place on the Supreme Court, securing—at least for the time being—a woman's right to choose, marriage equality, affirmative action. Hell, President Clinton even took a victory lap and awarded the Mirrorball Trophy on *Dancing with the Stars*.

There was no travel ban or suspension of refugees. No firing of Sally Yates. No withdrawal from the Paris Accords. No raids on undocumented immigrants. No executive orders to expedite funding for a border wall or for mass deportations or to revoke funding for sanctuary cities. No revoking Title IX protections for transgender students. No attacks on voting rights. No Stephen Miller or Steve Bannon or Sean Spicer or Betsy DeVos or Jeff Sessions or Michael Flynn.

This fantasy world only worked for so long. Somehow, I found my way to a grudging acceptance. But six years later, I remain angry over Hillary's loss. Our loss. I will go to my grave regretting that this country missed out on what could have been a transformative presidency that normalized the sight of a woman, herself so capable and full of resolve, behind the Resolute desk.

Would a Clinton administration have been perfect? Of course not. Would there have been stumbles and errors and disappointments? For certain. But it would have been humane. Intellect would have won the day because this woman—a lifelong student whose political and personal identities have been forged in curiosity, preparation, and experience—would have defeated a would-be tyrant of a man who prides himself on not reading or studying or preparing. Science would have been trusted and prioritized, which might well have saved thousands of lives from the pandemic we could not have known was looming.

I still would have wept on 9 November 2016. But my tears would have come in the wee hours of the morning. They would have been of an entirely different kind—a river of relief and joy. When Hillary took the stage at the Javits Center, beaming in her crisp white pantsuit while shards of faux glass cascaded from the ceiling above, I would have wept for my marriage; for our daughter, son, and teenage niece. For my friends, colleagues, and students, and even for people I didn't know—those left behind, marginalized, forgotten. All of them: Queer, Black, Appalachian, Latinx, Muslim, undocumented, Asian, elderly, urban, suburban, rural, people with disabilities or those who are economically challenged.

I would have thrown my head back in laughter and released a roar of delight for the boy I once was—who searched for the courage to be himself, who saw that audacity in Hillary Rodham Clinton from afar, who knew in his eleven-year-old bones that this intelligent, fierce woman would someday be president herself. That the childhood dream he had patiently waited on—for her to shatter that highest, hardest glass ceiling—had finally become a reality.

Alina Stefanescu

Dialogue in Diptych with Emma Goldman

No mere substitution of one political party for another in the control of the government, not the masking of autocracy by proletarian slogans . . . but the complete reversal of all these authoritarian principles will alone serve the revolution.
—Emma Goldman

i get choosing to be childless.
alabama hates trees, bumblebees, single

mothers, those most in need
failed by the lie of meritocracy.

i mean after the rape, my mom said
what made this country greater than the
land she escaped was the choice

of legal abortion. she was what you
call weak. she died young. this country
killed her. good ole boys 'n' their gals
licked her bones

like pickled pig's feet. but she thanked
them to stay *worthy*, to keep from being
deported she worked like the dog

they believed her to be. to be stateless
is lying prone during assault and
never speaking of it. she did this

for her kids so we could stay or survive.
this is my inheritance. i will cry and then
do anything. i will do anything for free

until it kills me. and thank them.

I fought against disillusionment.
I strove to believe a cog in the machine
wasn't violence. Discredit my veracity
for the good of the whole, the immaculate
state's central deity. Ends justify means
at first vaguely. Then violence blooms
into custom. Today is the parent of
tomorrow's chattel labor. Silence
remains your signal of consent.
O passion for power, this present casts
its shadow far into the future. *Buy the
T-shirt.* The new Soviet bourgeoisie
starved workers while demagogues
preached rich distrust. Go on, deport
me. The means used to prepare the
future becomes the norm. Rob the
robbers to create new ones. *Buy the T-
shirt,* the central deity. Real history
is not data but the personal reactions
of participants. Bombard my veracity
for the good of silence's heritage.
Deport me. Revolution must be
the negation of existing values.
One dictatorship replaced an-
other *by the T-shirt*. This country's
inheritance is hierarchy. Those who
deport me must live with the ghosts
of the *bitch* you unleash

Cal Freeman

Poolside at the Dearborn Inn

I sit near the shallow end, reading
John Dos Passos' *The Big Money*
          and scribbling in a notebook
while my wife does laps. *He never drank, never smoked.*
          His mother said he was a good boy,
and he believed it, Dos Passos
writes of Henry Ford.

Swimming slowly and maintaining the shape
of the stroke is an art. The fact that septuagenarians
can stare down the blank and be happy while bathing
          ponderous bodies
is nothing if not inspiring. I'm 36 and can't stand the sight
of my sallow face in mirrors.

The Fords built this hotel
to serve an airport that never materialized.
          Harry J. Brooks'
death off the coast of Melbourne, FL,
          in 1928 put an end
to the Flivver plane. Friends described the old man
as spooked and distraught over Brooks.

This I learned from my grandmother, not Dos Passos.

She would sit poolside here every day in July,
eating green grapes and playing bridge
beneath a Canadian maple tree.

The autopsy of the Flivver plane found
that Brooks had jammed wooden toothpicks
in the vent holes of the fuel cap
to keep moist air from entering.

The toothpicks plugged the vent,
causing engine failure. Nobody found the pilot's body,

lost somewhere along those
        coastal shoals, mutilated
and incinerated, dispersed by swift
        gulf currents. Nobody found
José Robles, Dos Passos' friend and translator,
thought to have been
        murdered by Stalinists during
the Spanish Civil War, either.

Dos Passos' politics would drift rightward, toward Ford's,
in the years
        following Robles' death.

I've never made a flight
in an airplane, and I don't know
        that I'm particularly
anxious to. I would, though, like to take
        a trip in a dirigible. Bring one out here
            some time, won't you,
Dr. Eckemer, and give me a ride? Ford

would only go on three
        short flights in his lifetime, publicity stunts,
mostly, and never after Brooks'
        crash. *History is mostly bunk.*
I wouldn't give a nickel for all
the history in the world, he once said.
        The only history that is worth
a tinker's dam is the history
        we make today. I take my drink into the shadows

of the Georgian brick building and think
        again of my mother's mother,
Gwendolyn Morrissey-O'Neill,
        who, when I'd ask her
questions about Ford's goons
beating up her cousin Jim, a UAW organizer,
        in 1941, or read her excerpts from
the *Dearborn Independent*, would tell me
to lay off of them,
        they were a good family.

My wife is the last
to leave the pool. She tastes of gin
and chlorinated water as we kiss,
her breasts pale against
          her sun-kissed shoulders.

The swimming pool gleams
          in this waning light,
and I know these epicurean
          afternoons and sleepy evenings
will one day go on without us.

I'm thinking of the coiled
          muscles of a dolphin's body, arcing
just a few feet above the surface
          of the water and old and young people
alike pretending to stave off eventuality.
How all beauty is anachronistic, down

          to the springs of the diving board;
the sick tropes that knowing history
          is supposed to ward off
falsely ennobling the past, the splendor
of this courtyard, bermed by Japanese
maple and honeysuckle,
          mulch the color of the brick.

How Ford's aphorisms sounded
          both ignorant and profound,
which might ultimately be the litmus
for true poetic statement: can it be both stupid
and deep? I keep coming back

to my grandmother who chased
          her bastard children she said
were sired by the devil
down the block when the streetlights
came on, how she told me the Fords were
          a good family, to let them be.

She was always playing cards, here
or in her kitchen, solitaire or bridge,
          smoking Doral cigarettes

she never inhaled, blowing smoke
rings at the kitchen ceiling or into
the dusty leaves of birch and maple trees.

Shuffling decks with the
          indelible sound of a mourning dove
taking flight, smoke whistling
          from her nose,
the shape of the rings holding
          and flowering like epiphytes
on hot still days.

Danez Smith

C.R.E.A.M.

—after Morgan Parker, after Wu-Tang

in the morning I think about money
green horned lord of my waking
forest in which I stumbled toward no salvation
prison made of emerald & pennies
in my wallet I keep anxiety & a condom
I used to sell my body but now my blood spoiled
All my favorite songs tell me to get money
I'd rob a bank but I'm a poet
I'm so broke I'm a genius
If I was white, I'd take pictures of other pictures & sell them
I come from sharecroppers who come from slaves who do not come from kings
sometimes I pay the weed man before I pay the light bill
sometimes is a synonym for often
I just want a grant or a fellowship or a rich white husband & I'll be straight
I feel most colored when I'm looking at my bank account
I feel most colored when I scream *ball so hard motherfuckas wanna find me*
I spent one summer stealing from ragstock
If I went to jail I'd live rent-free but there is no way to avoid making white people richer
A prison is a plantation made of stone & steel
Being locked up for selling drugs = Being locked up for trying to eat
a bald fade cost 20 bones nowadays
what's a blacker tax than blackness?
what cost more than being American and poor?
here is where I say *reparations.*
here is where I say *got 20 bucks I can borrow?*
student loans are like slavery but not but with vacation days but not but police
I don't know what it says about me when white institutions give me money
how much is the Powerball this week?
I'mma print my own money and be my own god and live forever in a green frame
my grandmamma is great at saving money
before my grandfather passed he showed me where he hid his money & his gun

my aunt can't hold on to a dollar, a job, her brain
      I love how easy it is to be bad with money
don't ask me about my taxes
      the b in debt is a silent Black boy trapped

Justin Wymer

What Proof Need You of Love

With room enough and change the woman wept
a gracious fit. She had Dolly Parton hair
she'd left, let lay a tease of half-pearl spokes
and her accent wasn't right, she knew how
doctors always think the worst. When here
your eldest son can't hide that he's a dead
man to a few, and you can't trust yourself to think
in proper poses, leave the bank and show
up here, and make him do, and keep in mind
to use your jaw to say your *d*'s. Here there
I can't pretend she doesn't love him. Born awhile,
the two keep on remembering how this
will always happen.
                        In the room where clear
hoses hang, the rollout couch's vinyl scrapes.
The wall clock constant as a dull-swathe plough
the cemetery zinnias are shocked
to wake in, stamens stable. Sons should know
enough of birds to name them, whether wrong
or good, to make her stop her rippling hands
and bracelet ripping, to keep the prayers at bay.
I cannot say I think in nows: my home
is still and still is null, all the null
hydrangeas, the ones without some blue
or pink are green, she gets to thinking, and I
know then, so far away, I've still made death
unwelcome in her house.
                        Some hours pass. Where'd
she got to? A shoulder wasn't worth the risk
despite the one she had bred socket-sand.
A risk is not a risk when it hides two
inches below where no one thinks to look
to find and pick up, drop it in for tithe.
She can breathe just fine if careful. Don't strain.

She did think last night: the heart pill. The heart.
I will never say she "did" or "never
would," I am in the lobby, now on the sidewalk
gravel, around the bushes, she is coughing,
the bush is coughing greeny hydrangeas,
we are out picking hydrangeas, you don't
need proof it's proof enough we're holding hands
our violet nails dyed through, and you, are

Ashley M. Jones

Hymn of Our Jesus
& the Holy Tow Truck

—*after Mary Szybist*

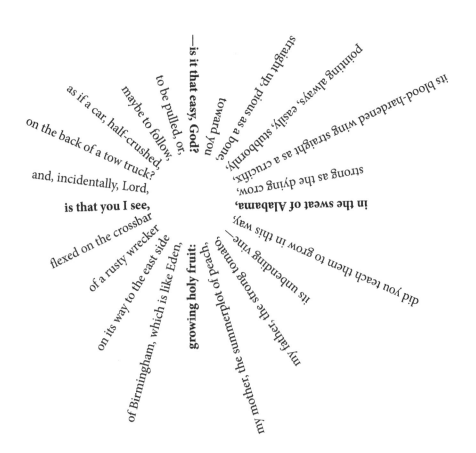

—is it that easy, God?
to be pulled, or,
maybe to follow,
as if a car, half-crushed,
on the back of a tow truck,
and, incidentally, Lord,
is that you I see,
flexed on the crossbar
of a rusty wrecker
on its way to the east side
of Birmingham, which is like Eden,
growing holy fruit:
its unbending vine,
my father, the strong tomato,
my mother, the summerplot of peach,
did you teach them to grow in this way,
in the sweat of Alabama,
strong as the dying crow,
its blood-hardened wing straight as a crucifix,
pointing always, easily, stubbornly,
straight up, pious as a bone,
toward you

Sonia Sanchez

Just Don't Never Give up on Love

Feeling tired that day, I came to the park with the children. I saw her as I rounded the corner, sitting old as stale beer on the bench, ruminating on some uneventful past. And I thought, "Hell. No rap from the roots today. I need the present. On this day. This Monday. This July day buckling me under her summer wings, I need more than old words for my body to squeeze into."

I sat down at the far end of the bench, draping my legs over the edge, baring my back to time and time unwell spent. I screamed to the children to watch those curves threatening their youth as they rode their 10-speed bikes against midwestern rhythms.

I opened my book and began to write. They were coming again, those words insistent as his hands had been pounding inside me, demanding their time and place. I relaxed as my hands moved across the paper like one possessed.

I wasn't sure just what it was I heard. At first I thought it was one of the boys calling me so I kept on writing. They knew the routine by now. Emergencies demanded a presence. A facial confrontation. No long-distance screams across trees and space and other children's screams. But the sound pierced the pages and I looked around, and there she was inching her bamboo-creased body toward my back, coughing a beaded sentence off her tongue.

"Guess you think I ain't never loved, huh girl? Hee. Hee. Guess that what you be thinking, huh?"

I turned. Startled by her closeness and impropriety, I stuttered, "I, I, I, Whhhaat dooooo you mean?"

"Hee. Hee. Guess you think I been old like this fo'ever, huh?" She leaned toward me, "Huh? I was so pretty that mens brought me breakfast in bed. Wouldn't let me hardly do no hard work at all."

"That's nice ma'am. I'm glad to hear that." I returned to my book. I didn't want to hear about some ancient love that she carried inside her. I had to finish a review for the journal. I was already late. I hoped she would get the hint and just sit still. I looked at her out of the corner of my eyes.

"He could barely keep hisself in changing clothes. But he was pretty. My first husband looked like the sun. I used to say his name over and over again til it hung from my ears like diamonds. Has you ever loved a pretty man, girl?"

I raised my eyes, determined to keep a distance from this woman disturbing my day.

"No ma'am. But I've seen many a pretty man. I don't like them though cuz they keep their love up high in a linen closet and I'm too short to reach it."

Her skin shook with laughter.

"Girl you gots some spunk about you after all. C'mon over here next to me. I wants to see yo' eyes up close. You looks so uneven sittin' over there."

Did she say uneven? Did this old buddha splintering death say uneven? Couldn't she see that I had one eye shorter than the other; that my breath was painted on porcelain; that one breast crocheted keloids under this white blouse?

I moved toward her though. I scooped up the years that had stripped me to the waist and moved toward her. And she called to me to come out, come out wherever you are young woman, playing hide–and–go seek with scarecrow men. I gathered myself up at the gateway of her confessionals.

"Do you know what it mean to love a pretty man, girl?" She crooned in my ear. "You always running behind a man like that, girl, while he cradles his privates. Ain't no joy in a pretty yellow man, cuz he always out pleasurin' and givin' pleasure."

I nodded my head as her words sailed in my ears. Here was the pulse of a woman whose Black ass shook the world once.

She continued. "A woman crying all the time is pitiful. Pitiful I says. I wuz pitiful sitting by the window every night like a cow in the fields chewin' on cud. I wanted to cry out, but not even God hisself could hear me. I tried to cry out til my mouth wuz split open at the throat. I s'poze there is a time all womens has to visit the slaughter-house. My visit lasted five years."

Touching her hands, I felt the summer splintering in prayer; touching her hands, I felt my bones migrating in red noise. I asked, "When did you see the butterflies again?"

Her eyes wandered like quicksand over my face. Then she smiled, "Girl, don't you know yet that you don't never give up on love? Don't you know you has in you the pulse of winds? The noise of dragonflies?" Her eyes squinted close and she said, "One of them mornings he woke up callin' me and I wuz gone. I wuz gone running with the moon over my shoulders. I looked no which way at all. I had inside me 'nough knives and spoons to cut/scoop out the night. I wuz a tremblin' as I met the mornin'."

She stirred in her 84-year-old memory. She stirred up her body as she talked. "They's men and mens. Some good. Some bad. Some breathing death. Some breathing life. William wuz my beginnin'. I come to my second husband spittin' metal and he just pick me up and fold me inside him. I wuz christen' with his love."

She began to hum. I didn't recognize the song; it was a prayer. I leaned back and listened to her voice rustling like silk. I heard cathedrals and sonnets; I heard tents and revivals and a Black woman spilling black juice among her ruins.

"We all gotta salute death one time or 'nother, girl. Death be waitin' outdoors trying to get inside. William died at his job. Death just turned 'round and snatched him right off the street."

Her humming became the only sound in the park. Her voice moved across the bench like a mutilated child. And I cried. For myself. For this woman talkin' about love. For all the women who have ever stretched their bodies out anticipating civilization and finding ruins.

The crashing of the bikes was anticlimactic. I jumped up, rushed toward the accident. Man. Little man. Where you bicycling to so very fast? Man. Second little man. Take it slow. It all passes so fast anyhow.

As I walked the boys and their bikes toward the bench, I smiled at this old woman waiting for our return.

"I want you to meet a great lady, boys."

"Is she a writer, too, Ma?"

"No honey. She's a lady who has lived life instead of writing about it."

"After we say hello can we ride a little while longer? Please!"

"OK. But watch your manners now and your bones afterwards."

"These are my sons, ma'am."

"How you do, sons? I'm Mrs. Rosalie Johnson. Glad to meet you."

The boys shook her hand and listened for a minute to her words. Then they rode off, spinning their wheels on a city neutral with pain.

As I stood watching them race the morning, Mrs. Johnson got up.

"Don't go," I cried. "You didn't finish your story."

"We'll talk by-and-by. I comes out here almost every day. I sits here on the same bench every day. I'll probably die sittin' here one day. As good a place as any I 'magine."

"May I hug you, ma'am? You've helped me so much today. You've given me strength to keep on looking."

"No. Don't never go looking for love, girl. Just wait. It'll come. Like the rain fallin' from the heaven, it'll come. Just don't never give up on love."

We hugged; then she walked her 84-year-old walk down the street. A Black woman. Echoing gold. Carrying couplets from the sky to crease the ground.

Allison Adelle Hedge Coke

Viscera

For Rachelle Cruz 4/27/2020

Our moms were widows before they met our fathers.
Their hair blue-black, their hands already chapped, caressed
by Inglis die-cast tooling   Bren light machine guns, Mauser
ammunition, or Browning   Hi-Power handguns, torpedo warhead
casings, or reining sorrels' leather when they made mountains home.
Their first loves shot, stabbed,   or lost in war.

While our fathers picked cotton   for a penny a pound,
steeped in dust friction-screamed like cats in winds untamed.
Rode fence to make it through school,   GI Bills or not.
Married our moms from wingman   blind dates,
worked side by side in the hospital in the peak of polio,
then made our broadcloth shifts by hand for school,
dragging thread through eyes, aiming needles   clean, while
our widow moms were current fried   in hospitals, asylums.

By then, they'd most likely lost three or four kids
                before any survived the early years.   Those of us
                who did, maybe never   told their names, or told
                so often we believed we remembered   them with us
                at the table they were never big enough to seat.

Our work permits in hand   at twelve, fields, like oceans,
called us.   Factories, registers, bars, counters, tables, horses—
but always the fields.   You know the deal, back gone. The former field-
worker retraining jump-started some of us   from post–middle
school labor vacancies   to college, by nearly thirty.

For those of us, widowed just like our moms, with no one
like our dads to pick up our after.   Who move through this

like walking rows, straight to the end,   straight for draws
on jugs, water, plain solutions tapped.

For those of us who must write, who can't sleep now,   who do know
people who have died,   are dying.   Who have always known
people who have died, are dying,   since the little ones who
preceded us as infants anyway   and all the way here, if no one
else nearby will, we will still   lose somebodies.

It's the viscera talking now, the nerves, guts,   bombs like sinew,
blue-red deep inside entrails, webs, mussed up neurons,
neural tissue, breaking brains, remains of hearts,   like Chiclets
chewed up, spit, forked,   forgotten.

Rosa Alcalá

Propriety

My mother turns off the kitchen light
before looking out the window
and half-hidden behind green apple
curtains, takes her nightly inventory
of the neighborhood. That one who asked us
last week for bread, her boyfriend rolls through
to collect the check. The father of one of the girls
drops a bag of groceries on the porch and
drives off. A scratch and thump means
the drunk above us is home. Every multifamily dwelling
has one. Count our own and we have
two. In my room I kneel before my bed
writing poems, and in the attic my mother
waits for my father (who earlier hurled a hacksaw
at my brother) to fall through the trapdoor of sleep.
Then she'll return to the costume
and sew all night. Another variation
on Spanish dancer. This is what sets us apart
from our neighbors, she tells herself. We work hard
to keep it together. Submerged in lavender I listen to birds
heckle me from the sage bush: It is not the eighties, your parents
are dead, it is noon. Let the family break apart, let
the neighbors look in. To see the frayed sofa? I ask,
panicking. The eggshells on the floor?

III
Blood and Bones

Nickole Brown

Thirteen Ways of Looking at a Saltine

1.

Perforations is what they are,
but I didn't know that word,
not back then. No, we just said
holes—thirteen of them, set up
like the board of that Cracker
Barrel game with a jar of colored
pegs to kill the time and quiet us kids
until the waitress brought the eggs.
Stamped in the wood were
the results: leave two pegs and *you're*
purty smart, it read. *Four or mor'n*
you're just plain eg-no-ra-moose.
Even then, I knew the score
for what it was—fun made
at how we talked, a joke for sale
in the gift store.

2.

Try and look: Not one
of those tiny salted peepholes
hardly lets you through to see
a thing. No, they were just big enough
for the boys to be boys, smashing together
a sandwich of them, peanut butter
made to look like thirteen worms,
like thirteen blackheads squeezed
from a preteen nose. *Bashing jacks*
is what they called it,
telling every boy that called
I couldn't come to the phone

because I was in front of the mirror
again, doing exactly that.

3.

Holes were something
I knew, all those bull's-eye
cans lined on the fence
not just *shot up* but *riddled*,
the spray of buckshot
ever wider with every inch
he sawed from the barrel
of a shotgun kept
under Mama's bed. When
the smoke and ruckus
was too much, I'd hide
in a Model A forgotten
deep in the weeds, curl
into a nest of rusted
springs and animal hair
burst from the driver's seat.
I'd test each little porthole
a bullet had made
in that old Ford, use my fingers
to dam the streams of light
bossing through doors
once made to close and keep
a passenger safe.

4.

What I didn't know then was
the holes are intentional, made to keep
a cracker pumped with yeast
from pillowing up—without them,
that Depression-era mix of not much
more than white flour and baking soda
would have no crunch, no hard edges.

5.

My grandmother took them
with butter, the unsalted kind in a red
carton, the kind whipped
white and soft. How delicate
she'd make each bite with all the manners
she could muster, making herself into

a cotillion-trained girl taught
never to yankee-up a slice
by slathering the whole thing at once
but to ready only what you can fit
in your mouth at a time,
buttering not the whole piece
but each individual bite, one by one.

6.

Hard to say if my grandfather tried
not to break them as he jammed
a pâté of finger sausages onto
his, the kind of sausages named
for the city of Mozart but never
pronounced that way, not *Vienna*
but *Vye-ee-nna*, a mechanically separated
little tin of God-knows-what,
perfect for bait fishing and made
delicious with a dash of hot sauce.
On the boat, I'd draw
my knees up on the cooler, pass him
one link after the next, watch him take
one for himself, another
for the hook.

7.

Listen. There's endless ways
to eat them, but the most basic choice
is this: salt side up or salt side down.
My tongue, always ready for a fight,
preferred the latter. Like the family
I love best, the bite is rough at first
but quickly goes soft, nearly falls apart
without even the need
to chew, not too unlike how I was taught
to take communion without the aggression
of teeth, letting what will forgive
dissolve on your tongue.

8.

My mama played
disco and ate hers with all kinds
of diet snacks, mostly cottage cheese,
but eventually a different something

could be found at the store, so she
brought home a taste of what
I'd never seen before: a cracker without
sharp edges, each scalloped and shaped
like a framed Victorian portrait on a wall.
I'd study them, say *Townhouse*, conjure
the brand name as if it might genie up
a place I'd live in some day with a pantry full
of fancy like this, each biscuit so burnished
it abandoned that factory-worker pallor
for something bronzed, something fresh
back from Miami in a white denim skirt.

9.

This is all to say
the first time I was called *cracker*
no one could've told me it was anything
than a jive made at what we ate,
and if it had anything to do with color,
it was only all those pale
waxed sleeves of those pale
crackers white enough to reflect
their nutritional content was that
of drywall. No one could've told me different,
convinced as I was it had everything to do
with the tan of those high-end crackers
we could hardly afford or regularly
find at our store.

10.

What I didn't know then was
how an industry would one day make
a nostalgia of it all, how we'd become the punch
line for those who would hardly make fun
of anyone else, white trash being dead last
in the race to make the workplace PC, a tough
case to make for difficult men who pass
as privileged without having much
to show for it at all. So the redneck
roast keeps going, all those jokes
about funeral casseroles, green beans
on the stove so long the Jesus
is cooked right out of them, that slop
slopped together with cheese that's not

really cheese, the kind that also comes in a box,
all of it topped with a crumble crust of
cheap. But I know what it's like to swallow
it down when those new graves are dug,
just how long it takes for anything to grow
over that red gash in clay earth.

11.

Etymology says *whip cracker,*
and on my best days I see that exhausted
draught horse, swaybacked and crusted
with the black scat of fleas, some grandfather
from way back down the line plowing
those merciless fields and snapping
that stinging tip. Worse, I imagine
that obscene whip cracking over
another human being.
Once, when I asked my grandmother
where our people were from, she said
not to worry my pretty little head
*cause we weren't nothing but a bunch
of chicken thieves,* meaning we were
poor, as in *dirt,* as in *no pot to piss in
nor a window to throw the piss out,*
meaning we were tenant farmers,
poor enough to hardly own
ourselves, much less anything or any-
one else. But still, it's near impossible to
escape the report of that whip, to figure
who might have held it or what
back of what living being
was ripped to shreds.

12.

So screw Paula Deen and the clack
of her too-white teeth too big
for her foul mouth: what we made of simple
flour and water and salt was never meant
to be a show. In the clamor of it
all, we forgot how those plain crackers gentle
the stomach like nothing else can
when you're sick, a bite to try
when nothing else will stay down. And mercy
if they don't thicken even the most

watery soup, making the buy-one-get-one
from a can into something that might
actually fill you and keep you
from hunger.

13.

Believe me when I say
they're still there at the bottom right
of the bottom shelf, and damn it
if they still cost less than just about anything
else at the store. And please: don't tell me
how useful they are, how comforting still:
I remember: of course I know. I do.
I know. But I also know if too many are eaten
dry, the roof of my mouth will be torn
to rags, and rightly so. Worse, I'm ashamed.
And oh, how ashamed and ashamed of how
ashamed I am. I roll my cart past now
without looking down to them, and never
do I buy them anymore.

Tony Sweatt and Robert Gipe

On Mute

September 20, 2021
Robert Gipe: In 2003, Dr. Tony Sweatt and I interviewed his grandmother, Missouri Cottrell, at her home just outside Harlan, Kentucky, where Tony and I both live. Among other stories, Ms. Cottrell told us how as teenagers, she and her brothers ran a poker game for coal miners as a way of making money.

Tony Sweatt: My grandmother's mom passed when she was a young girl. Her dad left my granny and her younger siblings and moved up the street with another family, leaving them to fend for themselves. They started running a poker game, making money off the miners. During her story, I remember laughing at the thought of a young girl running a card game. However, after getting the whole story of what led to her running the game, I remember experiencing sadness, anger, disgust, surprise, and finally the joy that came from knowing my grandmother was a resilient Black woman.

RG: Ms. Cottrell's story was adapted for *Higher Ground,* a 2005 play sponsored by the Southeast Kentucky Community & Technical College Appalachian Program. Over two hundred people were involved in the creation of the play, which focused on how we might apply our community's strengths to combat the opioid crisis.

TS: I was raised by my grandparents for the most part until age eight. My granddad was a coal miner, worked at a gas station, and collected rent for Mr. James Turner. My grandma was a nurse's aide. My grandparents had nine children, and I made ten. I was reunited with my mother at eight years old. Early on, my mother was a nurse at UK and then in Harlan. Shortly after rejoining my mom, she quit her job and we went on welfare. To this day I am not sure why she quit. We never talked about financial matters. I graduated Evarts High School in 1988. My first full-time job was in the military. I got out of the army December 23, 1991, shortly after the first Desert Storm ended. They gave soldiers early outs to go to school. I made more money taking computer repair at the vocational school on the GI Bill than some of my friends were working. I remember guys saying, "Hey Sweatt, [so-and-so] is hiring," and I'd be making more money going to school. Why would I quit school? It's like the old-timers say: "That would have been hustling backwards."

RG: When I met Tony, he had finished his associate's degree at Southeast and was working on his bachelor's degree in human services and counseling at Lindsey Wilson College's Harlan-based program. He did his interview with his grandmother as part of my Appalachian Studies class at Southeast and then came to work on the Harlan County Listening Project.

TS: With the Listening Project, we went out into our different communities to find out what folks' perceptions of our biggest challenges were, and once we identified those challenges, we wanted to develop that into a community play to share what people were saying. We said, "We want to hear your story. We don't care where you're from and if that story is happy, tragic, or sad. We want you to talk about what you want to talk about." We didn't go in there with an agenda and say, "OK, we're just going to talk about the opioid problem." We gave them the opportunity to say what they saw hindering us from being a healthier community. The group that did the interviews, many of us were addicts, recovering addicts—we were the misfits. We interviewed addicts, recovering addicts, educators—over two hundred interviews. That opened my eyes up. It wasn't just me going through this struggle. This is a whole community.

RG: The Listening Project and the first Higher Ground play led to fifteen more years of community engagement and art-making grounded in maximum participation of the broadest cross section of the community. Over a thousand Harlan Countians have been part of creating more plays and public art, and we have traveled together to present that work—which has addressed community experience with race, strip mining, harm reduction, gender, sexuality, and other topics—at conferences and gatherings. And the work continues.

TS: Everyone has a story. [People] felt honored when we approached them to hear those stories, especially if they considered themselves poor, first generation, low income, living in poverty, and all that stuff—they were like, wow, they want to hear what I think. [Robert and I] crossed paths at a time when I could have gone either way. This work connected me with people. It helped me build confidence within myself. I think about the community college—what it was and still has the ability to be. It can be a game changer.

RG: I was hired by Southeast Kentucky Community & Technical College in 1997. At that time, the president of the college, Dr. Bruce Ayers, had the idea that our community college would be more welcoming to coalfield students and their families if the school celebrated and integrated the culture of the community. My mandate when I was hired as program director of the Appalachian Center was to use Appalachian culture to make people feel welcome at Southeast. The work that followed was my interpretation of that mandate.

TS: I was hired by Southeast in 2005 as an interactive television facilitator. In 2006, I received my master's degree in human services and counseling, and in 2008, I accepted a job with the Office of Vocational Rehabilitation. In 2009, I came back to Southeast as director of enrollment. I successfully defended my dissertation and received my doctorate degree from Eastern Kentucky University's Educational Leadership and Policy Studies doctoral program in December 2017. Since then, I worked two years with Partners for Education with Berea College and am now the managing director of the Appalachian College Initiative with Teach for America Appalachia.

RG: For many years, Tony was not as involved in the work of Higher Ground. But in 2021, Tony came back to help a new generation of Higher Ground leadership create a play about the pandemic; the demonstration in Harlan that took place in the wake of the Ahmaud Arbery, Breonna Taylor, and George Floyd killings; and the 1970s erasure of Georgetown, a Black community in Harlan.

TS: As a youngster, I grew up on stories of folks that migrated to Detroit, Chicago, Philadelphia, and Cincinnati and came home every payday just to party in Georgetown. But by the time I got old enough, Georgetown was gone.

RG: An early draft of the 2021 play *Higher Ground 9: Shift Change* included these lines:

> LEENA: Summertime, I eat a tomato a day, buy vegetables from roadside stands and farmers' markets. This August I was getting a five-pound bag of green beans a week, cooking some with taters, bacon, and onions, but stringing up most of them to make shucky beans.
> HANK: Summertime to me is getting out and running the roads. Going to Dollywood. Maybe go see the Cincinnati Reds.
> ACEY: There wadn't much of that running this past summer. That corona kept us all at the house.
> COTTON: That governor kept us at the house.
> MYRA: And those protests kept picking up steam. Lid blew off in Louisville. People reminding people how Breonna Taylor got shot in her bed by the police.
> COTTON: That woman was up to something. You know she was.
> ACEY: I don't believe she was. And it don't matter. She shouldn't have died like that.

RG: There were about fifteen of us on the script committee, but I was one of the main ones editing the script into something we could perform. Tony had issues with Acey's response to Cotton and sent me a rewrite:

> COTTON: That woman was up to something. You know she was.
> ACEY: Cotton, that's your "go-to" line every time a Black person is killed. You said Tamir Rice was "up to something" when he was killed in the park with a toy gun, but when Kyle Rittenhouse was accused of killing two people and went home, you didn't say a word. You said Walter Scott was "up to something" when he was pulled over and killed for having a busted taillight, but I didn't hear a thing when James Alex Fields Jr. ran over and killed Heather Heyer in Charlottesville. How is it okay for Blacks to be killed for MAYBE being "up to something," but white people who we can see are "up to something" still get their day in court? But you know what, that's my fault.
> COTTON: How is it your fault?

ACEY: An old man told me a long time ago that "it doesn't cost a thing to listen." And ever since I met you, I have allowed you to spit those insensitive comments without challenging your idiotic view. Therefore, from here on out, when you approach me with that bull crap, I consider it my duty to voice my opinion whether you like it or not. As a result, one of two things will happen: either you will at least look at it from my point of view or you will stop talking to me. I'm fine either way.

RG: I thought a long time about what to say to Tony, because I thought Acey's briefer response in the earlier draft is so often what happens in real life. We don't say what we feel in the moment. And we had other characters talking about how difficult it is as a Black person to show your emotions in front of white people for fear of being labeled the "angry Black person." But who am I, a white man, to tell Tony, a Black man, what African American character Acey would say in response to Cotton, an openly racist white man, in that moment? Before I could respond to Tony's rewrite, we had a script meeting on Zoom. There were about ten people on the call, including Tony. The director, Keith McGill, asked Tony how his rewrite was coming. Tony gave a summary of his rewrite, and another cast member on the call said he had a friend in Louisville saying Breonna Taylor was mixed up in drugs. A cast member who'd had their own run-ins with violence at the hands of law enforcement jumped on that cast member, saying it doesn't matter whether she was or wasn't—she doesn't deserve to get shot in her bed. The scene from the play was playing out in real life on our Zoom call. When I talked to Tony later, he said he had muted himself during the confrontation.

TS: I'm not a big social media guy. I'm getting to where I hate it. I get on there and I see people that I have respected, former teachers and folks that on the surface are good people. But they have been given the power to freely say openly hurtful things. I think back to First Lady Michelle Obama—when they go low, we go high. But damn, man. Sometimes that shit gets old. I think the reason I muted myself is cause the old me would have talked to him in an intentionally disrespectful way, and I may have called him out his name in hopes he wanted it to escalate to the next level. But in this transition I'm going through in life, I'm trying to be a productive, positive citizen. The somewhat intelligent version of me must pause before responding to ignorance. It reminds me of when I got a DUI when I was at the college. Dr. Ayers came to see me. He was compassionate with me, but he also let me know that on the Harlan campus, "You are the face of this college. And so, we cannot have this—the face of our college in the paper for negative things." That right there let me know I had to change what I was doing because it was bigger than me. I'm in a position now where I have to ignore ignorant statements. Or if not ignore it, I have to take more time to make a conscious effort to respond.

RG: In the end, Tony and I had Acey say very little to Cotton, but turn to the audience and share his thoughts with them. Here's how the scene was performed:

COTTON: That woman was up to something. You know she was.

ACEY [WITH ANGER IN HIS VOICE]: I don't believe she was. And it doesn't matter. She shouldn't have died like that.

COTTON: Aaaa, you don't know what you're talking about. I heard she was mixed up in drugs.

ACEY: She was an EMT. A first responder. You support first responders, don't you?

[COTTON MAKES A GESTURE EXPRESSING HIS DISDAIN. ACEY STARTS TO SPEAK, RESTRAINS HIMSELF. LIGHTS SHIFT. ACEY ADDRESSES THE AUDIENCE.]

ACEY: "Up to something." Breonna Taylor was "up to something." That's what that man says every time a Black person is killed. He said Tamir Rice was "up to something" when he was killed in the park with a toy gun. He said Walter Scott was "up to something" when he was pulled over and killed for having a busted taillight. But he didn't say a damn thing about what Kyle Rittenhouse was up to when he killed two people and went home, when James Alex Fields Jr. ran over and killed Heather Heyer in Charlottesville. How is it okay for Blacks to be killed for MAYBE being "up to something," but white people, who we can see are "up to something," still get their day in court? But I didn't say that to him. I put myself on mute. Why do I do that?

TS: I think by turning to the audience, you're letting them know what you're struggling with. There's no greater struggle than the one that goes on within, and the Black man struggles with that daily. It gets hard.

RG: I liked the solution because rather than forcing the audience to choose sides in a confrontation between Cotton and Acey, it becomes an opportunity for them to participate in Acey's decision-making process. Our director, Keith McGill, who is from Louisville, talked to the cast member who made the hurtful statements, and there was reconciliation amongst the cast.

TS: You know I thought maybe at one time y'all might ask that cast member to not be a part of the play, but you can't do that. I told you years ago, it don't matter to me if they got KKK tattooed on their forehead. That lets me know who they are. And what did Maya Angelou say? "When they tell you who they are, believe them." So I don't want to censor or mute you. You continue to talk, so I know who you are. As my granny says, that lets me know I need to feed you with a long-handle spoon. Or not feed you at all.

RG: The kind of cultural work we are doing at the community college has gotten harder over the last five or six years. Budgets have constricted. Positions in the humanities have not been filled when people retire. Adjuncts replace full-time faculty. Engaging people in critical reflection on the present and history of our communities has not been made grounds for punishment in Kentucky, but it has been elsewhere. Higher Ground has had to raise a larger percentage of its budget through external sources to survive. In 2016, I wrote a federal grant proposal for our work and the college was awarded $596,000 in federal dollars. But somebody held it up. Maybe a US senator.

Maybe a US congressman. I was never told. But my administration suggested I clean up my Facebook because something on it had given offense. I censored myself to protect the workers I feared would lose their jobs if we didn't secure that grant.

TS: That was the whole thing Rob never wanted to get into. He was always committed to the work from the ground level and left the politicking to the senior administrators. It is harder today for people to remain neutral.

RG: It is. We have worked very hard in our cultural work for multiple points of view to be represented, to be about conversation and not dogma. But even talking about the issues that divide us has become too "political" for some.

TS: The truth is that white, European American, heterosexual males hold power and set the parameters for interaction in our institutions. For muted groups to "fit in," they have to change the way they act and talk, which results in a loss of power. Injustice is a direct result of the dominant group's concerns being attended to while the concerns of the marginalized people are muted.

RG: Arts and humanities budgets get cut and we are told our work is frivolous or nonessential. But when cultural work is done right—when it is engaged with all the different types of people in our world—it is extremely potent. And I think the budget cutters know that.

TS: If we are going to heal our wounds and come together as a nation, we must invest in honest conversation with one another. We cannot be a nation of individuals with the idea that I can overcome if I pull myself up by the bootstraps. The song is "We Shall Overcome," not I.

George Ella Lyon

Where I'm From (2018)

I'm from the cries of families / sundered at our southern border / while Lady Liberty faces a filthy sea. / I'm from "all [white able-bodied well-off hetero] men are created equal" and "Here / Puerto Rico, have some paper towels!" // I'm from our Predator-in-Chief / who brags about grabbing pussy / and mocks a woman who was sexually abused. // I'm from countries we bombed or clear-cut / or destabilized to get what we wanted. / I'm from the Seven Deadly Sins / confused with the American Dream. // I'm from the whole Pilgrim whitewash / our refusal to admit the land we stole / from the Indigenous we slaughtered, the Africans / we chained to build our wealth. I'm from / their descendants, gunned down on the street. I'm from / children ripped from their parents' arms / when the ship docked, at the auction block / in the field. I'm from their blood and bones / feeding the ground I stand on.

Emily Skaja

If Anyone Should Fight to Breathe

It's him: the two-bit mayor of the dead
flagged against a balustrade, live all night,
the world on fire. *Conspiracy*, he said.

Reading the retweets, never the thread,
relaxed, imperial in black and white,
it's him: the two-bit mayor of the dead.

His crown of bones, his genius-heavy head,
he's Jesus—he can see it—hosed in light,
the world on fire. *Conspiracy*, he said.

The ashes of the hundred thousands dead
are in the air he tries to breathe. He fights—
it's him: the two-bit mayor of the dead—

he's gasping *I can't breathe*. FAKE NEWS! he said.
Stand back, stand by, fine people on both sides,
the world on fire. *Conspiracy*, he said.

He can't count deaths, he's counting votes instead.
The biggest hoax you've ever seen! He's right—
it's him: the two-bit mayor of the dead.
The world on fire. *Conspiracy*, he said.

Laura Secord

Bringing the Monument
Down *Birmingham, AL*

April 26, 1905   They placed this tower, made clear
who'd wield the power in this new town.
White. Erect. It seized the grounds.

May 31, 2020   The people tried to pull it down.
Ropes and chains and cries of pain failed to topple
supremacy's idol. Not protest tags or broken glass or flame.

June 1, 2020   Curfew's darkened silence. A flatbed hearse awaits.
Above magnolia trees, two men work to ablate
this symbol looming to curse the nonwhite race.

White man with pry bar. Huge crane. Chisel in hand,
a young Black man—curly beard, hard hat and 'Rona
mask—works to loosen the capstone. He makes his last chip.
The obelisk twists away.

No song, no celebration, no comrades to cheer,
a sole brown witness, with chisel, stands his ground,
as the tower of Jim Crow power, in swaddled straps

drops from sky to waiting ground. A singular
witness, staring as repression's pinnacle swings.
He dislodged it. Silent fist pump. For the moment,
        his spirit sings.

A. H. Jerriod Avant

If I May Be Frank

i am a ghost
out of yo' control
back for some
shyt, i can't even
use and my unlawful
breathing is its own
reward. the deep
south brims with
lost things and the
stolen property and
bodies of dead people.
my chest be a graveyard
of folks white folks
wouldn't've buried.
best i can i stay
funked out in these
southern spaces.
build homes on
land, white folks
stole enough times
they done forgot
whose is what
and won't ask
you to move to
cause you to be
gone. their lip-
service to peace
leaks ornery fumes
of corpse-infused
river water, pounded
by hot rain. pig guts
that barely drown
out honeysuckle
and the weighted

branches of ripened
peach trees. wrinkled
witnesses hide in
rot and sit silent
as pecan groves,
foul as the blue news
people tell with joy
blotched 'cross a
mob of white faces.

Sandra Beasley

My Whitenesses

Whiteness as my body's
spent currency:

hair that holds no melanin,
which I pluck out;

an overlong fingernail
that I tear away;

what once blistered,
collapsed flat to my heel.

And what then?
Skin picked, flicked

under my bed—
strands dropped to tile—

the keratin crescents folded,
tucked in couch-crevice.

My performative strip
of self still

trashing up the place.
Down by Richmond,

how you pronounce a thing
sets stake in the land.

Do you elaborate
a tribe's original *Pow-hite*?

Or does 300 years
of muscle memory

guide your tongue?
Po' white Creek.

Po' white Parkway.
One man claims *cracker*

as absolution,
as proof of brotherhood.

Another man claims *cracker*
because someone,

back three *great-grands* ago,
cracked a whip.

Virginia, my ghosts
need gathering.

Come to the table
and sit, goddammit. Sit.

Keith Leonard

Statement of Teaching Philosophy

My students want certainty. They want it
so badly. They respect science and have memorized
complex formulas. I don't know
how to tell my students their parents
are still just as scared. The bullies get bigger
and vaguer and you cannot punch a cloud.
I have eulogies for all my loved ones prepared,
but cannot include this fact in my lesson plans.
The best teacher I ever had told me to meet him
at the basketball court. We played pick-up for hours.
By the end, I lay panting on the hardwood
and couldn't so much as stand.
He told me to describe the pain in my chest.
I tried. I couldn't find the words. Not exactly.
Listen, he said, *that's where language ends.*

Kwame Dawes

Work

Five days to go: Working for the next day
—Bob Marley, "Work"

Look at this man's hands, look
at the toughness in his fingers,
the way his nails darken at the edges,
the way his skin is marked
by old scars, the way his palms
are leather-tough—a grater of skin
if he drags those palms over
your arm. Those hands still
remember the smooth shape
of wood, the grooves where
the blisters would settle and then
harden to toughness; the handle
of the clumsy seed planter, bouncing
on the uneven grooves, planting,
planing. Sometimes it is easy
to not know that on the plantation,
out there on James Island,
every morning, seven days a week,
a bell would sound out, and that
bell would mean that thirty minutes
was left before you lined up
by the fields to start to sweat.
And you would work all day
to pay rent on the wood shingle
and mud chimney that they
had given you. And if you missed
a day, your family would lose
shelter. That is work. Work is
keeping the wolves from your door,
work is the left foot following
the right, the sickle swinging,

the dirt on your skin. Work
is always being behind, always owing
somebody something. Work
is payment in June for debt
from last December, when the cold
reached into your gut, held
you down. Work is one pair
of shoes all season—barefoot
grown man all summer long,
and mules for the freeze
all winter. Work is the day
you think you are grown enough
now to run, to run from this
constant falling back, only
to find that big-bellied white
man with a shotgun saying, "Here are
some stripes, nigger, nice stripes
to help you work better—now
you get three meals a day;
now you get a bed to sleep on,
boy; now you got something
to live for." Work is all
a nigger has for sure, and work
tells you that nobody, nobody
is going to give you something
for nothing; work is like breathing—
and every breath is a loan
that you can never pay back.
Work is all a man has,
and work is nothing, nothing
at all; every day is work, work, work.

Reginald Dwayne Betts

In Alabama

IN THE ███████ ██████ MIDDLE ██████ OF ALABAMA

████████

v

THE CITY OF MONTGOMERY

The Plaintiffs ████ ████ impoverished ██████ jailed by the City ██████████ unable to pay ████████ traffic tickets ██████████ pay ███ ████████ or █ sit ████████ in ███ jail █████ $50 per day ██████ Plaintiffs ████████ unable to pay ████████ each █ sent to jail ███████████ ██████████████ ████ █ they could ████████ work █ off █████ debts █████ $25 per day █████ ██████ ████████ cleaning the ████ City ████ scrubbing feces and blood from jail floors ████████

The treatment ██████████████████████████
████████████████████████ reveals ██████████████████████ the
City ███████████ against ███████ its poorest ███████████████████
███
████████████████████████ jailing people if they ██████ poor ███████████
███ ████████
████
███
██████████████████ Plaintiffs seek ███████████████████████████████
fundamental rights █████████████████████ they suffered █████████ .
██ the
City s █████████ unlawful ██████████ ██████████ ███████████
█████ ███
██
██

It is the policy ▮▮▮ of the City ▮▮▮ to jail people

It is the policy ▮▮▮ of the City to jail ▮▮ people ▮

It is the policy ▮▮▮ of the City to hold prisoners ▮▮▮ until ▮▮▮ extinguished

It is the policy ▮▮▮

It is the policy ▮▮▮

Plaintiffs seek ▮▮▮ relief

▓▓▓▓▓▓▓▓ a 23-year-old woman ▓▓ mother of two ▓▓▓▓▓ ▓▓▓▓▓▓▓▓▓▓▓▓▓▓ ▓▓▓▓▓ ▓▓▓ ▓▓▓▓ police officers came ▓▓ ▓▓▓▓▓ arrested her ▓▓▓ she owed the City ▓▓▓▓▓ ▓▓▓▓▓ Officers took ▓▓▓▓ away ▓▓ her two children ▓▓ ▓▓▓▓▓▓ she ▓▓ too poor to pay ▓▓▓▓▓▓▓▓▓▓▓ . ▓▓▓▓▓▓▓▓▓▓▓▓▓▓▓▓▓▓▓▓▓ ▓▓▓▓ told ▓▓▓▓▓ she would ▓▓▓ serve ▓▓▓▓▓▓▓ ▓▓▓ ▓▓▓▓▓▓ taken ▓▓ to ▓▓▓ jail ▓▓▓▓▓ ▓▓▓▓▓▓▓▓▓▓▓▓▓▓▓▓▓▓▓▓ ▓▓▓▓▓▓▓▓▓▓▓▓▓▓▓▓▓▓▓▓ ▓▓▓▓▓▓▓▓▓▓▓▓▓▓▓▓▓▓▓▓ ▓▓▓▓▓▓▓▓▓▓▓▓▓▓▓▓▓▓▓▓ ▓▓▓▓ Desperate to get back ▓▓▓ children ▓▓▓ ▓▓▓▓▓▓▓▓▓▓ labored to clean ▓▓▓ ▓ jail bars ▓▓▓▓▓▓▓▓▓▓▓▓▓▓▓▓

a 58-year-old disabled resident

arrested

took into custody

kept for three days

informed he would

be released if someone pay

asked for mercy

The court

ordered him to serve 44

days

██████████████████

██████ 38-year-old father ████████ ████ lives ██

███████ with ██████████ his children ███████

█████████████ went to ██████ police █████████ after he

learned ██ he had ██████ warrants ████████ ████ traffic tickets ████

████████████████ arrested ██ placed in █████ jail ██████

███████████████ kept overnight ████████████

████████████████████ he owed

the City ██████ $1,600 ████████████ █████████

██████████████ The judge ██████

ordered him jailed ████████████████

██████████████████ told ██████

██████ released if he █████████ served 23 days ████

████████████ told ████████ he could work off his

debt ████████████████████████

████████████████████████████

██████████████████████

██████ did not want to clean ██████████████

██████████ blood and feces ████████ desperate ████

█████████ agreed to clean ██ blood and feces from the jail floors ██████

██████████████ lost his job while he sat in █████ jail ██████

Request for
Relief

WHEREFORE Plaintiffs request ██████████████ relief

Respectfully submitted

Tyrone Williams

D.D.I.Y.

Unlike cops and cabs
always on their way
he is already waiting

in a parking lot
with his Mercury
in idle, coughing

exhaust as he takes
another long drag
on a Camel,

squinting at
a racing form
until a door

swings open
and a cart
crammed with groceries

and the straggling
arms and legs
of kids trying

to hitch a ride
exits the store,
followed by

a woman already
nodding toward
the jitney rushing

forward to help, his arms
the trunk and passenger
doors wide open.

Darius V. Daughtry

Ghazal for Grandma's Hands

Floors, windows, toilets, pots and pans
painted lush landscapes on the back of Grandma's hands.

Snowbirds squatting spot the spotless
work on baseboards and basins scrubbed by Grandma's hands.

Warrior woman worked for pennies traded for
beans and fatback that became magic in weary hands.

So much time spent back-bent, akin to those
with cotton pricks and tobacco stains on humbled hands.

Too many centuries worth of work spent
with body and spirit broken by some soulless hands.

Mop, sweep, change bedpans and sheets;
seems sewage and shit always found Grandma's hands.

I ran away from labor like hers;
away from brittle, scarred and calloused hands.

Thought my mind would save me,
make me more talent than the toil of my hands.

Did she ever know the brilliant
she could be with paper and pen in them hands?

What if she, I often wondered,
had poems and portraits in those hands?

I wished for more than Borax and Brillo pads
as familiar tools in ever-aging hands.

But homes were built—brick laid, lives planted
and nurtured with the wisdom cemented in her hands.

What an empty man I would be if
not for the rugged grace of her weary hands.

Switches picked and correction flicked
from wrists with precision; love in splintered hands.

I admit to being less than;
wish my work earned even one of those calloused hands.

But, I say, "Darius, feel no shame;
you sparkle like all the work of Grandma's hands."

Cheryl R. Hopson

Family Musings, Matriliny, and Legacy

I as a Black Queer feminist poet, professor, and scholar seek the roots of my ascension from lower middle class to a shifting and commingled middle and intellectual class, through an exploration of my maternal line.

My mother was the beneficiary of a financial inheritance from her maternal great-uncle Walter that provided for her education and left her with a sum of money.

What I have construed from decades of being my mother's daughter is a tangible material and psychosocial link between my own ambitions, achievements, and class locations and those of my mother—as well as those of her great-uncle Walter. Second to this, I have come to recognize the significance not only of Walter's financial gift but also of the *man* himself to my mother and her family and thus to me.

Family lore tells that my mother's great-uncle, my maternal great-great-uncle Walter, was the first African American millionaire in our hometown. As a young man Walter worked for the railroad, later opened the first African American real estate company in our city, and, by virtue of the fact that he could pass for white, was able to secure a beautiful home for himself and his wife (remembered as being "very elegant") in an all-white neighborhood of the city. Today, one of Walter's beneficiaries and executors, my mother's cousin and his wife, remains in the home. (There is still a noticeable familial pride in the fact that my great-great-uncle could pass for white and therefore play the trickster by purchasing a home in a segregated white community.) I as a girl and a young woman must surely have imbibed both the internalized colorism inherent in the complex displays of racial and ethnic pride in my mother's family and the resistance in my great-great-uncle's actions. Much of my mother's family, my grandmother's immediate family in particular—that is, my great-aunts and great-uncles—were very light complexioned, in part because my great-grandmother, like her brother Walter, both born in the 1890s, were mixed race; their father was an unknown (to me) local white man.

As a Black feminist and as a poet, I love the idea of rendering nonsensical and farcical this country's long history of the "one-drop" rule concerning race. I also appreciate any attempt to demonstrate the absurdity of the idea of a "pure" white American, as well as that of a monolithic Blackness. Great-uncle Walter's financial gift to my mother (and her many siblings and cousins) provided a legacy of thinking ahead to, and accommodating financially and in other ways, future generations of his family. This and more is his legacy as an African American man and a great-uncle to my mother. This and more is his legacy to me. This and more is his legacy to an unnamed number of family members past, present, and future. This gift and foresightedness is his legacy of resistance demonstrable in his choice of location for his home.

After all, it was in accounting for future generations of his family that he perhaps in full knowing was also accounting for me. What follows demonstrates in some measure the magnitude of my great-great-uncle Walter's generosity and foresight and the gratitude I have for him as a model.

I was born to a young married African American couple who were already parents to two daughters, aged fifteen months and forty-eight months, and whose marriage was in shambles at the time of my birth in the spring of 1973. I entered my parents' life when my mother was twenty-one and my father was twenty-three. Not long after my birth, they finalized their divorce.

In quick order, my twenty-one-year-old mother became a newly divorced single mother of three daughters all under the age of five. Add to this the fact that my mother was a Black woman who, at the time, had only a high school education and already a few years of seasoning as a full-time student, wife, and mother. Again, this was 1973–1974, when the social movements of the late 1960s and early 1970s, including Black Nationalism, Women's Liberation, and Gay Liberation, were part of the national consciousness and a backdrop to the domestic life in which my still beautiful and ambitious mother suddenly found herself. My mother, now on welfare to help shelter and feed her daughters, was not supposed to succeed, and neither were her daughters.

According to national narratives that predominated from the 1960s onward—narratives imbibed by others—Black women *as* mothers were pathological and thus dangerous to their families. Worse still, the narratives continued, Black women emasculated (and thus ran off) Black men, and this accounted for the high rate of absentee Black fathers. My mother was well aware of and susceptible to these narratives as a newly divorced single mother. My mother was supposed to be a statistic. The interconnected and systemic material reality of existing as a Black single mother in a racist, sexist, misogynist, hetero-patriarchal, and white supremacist as well as Black masculinist US society and culture must have dawned on her daily, as it does me, and surely must have manifested in her life. Take as just one of multiple examples the day in 1985 when a family court judge, a Black man, decided that my father must pay $50 a month in child support to my mother for "three growing daughters," she said in dismay. The judge, according to my mother, sympathized with my father and intimated as much as he issued his judgment. Still.

My mother rejected subsistence living, refused to sublimate self to motherhood and poverty, and ignored the everyday mini-cuts of Black masculinist sexism and bias, as well as liberal and progressive white America's oppressions, projections, biases, and stereotypes—such as the stern and sexless matriarch, the lascivious and irresponsible "welfare queen," and the always angry and irrational emasculating Black woman. Instead, she insisted on being herself—a newly remarried mother of now four daughters, with educational and professional ambitions, a zest for life and hard work, and a penchant for romance. What I remember growing up is a mother who worked and attended school simultaneously from the time I was eight years old. Like many Gen-Xers, my sisters and I grew up as latch-key kids. We got ourselves off to school, returned home to cook dinner and tidy, tackle homework, watch television, and then prepare for a repeat of the process the next day. My mother and stepfather worked full time, and my mother attended school part-time for much of my childhood. In fact, one of the jokes of my mother's family was that she was a perpetual student.

My mother graduated with her bachelor's in 1992 (and I graduated from the same college in 1995) and earned her master's in 2000 (as did I from the same university in 1997). Over the span of my childhood and into my early adulthood, my mother went from being a certified nursing assistant to a registered nurse to a nurse practitioner. She saw her income more than quadruple in the process—and most assuredly experienced an escalation in her sense of her own competence, intelligence, and ability. Still.

By the age of thirty-five, I had a PhD in English, a great love affair that would blossom into marriage a decade-plus later, and *massive* amounts of student loan debt from nearly twelve years of postsecondary education. I also had a visiting professorship in English lined up at my alma mater, a private and historically white liberal arts college one town over from where I grew up.

The year was 2009, and I was at a professional zenith but a personal nadir after the sudden loss of my two older sisters in the previous two years. However, student loans and no financial safety net meant that I had to work, undiagnosed and untreated trauma and all. What I remember most from my childhood when I learned about my mother's wealthy great-uncle was my profound sense of regret as a girl and a teenager that the money from the trust Great-uncle Walter established did not extend to me. While my mother and I attended the same private and very expensive college, her great-uncle covered her tuition. When I applied to the same college, I did so without any forethought as to how I would afford it. I simply thought that because my mother could afford to attend our alma mater, it followed that I could too. The beauty and hilarity of youth. You have to love it.

Uncle Sam, my mother, and I covered my tuition, but just barely. My mother worked overtime at her job, and I worked extra shifts at whatever jobs I happened to have throughout my college years, and together with the aid of student loans and a wealthy white woman who became my benefactor in my sophomore year, I managed to graduate from the same college as my mother. Today, I try to imagine a life without the debt from a decade-plus of study underwritten in part by Uncle Sam. It is a stretch. Still.

The recently departed coach Barbara Sher says to imagine the most impossible dream you have for yourself and go in the direction of that dream, piece by piece until you manifest it. My dream is of an existence in which I do not have the financial and psychic burden of debt accrued because I attempted to educate myself and better my station. However, this student loan debt is not my legacy. The story of the debt is, perhaps.

As a girl, I bore witness to my mother's struggles both as a divorced single mother and as a remarried mother of four who worked full time and attended first undergraduate and then graduate school. Like my mother, and like her mother before her, there is grief as well as triumph in our genetic makeup. Like my mother, I still take pride in the fact of our matrilineal millionaire ancestor. We have in our family lineage a Black man who, despite the terrors, restrictions, and constrictions of a deadly and racist white supremacist nation, and because of his own tenacious spirit, fortitude, ingenuity, and foresight—aided most certainly by his white-passing complexion—managed a life well lived and provided for his sister's grandchildren's education, one of whom was my mother.

Well done, great-great-uncle. Well done.

Randall Horton

: the making of {#289-128} in five parts

*

you will be arrested & sequestered
as property of the state as {#289-128}
                a beetle
                in a darlingtonia
might be more accurate.

*

each day/month/year builds to a question
   the response known before the query
again   & again
                disbelief is futile
on rehabilitation
you wait   & . . .   wait—

*

at some point repetition sets in:
   boiled egg, farina, white bread, bland coffee
for breakfast   reminders
of what   you have become {#289-128}
a nonbeing   from which
escape or release   is a fairytale.

*

the rec yard never alters its landscape:
dirt track, hoops, weight pit, fisticuffs—

*

the changing same . . . ?

Nabila Lovelace

Ars Poetica

prison labor meshes   your gym shorts

prison labor freezes   your frozen potatoes

prison labor lacquered   your new door

prison labor saved   your neighbors' burning house

prison labor twines the book
          you read this from

prison labor fed your cat &
          your favorite street strays

prison labor plasticized your emergency float under-
          neath your ass in an airplane seat

prison labor made your pay go up

prison labor bought your bosses'
              bosses'
              bosses'
              boss
       a league of new cars
    then made the nylon
seatbelt
     to strap each of his engines
        in place

prison labor stitched the collar to your golf
                shirt

prison labor pelted the priests' robes

prison labor hexagoned the stop signs
                in our school zones

                prison labor sculpted breasts   from young chicken chests
                        to top our brioche buns

prison labor shaved cloth trimmings
                from across the bottom of our couches

prison labor shined the polyurethane that water-
                proofs my Nike's tongue

                        everything we buy   supplies metal for cages
                        aren't we ready   for something else?

Pauletta Hansel

I Confess

July 5, 2019

These days I think too much
about assassination, and let me just say
I have come down against it every time,
swatting it away, a plague-ridden fly

in my otherwise mild and law-abiding imagination,
and I do not accept the legal argument
that targeted killings are a country's form
of self-defense, regardless of whether the target

will ever see the inside of a detention center,
and be faced with deciding, like thousands
of seven-year-olds, should the assigned Mylar blanket
go over or under, on the mud-caked concrete floor.

Every time, I rise up on the right side of the question
though I have gone so far as to research the word:
From the Arabic, hashshashin, the Assassins of Persia,
perhaps so-named for the necessity of getting high

before slipping in the blade. (In private,
some Border Patrol agents consider migrant deaths
a laughing matter; others are succumbing to depression,
anxiety, or substance abuse.)

How, with or without the name, the act
is older than our ability to write it down.
How, way back in the Old Testament,
there it was alongside the begetting and begats.

How in the Roman Empire, strangling in the bathtub
was the method of choice for murdering one's king,
while, as you might expect, in Japan it was the sword.
Here in the US we, as always,

prefer the gun, and let me just say,
I do not and will not own one.
I confess only to the image in my mind
of the mongrel dogs of history lapping at the wound.

Wendell Berry

Questionnaire

1. How much poison are you willing
   to eat for the success of the free
   market and global trade? Please
   name your preferred poisons.

2. For the sake of goodness, how much
   evil are you willing to do?
   Fill in the following blanks
   with the names of your favorite
   evils and acts of hatred.

3. What sacrifices are you prepared
   to make for culture and civilization?
   Please list the monuments, shrines,
   and works of art you would
   most willingly destroy.

4. In the name of patriotism and
   the flag, how much of our beloved
   land are you willing to desecrate?
   List in the following spaces
   the mountains, rivers, towns, farms
   you could most readily do without.

5. State briefly the ideas, ideals, or hopes,
   the energy sources, the kinds of security,
   for which you would kill a child.
   Name, please, the children whom
   you would be willing to kill.

Marcus Wicker

Reparations Redefinition: Bond

verb • The systematic lapping of brick in a wall.

                    Or shingles on the portico
of a two-faced estate—
                    Asphalt, wood, or rock
elements laid lip to incline.
                    Schindle from the German.
Meaning roof slate, sun-
                    baked. Meaning blacktop
underlayment, AKA
                    stacks of neighbors of
hoods adjacent to
                    chipper compatriots
waving from upper-
                    crust palisade schools.
Shade built for some.
                    Others made to serve
as holey canopies.
                    What trenches me
around this coal pit grist,
                    these deserted hallways,
is a maze
                    I can't rightly name.
In ancient Chile,
                    Fitzroya roof tiles were
exchanged to settle tax
                    balances.
Under this new definition,
                    every Black family's owed
one Fly Ash concrete
                    basement.

A harbor. Bulldozer
                  at bare minimum.
A telescopic fire escape—

M. L. Smoker

It Comes Down to This

The man who owned the only saddlery shop in
town refused, until the day he died, to sell back my
grandfather's grass dance regalia. When the shop owner
was still alive, the wiry hairs on his knuckles stood on
end each time a new wind blew down Main Street. Later
he grew to call this "cancer," but I will always call it *he
should have known better*. His wife, in some form of
mourning, says she too won't sell us a single piece, even
if we can prove with old photos of my grandfather that
it was his. Instead, she says we have to buy the whole
shop, leather-crafting tools and all. (I heard it said once
that her husband made her promise this on his
deathbed, but who can say for sure.) Last month, on a
below-zero midnight, the building next door burned to
heaps of wreckage and ash, a brick wall separating the
flames from a glass case that holds my family's heirloom.
They called this "luck," that the whole block didn't go
down too. *I call it what's ours is ours.*

Kelly Norman Ellis

Work History

My grandfather had one hand, two degrees, one wife, six daughters, one farm, one house, two stores. He grew corn, peanuts, greens, beets, watermelons, and okra. He raised pigs, cows, a goat, a few chickens, and several horses.

My grandmother had one husband, one house, two stores, two hands. She was pregnant seven times. She had one miscarriage (a boy) and six live births (daughters). She taught school. She tutored children. She washed dishes, washed clothes, and washed her children's hair. She bathed babies, made formula, and changed diapers. She stirred hundreds of pots of grits, greens, and purple hull peas. She baked hundreds of hens, pans of cornbread, and oyster dressing.

My grandfather was a high school social studies and history teacher, football coach, sports referee, farmer, high school principal, and the first Black alderman in Forest, Mississippi.

My grandmother was a wife, a mother, a teacher, and a writer. My grandmother owned hundreds of books. My grandmother read Eudora Welty. My grandmother read Gwendolyn Brooks.

My grandmother drank hot tea (not coffee). She smelled like VO-5 hair oil, the almond scent of Jergens lotion, and Ivory soap. She stayed up after her children went to bed and wrote stories into the night.

My grandfather smelled like Aqua Velva and C. F. Young Pomade. Some days he carried the scent of watermelons and the earth he grew them in. He always smelled like sweat and Mississippi air.

He drank slender cold bottles of Coke-Cola and huge pitchers of ice water. He had one prosthetic hand he wore to school and a silver hook he wore to the fields. He wore a cowboy hat to both.

She wore her hair curly and her dresses tasteful. She wore a single gold wedding band on her left hand.

My grandparents cooked hundreds of hamburgers for hungry football players my grandfather brought to their home after practices. My grandparents taught thousands of Black people.

My grandfather coached hundreds of football and basketball players.

My grandfather registered to vote every year. My grandfather was denied. My grandfather was told he failed the Mississippi Constitution examination. My grandfather taught Mississippi history. The Mississippi State Sovereignty Commission kept a file on my grandfather. My grandfather didn't care.

Every summer for three years, my grandfather took graduate classes outside of Mississippi because Jim Crow would not allow him to study at Ole Miss or Mississippi State.

In 1955, my grandfather received a summer fellowship to study at UCLA. He and my grandmother drove across the country with four little girls. They carried *The Green Book* in the front seat. Jim Crow followed them all the way to Texas. *No Mexicans, No Negros, No dogs.*

My grandmother sat a manual typewriter on the kitchen table in their California apartment and listened to my grandfather's ideas and typed into the night. She crafted paragraphs and inserted commas. Organized his ideas. He talked. She wrote.

My grandparents wrote papers together.

My grandmother wrote poems and stories in her head.

My grandfather received his master's degree in education through the GI Bill and despite Jim Crow.

They owned land. They owned one catfish pond and one barn.

He was born in 1922. They eloped in 1943. A grenade blew up at boot camp in Missouri and took his hand in that same year. He was discharged from the army.

She was born in 1923. They eloped in 1943. A grenade blew off her young husband's hand in boot camp in that same year. She left her freshman year at Lincoln University and tended to her husband.

They returned to Mississippi. My grandfather started college at Tougaloo. My grandmother wanted to be a journalist and travel the world.

My grandmother gave birth to my mother in 1944 on the anniversary of my grandfather's injury. My grandmother was mostly pregnant for seven years.

They owned a café in Tougaloo. My grandfather sold peanuts, Coke-Cola, and hamburgers.

My grandparents uplifted the race.

He taught social studies and Mississippi history. She taught English. He was a football coach. They joined the NAACP. He was the president of the NAACP. Someone set their yard on fire. I don't remember which year.

My grandparents' grocery store opened in 1969 in Forest, Mississippi.

I was five.

My aunts were in college and one was in law school at Ole Miss. They all came home to help stock the store and dust shelves. The auntees gave me my first job stamping prices on canned goods with a handheld silver machine.

My grandparents named the store in honor of their six daughters: Cheryl, Constance, Charlotte, Cynthia, Clarice, and Carolyn: The Six Cees Superette. Mama created their first slogan: "We don't want all the business, just yours." My aunt Clarice put her art major to work and penciled signs for sales and bargains: "Whole Chickens 39 cents a pound!"

My mama and aunts worked the cash registers, mopped and swept floors, bagged raw chickens from the chicken plant, dusted shelves, drank Tabs and ate chips, taught me to give change, counted hundreds of dollars in food stamps, bagged hundreds of groceries, and then slopped pigs, pulled and picked greens, chopped okra, fried corn and pork chops. Braided hair, studied for finals, wrote papers, dated cute guys, got arrested for protesting Jim Crow, married their boyfriends, grew Afros. Graduated from Tougaloo, Jackson State, Millsaps, and Ole Miss.

My grandmother kept a credit box. My grandmother cut cheese, bologna, and hog's headcheese for men in overalls and women in head scarves. If they had no money, she logged what they owed on little receipt pads and stored them in the credit box. My grandmother drew pictures on cotton pillowcases and taught me embroidery stitches. In between customers, she taught me running stitches and French knots. My grandmother smiled when the Choctaw women gifted her necklaces to thank her for her many kindnesses. My grandmother refused to sell beer or Listerine to the old white man who wandered in on weekend nights drunk and stumbling.

My grandmother stood behind the main counter every day (except Christmas) for twenty years handing out change and kindness.

On Saturday nights, men and women filed in and bought Miller High Life and Pabst Blue Ribbon. My grandparents sold them Winston and Salem cigarettes. My grandmother let the teenagers crowd around the Coke-Cola cooler, drink pop, and listen to WOKJ.

My grandparents made a home for Black joy.

My grandparents were freedom fighters.

My grandparents built an office next to the store for my aunt's new law practice.

My grandparents built a home for Black justice.

My grandfather was principal of the Black high school for twenty years. When the Black and white schools merged in the name of integration, the school board appointed my grandfather principal with a white boy all of 28 years old as superintendent to supervise him.

The NAACP sued.

My grandfather retired.

My grandfather ran for alderman of a small city.

My grandmother took me inside the voting booth the day she voted for my grandfather. She said, "See your grandfather's name? Now move the lever." She said, "Now, you have voted for your grandfather."

My grandfather won.

My grandfather barbecued a goat and fed his family and friends to celebrate. My auntees made potato salad and homemade ice cream.

My grandfather developed diabetes.

My grandmother developed cataracts and glaucoma.

My grandfather lost his foot to diabetes.

My grandfather fell and broke his neck.

My grandfather died in 1981.

My grandfather was 58.

My grandmother was depressed. She was 57 years old. My grandmother wrote poems about my grandfather.

My grandmother became a journalist.

My grandmother wrote a column for the *Scott County Times* called "Slaughter News."

My grandmother opened a library named after my grandfather.

My grandmother filled this library with hundreds of books. My grandmother filled the library with books written by Black people.

My grandmother archived slave schedules from plantations and vintage photographs of Black life.

My grandmother was a library.

My grandmother was a museum.

My grandmother taught hundreds of children to read. My grandmother wrote plays about Mary McLeod Bethune and Ida B. Wells.

My grandmother met Alex Haley and traveled to England. My grandmother sent her granddaughters postcards from Stratford-upon-Avon.

My grandmother discussed *Their Eyes Were Watching God* with her granddaughters.

My grandmother had a cancerous tumor in her head.

My grandmother started to go blind. She worried she would not be able to read books or write stories.

I told her she would be like Milton. I said I would read books to her.

My grandmother was 68 years old when she died.

My grandparents were race people.

My grandparents were freedom fighters.

My grandparents are buried next to each other in Tougaloo, Mississippi.

My grandparents are resting places for Black joy.

Kevin Young

Ode to the Hotel Near the Children's Hospital

Praise the restless beds
Praise the beds that do not adjust
    that won't lift the head to feed
    or lower for shots
    or blood
    or raise to watch the tinny TV
Praise the hotel TV that won't quit
    its murmur & holler
Praise the room service
    that doesn't exist
    just the slow delivery to the front desk
    of cooling pizzas
    & brown bags leaky
    greasy & clear
Praise the vending machines
Praise the change
Praise the hot water
& the heat
    or the loud cool
    that helps the helpless sleep.

Praise the front desk
    who knows to wake
    Rm 120 when the hospital rings
Praise the silent phone
Praise the dark drawn
    by thick daytime curtains
    after long nights of waiting,
    awake.

Praise the waiting & then praise the nothing
    that's better than bad news
Praise the wakeup call
    at 6 a.m.
Praise the sleeping in
Praise the card hung on the door
    like a whisper
    lips pressed silent
Praise the stranger's hands
    that change the sweat of sheets
Praise the checking out

Praise the going home
    to beds unmade
    for days
Beds that won't resurrect
    or rise
that lie there like a child should
    sleeping, tubeless

Praise this mess
    that can be left

Luther Hughes

My Mother, My Mother

When I was a child I would run
through the backyard while my father
yanked dandelions, daisies, thistles, crabgrass,
mowed, rearranged the stones around the porch—
the task of men, though I didn't know.
Blushed with cartoons and chocolate milk
one Saturday, I found a bee working
a dandelion for its treasure the way
only God's creatures can, giving
and giving until all that is left
is the act itself—*and there's faith, too,*
my mother used to say in her magnolia lilt.
It comes as it comes—there's a road to follow.
When I swat the bee, I plea in triumph.
My father, knee-drenched in manhood,
grins and his gold tooth glistens a likely tale.
And when the bee stings my ear,
I run to him screaming as my mother
runs outside hearing her only child's voice
peel back the wallpaper. She charms my ear
with kisses. This afternoon, I notice a bee
trapped inside the window as my mother
on the phone tries to still her voice
to say her mother has died. I wonder if he can
taste the sadness, the man on TV tells the other.
The bee is so calm. The room enlists
a fresh haunting, and the doorframe distracts.
To believe her when she says—
as the bouquet of yellow roses on the dresser
bows its head and the angles of my clay bloom
with fire—*it'll be okay*, is my duty as son.
My mother sits in the hospital in San Antonio,
motherless—my mother is now a mother
without the longest love she's ever known.

My mother who used to wake up
before the slap of sunrise with my father
to build new rooftops. My mother who wrote
"I pray you have a great day"
on stupid notes tucked in my lunchbox.
My mother who told the white woman
in Ross to apologize for bumping into me
as I knocked over a rack of pantyhose.
My mother who cried in Sea-Tac airport
as I walked through customs, yes-ing
the woman who asks, Is it his first time
moving from home? My mother who looks
at me with glinted simper when the pastor spouts
"disobedient children." My mother who was told
at a young age she'd never give birth,
barren as she were. My mother, my mother.
What rises inside me, I imagine inside her, although
I've never had a mother leave this earth.
I've never been without love.

IV
Every One of Us: Owned

Steve Scafidi

After a Hard Time

Just getting away from the town enough
to only barely hear the industry of hammers
and engines muted in the distance by
wind in pines and crows chasing a hawk
is essential every day of a man's life.
I am up on the hill behind the cabinet shop
where I work, where, out of money,
I should be working now. It is all hidden
by the tall hay and the pine trees. It is
Sunday, the day most sacred to the half-crazed
and the desperate. Furious for death. I don't
ever want to be furious for death again.
Falling for miles like midnight snow.
Give me the sudden false spring of a Sunday
in February. Give me the honeybee wobbling
through the air stunned with life unexpectedly.
Golden and doomed and going through it.
How have you made it this far my friend?
Honeybee, show me, show me how you do it.

Julia Bouwsma

Etymology of Land

1. ground, soil

    A. May-born, I carry a low grime beneath my fingernails. Lineage swings its pickax

       to the ground. Stroke after stroke, it refuses to lift its head. I come
       from a people ordered to dig their own graves. My first instinct is to flee

    B. to the garden. My first instinct is to close my eyes, tell myself, *This is your bed.*
       Now lie in it. Before this land, my body was my first terrain, a soft yielding to
       dig and blade. Mud that squelches lets anyone in. I did not remember my shape

    C. and so I could not reclaim my shape, my body an emptiness I brought
       with me everywhere. I was numb, without roots, was always making myself
       a geography for someone else. The only alternative

       is to run. How quickly our bodies become the rituals required to leave it—
       a gathering of keys, a slamming of doors.

2. the surface of the earth and all its natural resources

    A. Because I was raised on the old ballads. Because my father's drunken mouth
       sang hills and riverbanks as archetype whiskeyed his teeth, softened

       his bones. Because moonshine shimmers the river white. Because the man
       standing beside his lover on the bank will never escape the circle his fingers
       make as they wrap her throat and tighten.

    B. Turn flesh. Turn moonlight. It's under here somewhere. Turn blood. Turn soil.
       I learned the words to all the songs. Later, to fill in the blank spots,
       I mixed them up, mixed them together.

3. *definite portion of the earth's surface, home region of a person or a people, territory marked by political boundaries*

    A. Auntie insists there's no difference between shit and mud.
       It's all caca to me, she says, but we come from a people not allowed
       to own land. And a grave could be called a home. A skin could be
       called a grave. An archeological excavation site is long enough
       to lie down flat inside, arms crisscrossed over chest.

    B. Consider me a surveyor then. Razor blades my plumb rule.

       The familiars of fence posts are scars. The familiars
       of blood, tendons, nerves are hardpan clay, root rot, grubs.

    C. Consider me cartographer. I was only drawing a map.

    D. Yellow fat under the thigh. I cut. I dug. What you can't forget
       and can't recall, you furrow. Consider me farmer.

4. *the solid part of the surface of the earth*

    A. This *here* then, this wooded hilltop, where I rut myself across the surface

       until the surface ruts me. Where I open and blackfly slicked. Where I all sweat
       and waistband. Where I bend and bend and the earth

       like the open page bends, red and knotted, back. And all our ghosts
       like the earth bend, red and knotted, back.

5. *an open space*

    A. Our meeting place, our confluence: Here we steel ourselves for love
       and everything we love is stolen. Here the labor never ends, our feet
       not the first nor the last. We practice becoming *solid*. We dig
       our spade in, dig our hands in. Sink or claw. Chop then wobble
       our weight against the blade. Hack at the roots. Plant the crop.
       When it blights, spoils, plant it again. Here it doesn't take long

    B. to hit clay. To hit the sticking point. The gray, the hard, the edge
       of memory, the salt taste like skin peeling the runnels
       of our mouths as we work—

6. enclosure, church

    A. What is the opposite of confession? This whole hillside bleeds
       water. I spill at the edges, suffer a loose tongue, but I'm not asking
       for forgiveness. My love tells me he's dry as a well

    B. in summer drought. He chisels and sands the spine of each beam
       for our house, back bent to the rhythm of his hands. He pops another beer,
       creases his mouth shut. I know there's a dark well thrumming beneath
       his organs, artesian. The dog bites the other dog and after staples,
       antibiotics, we assume she's fine. Only two years later do we find it—
       a hard lump. Infection walls itself off

    C. corner by corner, post by post. It becomes our home.

    D. This hardness holds us close.

7. "fallow land"

    A. Lupine, also known as bluebonnet, is poisonous to sheep, cattle, horses, dogs.
       Our neighbor loathes them so I dig his up, replant them in my own yard where
       they wither without water.

    B. Each night it rains a dirge of torn sheets. In dreams I let myself go, wander
       naked as the pocked moon, round as a bloated tick. My fat and hang lead
       the way. I am always running—shame an afterthought

       to the tangle of tongue in hair. A feral singing through the trees.
       The taste in my mouth like a substratum

    C. I wake from, scent of loam still on my teeth.

8. "wasteland"

    A. Story says this is how our hill was born: a girl wandering the woods
       found a soft spot to bury a sorrow. A sorrow swells just as well in hardpan
       or loam. This one grew between rock and bone. Grew like tumor or longing or
       absence. Grew like a child, skull pointed toward the rusted gate. Grew
       like maple roots creeping, like fingers

       reaching, like apple blossoms in a clutch of branch, a silence tucked into another
       silence, flat and wide and hollow as dry rot. This sorrow grows
       until it's just a space where a sorrow used to be—

worms in, worms out. In winter it folds its naked self over itself
until the cabin posts heave and the doors won't open right,
won't close right.

9. In the American English exclamation "land's sakes," land is a euphemism for Lord.

    A. I walk restless until my steps become the road.

    B. Each spring the mud belly-ups a new harvest of trash: bottle of piss, shirt
       sleeve, tarnished silver spoon, old man's face translucent on the delaminated
       film of a lost driver's license. This land is riddled

    C. with the expunged. We all walk on carcass and jawbone, a fist of chewing beetles.
       We all sink our shovels in and slice another cache of dust. This land is abscess
       we refuse to drain. This pus this blood this rock this tooth

    D. it mines us, it erodes us.

    E. Let it. If I'm home it's because I no longer have to carve it

    F. into my flesh.

Crystal Wilkinson

O Tobacco

You are the warm burnt sienna
of my grandfather's skin
soft like ripe leather.

I cannot see you
any other way
but as a farmer's finest crop.
You are a Kentucky tiller's livelihood.

You were school clothes in August.
The turkey at Thanksgiving.
Christmas with all the trimmings.

I close my eyes
see you tall
stately green
lined up in rows.
See sweat seeping
through Granddaddy's shirt
as he fathered you first.

You were protected by him
sometimes even more
than any other thing
that rooted in our earth.

Just like family you were
coddled
cuddled
coaxed
into making him proud.

Spread out for miles
you were the only
pretty thing he knew.

When i think of you
at the edge of winter,
i see you brown, wrinkled
just like Granddaddy's skin.

A ten-year-old me
plays in the shadows
of the stripping room
the wood stove burns
calloused hands twist
through the length
of your leaves.
Granddaddy smiles
nods at me when he
thinks i'm not looking.

You are pretty & braided
lined up in rows
like a room full of
brown girls with skirts
hooped out for dancing.

Marci Calabretta Cancio-Bello

Poem in Furrows

Not like my grandfather's labor, smoking pork
or selling horses, barebacked and bronze.

Nor like digging soil for a handful of lima
beans swaying on the stalk, hard and ready.

But it is work of a kind, the way we rake words
into the light like potatoes, threads at our elbows

dampening into sweat against the ribcage,
bushels behind us full of pearl onions or stones.

James and Tina Mozelle Braziel

Necessary Weight, Necessary Time

Weight

My hands hurt all the time now. I sleep on them in ways that pull my arms ready to strike nails with a hammer, push the bar of a chainsaw through the dark rings of a tree. I get up—can't sleep good like this—tell my hands to relax, and tell myself, "The nails will get driven tomorrow. The firewood will get cut, and we'll be warm in winter." The rest of the night I'm half-dreaming under a moon our skylight shows as a bright nickel in one corner, hours later as a dime above my feet, but the ache won't quit.

My wife, Tina, and I live in a glass cabin we are building by hand in rural Alabama because we don't have money enough to hire someone to do it. Eight years in, what is necessary is what shapes our life.

We purchase drinking water five gallon jugs at a time for our cooler. We haul water for cleaning purposes from the local water authority 250 gallons, 1 ton, at a time in an IBC tote on the back of Ruby, our '98 Dodge truck. Ruby manages somehow to chug up the hill. Then the ton is gravity fed through garden hoses to a second tote that sits on stilts next to our cabin. Takes four hours for it to drain out.

I fill blue plastic jugs, carry them inside, and pour the water into a ceramic jug with a spigot so our hands can be washed, our teeth brushed. The bucket underneath the sink has to be emptied several times a day. I heat water on the stovetop and pour it into a stainless steel basin to wash dishes, and into an old cowboy bathtub so we can be washed. Because even a half-full tub is too heavy to carry outside, I scoop the old water out with a plastic cup. Three weeks later, I'm driving Ruby back to the authority for a refill. So I know the time it takes to haul and carry water. And I know the weight of it, how much is needed to wash hands and clean a body of the dirt and sawdust and sweat of each day.

When I'm in B town and turn the faucet on in a store restroom, or in someone's house, water shoots out so fast, I jump. I try to wash my hands quick to stop it from disappearing. And I wonder about the ones who don't have running water like me. I bet when they turn on a faucet, they jump, too. I bet they turn breathless, anxious because of the rushing and the waste. Tina says, "Inconvenience pushes us to conserve." I tell her, "Convenience leads to neglect," of water and of those who struggle to have enough. Let me ask you, when you turn on a faucet, do you ever think of the weight of water?

Do you ever think about the people who can't get water easily? They're struggling to get enough food, I promise, struggling to find heat and shelter.

At night in my half-dreaming, that weight stays with me. Wherever it lifts into a lightness is where Tina is. The cabin we are building wraps our love around our necessity—we are lucky in that way.

My pop built the house I grew up in in rural Georgia. He put up the barbed wire fence around his farm, all two hundred acres of it, by himself—posts dug, strands of wire pulled. When I was old enough, I helped him with the mending—cows love to wreck fences for the taste of grass on the other side.

In high school I worked in melon fields for the county farmers. It was hot in June and July walking those rows. What I found there was this: Didn't matter my age or yours, didn't matter how much money my parents made or yours made or you made, black or brown or white skin didn't matter because the sun overtook all concerns. It blistered us all the same. Made us all thirsty. The length of a row mattered. Getting to a jug of water at the end of that row mattered. And us working together mattered, picking, tossing, stacking melons to be thrown later to a packer standing in a truck bed who took the melons weighing twenty, thirty, forty pounds made of red water and black seed and sugar. The packer set them on a bed of hay into a perfect green pyramid for market.

I never understood when I stepped outside those fields the hate of every color of skin that wasn't white. And the quick blame in conversations in town assigned to people for what they didn't own. What I found in these prejudices was the disregard, the discounting, the way to not know a person.

But down the rows we knew each other because we counted on each other. There was something about the willingness to do what was not easy—we saw that and respected that. There was something about the time spent laughing as a way of shrugging off the sweat of our labor and the hot of the sun and whatever else was hard in our lives. And there was something about just spending time. The work was in no way pleasant, and the only reason we were out there was to get paid cash at the end of the day, but the act of working made us depend on each other and that made a bond.

My pop is in his eighties, but he still mends fences. I help him when I'm down in Georgia. I am in my fifties. Work has become an ache I can't sleep away. So let me ask you, do you ever dream at night about the work not yet done? Back in the melon fields in June and July, I could not get the sand out of my sleep. Sometimes now the grit shows up with a nickel moon and restlessness. Sometimes the hands of those in the rows I worked with appear with palms rubbed smooth by field dirt to lift and carry me through the heat. Sometimes I carry them. And sometimes it is Tina's hands. They put the next board in place in our cabin. I cover her hands in mine. Then she walks over to the woodstove, starts a fire on this hearth.

Time

When the time clock clamped down, I jumped, feeling a tug on the card stock. I lifted it and ran my finger over the impression 6:28 a.m. left before I slipped the card in a slot with my mom's and my brother's, a slot marked with our last name.

For $3.35 an hour, my brother and I cleaned the clinic, where the doctor treated people without insurance and even if they hadn't paid their last bill. We dusted and straightened magazines in the waiting room filled with Naugahyde furniture patched with electrical tape. We carried trash to a plywood platform out back and scoured examining room sinks and restroom toilets. That was supposed to take up every minute Mom drove the school bus, picked up our classmates, then returned to pick us up. While we sat in our fourth- and fifth-grade classrooms, she worked at the clinic drawing blood. On Tuesdays and Thursdays, she drove to Anniston to get certified as a medical assistant.

Me and my brother were practiced at doing chores, but we hadn't learned how time becomes money. What mattered to us was clocking out, so we could slide down the metal banister that ran beside the gurney ramp and wage rubber-band wars from the enormous supply we found in a cabinet. Peering into the rusty drawers of the 1950s examining tables and imagining bodily things plopping into them mattered to us. I had read *Cheaper by the Dozen* and felt inspired by the father's job as an efficiency expert. Figuring out the fastest way to do things mattered to me too.

Our first checks were so small Mom asked to see our time cards. Then she sat us down to talk. She explained that it was necessary to be thorough and double-check our work even if it took longer. Every additional minute was necessary. Our family needed the money while she was in school. "Ask for more work if you get done quick," she said.

So I asked the doctor and nurse who lived in the apartment attached to the clinic what else I could do. That meant folding mounds of clothes, filmy boxer shorts I'd never encountered before, and polishing row after row of nursing shoes laid out on an examining table. Somehow that time weighed more, took longer than ever.

*

"How much time will it cost you?" asked Dad when I told him I wanted to buy a Swatch watch. To me, a Swatch was a good value because I would wear it every day forever. And it would make everything I wore cool: my cutoffs, dresses my grandmother made, and my culottes, which I spelled *cool-lots* because it meant lots of cool. To Dad, a Swatch was an overpriced bit of plastic.

"Take my broken lawn chair," Dad said. "The way I figure, I could buy a brand-new one that's ready to go for three hours of driving piles while sweating through my jeans. Or for only fifteen minutes of work I can buy a roll of webbing and spend twenty minutes of reweaving the seat myself."

"Time," he warned, "is the real cost. Money is nothing but a middleman put there to fool you."

I didn't think his question fair. Dad made so much more than me in an hour. He pointed out that I didn't pay lot rent for our trailer or a truck payment or insurance or power bills. He could and would have gone on, but I cut him off, knowing what I owed him.

I didn't buy a Swatch. My brother did. He saved up just enough for the smaller one. When his friends laughed at him for sporting the "girl" Swatch, he gave it to me. But it didn't make me or my outfits cool. It didn't "go" with everything. When I did wear it, I became time obsessed. I kept trying to fit in as much as possible before the hour was up. That made me anxious and often late, so I swore off wearing watches altogether. They cost me too much ease.

*

While washing my hands under a restroom faucet, my efficiency fetish kicks into high gear. I look for the paper towels or the hand dryer, figuring out how fast I can get out of there. Intent on defying the stereotype that women take forever, I race men standing in lines for restrooms and Porta Potties. And I win.

Because I'm right-handed, I always reach for the knob on the right, the cold water. I don't even think about using hot. That would mean waiting for the water to warm. But winter mornings, before I can get the woodstove burning hot enough to lift the temperature in our glass cabin above the fifties, I wash my hands in warm water. Water Jim has poured into a pot, heated on the electric stove, then poured into the jug with the spigot. He does all this so my hands won't ache with cold. I marvel at this act of love, at the care and time Jim spends on a simple luxury, one I don't afford myself even when it is much easier, much more efficient, while standing at a faucet.

As that warmth eases me, I wonder about the question of cost. Maybe Dad and I, all of us really, began at the wrong end. How much does it cost to work forty-plus hours a week, often at two or three jobs, and make less than a living wage? How much life, how much well-being, how much potential? How much time should it cost to put a roof over your head? To feed yourself and your children? What is fair?

All I know is work shouldn't cost anyone time to sleep, to dream, the time to care for the ache of another's hands.

Rodrigo Toscano

The Zone

"Panama"
can choose to be
just-Panama
or re-join "Colombia"
in Westphalian 1648
state's sovereignty treaty
legacy modality
or join the Triple Alliance
"Canada" "U.S." "Mexico"
administrative zone
which is a way to say
why "Honduras" now
in this day and age
the region's growing hotter
and hotter crops failing
narcos dominating
new generations which is
a way of saying
"Haiti" at breaking point
won't work as is
folks shriveling there in
zero to scant industry
in need of flotilla
organized and administered
millions out and into
The Zone as with "Guatemala"
sub-administered by
administered "Mexico"
work the pipelines
thousands of aqueducts
water to and fro
like Louisiana rain
to California
Jalisceño blue tequila

to Peoria and Winnipeg
steady work fair work
in The Zone no need
for hideous face tattoos
and special ops
not to mention
failed "Canadian"
nor "American" poets
touting Westphalian
liberal-democratic horizons
cloaked as "democratic socialism"
socialism—is *para*-national
at the end of the day
tribal lands allow pipelines
of water to flow
across vast territories
while new train tracks
get laid down eagerly
not self-driving trucks
belching CO2 and resentment
haulin' veggies and granma
back to town this town
your town's local admin's
intensely responsive
tempered by Northern Zone
general imperatives
takes the wind out of
tiki torch supremacist
carnivals and "anti-racist"
corporate peddlers in
permanent Westphalian
mode of inclusion into
neoliberal tribalism of
the 1% (actually less)
with same cheery tale
again and again
"American" poets
mute servants to system
quilting idealisms
into patchwork of
safe-spaced silos
border enforcement
at the end of the day
genre and expectation like

is this a legit poem
about "Panama"
or "global warming"
or the truculence of
sub-sub Westphalian
fatigued nationalism
pickin' and pokin' at
every nook and cranny
of instrumental nostalgic
Best American ____
Best Canadian ____
Best Mexican ____
empirical mass ornament
gray verses sung to
scratchy music score of
B-movie for *inter*
(Westphalian) nationalism's
finance driven identities
plus sub-sub identities
dragooned by
Anarcho-Tyranny as
that is *the deal*
before the establishment
and careful conducting of
The Zone

Vicente Yépez

Unskilled Labor

—Northwest Arkansas

When the clock hits eight, my parents rise
for the night shift. They stretch sore muscles
and wash their faces before getting dressed.
As I prep the kitchen—gather bread, cheese,
milk for midnight protein shake
lunches—my mother approaches me, hands
extended. Jálame el pulgar, she requests.
My mother—who had been an accountant—
winces as I pull the locked digit into place.
Meanwhile, my father lowers himself
onto the sofa and laces steel-toed boots,
necessary protection
for what once were policemen feet.

Before departing, they do their homework—
I am/You are/He is/She is/
They are/We are/
I am—
Unable to comfort them,
I do what little I can:
I feed them. Coffee and sandwiches,
the only work I can do
without language.

Nandi Comer

"Están Haciendo Trabajos Que Ni Siquiera Los Negros Quieren Hacer"

—President Vicente Fox, Mexico

1.

Ay diós! We are in the computer lab when I hear it.
A voice purr from a mouth, stain the air. I hear it
whine over our keyboard keys like a sad mosquito

come too late in the season. *Ay diós me tienes aquí.*
It is grading time and we teachers crowd
into the school's only lab the way teachers

with grading must. *Me tienes aquí trabajando.*
We all have a load. We all face our computers
and pick at our students' labor.

We check boxes and the room stays so quiet until
Ay diós! me tienes aquí trabajando como un negro.
Her sigh and groan. I hear it.

Me tienes aquí trabajando como un negro.
Others hear it, *me tienes aquí trabajando.*
I don't have to look up to see who said it.

I never have to look to see who's saying.
Como un negro I am always. *Como un negro*
the voice crawls to me. *Como un negro trabajando.*

2.

Ay Nandi, no seas así. Aquí en México no hay racismo porque no hay negros.

3.

You have me working like a slave.
You got me working like a nigger.
Me tienes trabajando como un negro.

Never in my cotton pickin' years.
You alligator bait, you fortune cookie,
you Indian giver. How to let the tongue
do its work down my leather-skinned back?
What offense was not meant, is dealt

is taken. Dig into the weighty work song:
dirt, laundry, landscaping. Widen
a crater for all the sounds:
wetback-gypsy-coon-coolie.
Slack limp words, pitch them
down the center *O*
of job. Let the work fall in.

Ciona Rouse

Yes/And

Too early in the blue hour, the starlings screech their yes/and:
needing to gather but not leaving all together. When I say starlings I

think poet. And I wish sometimes to silence my flutter and remember
this is not a competition. We wear almost the same size memories: I sat on the

porch with my grandma tossing green strings from beans into the wind
our brown hands wet and dripping. You joy-shiver now next to me in that

knowing way when you remember how thick her white laughter sang
along the waves of summer sun—your grandma, shucking tales and beans. Of

course. We know the same soil. We both hold jessamine secrets. But I hate

when you say you don't see my black. As
if you don't see me. What about black makes it

so hard for you to see? No, it's not a competition. Every one of us played.
And owned. In all of our colors. What are we even doing with

all of these little boxes on our doorsteps? Little boxes with the
smile on them? Sometimes I flutter frustrated at our silence about how little

they pay taxes. As we, with our needing and our lament of debtors' calls, wag fingers
at each other. Every one of us: Owned. All in the red. Of Blue Cross. Of Exxon. Of

Amazon. And still when I mention the forest, you recall fondly the
time of complete freedom and a good climb, for which you pine and pine.

While I, weeping, place a hand on their chests, forgiving all the live oak trees.

Marcelo Hernandez Castillo

Wetback

After the first boy called me a wetback,
I opened his mouth and fed him a spoonful of honey.

> *I like the way you say "honey,"* he said.

I made him a necklace out of the bees that have died in my yard.

> How good it must have felt before the small village
> echoed its grief in his throat; before the sirens began ringing.

How fallow their scripture.

Perhaps we were on stage which meant it was a show,
which meant our only definition of a flower was also a flower.

I waved to the crowd
like they taught me,
like a mini-miss something.

> *Thank you.*
> *Thank you.*

Yes, I could have ripped open his throat.
I could have blown him a kiss from the curtain.

> I wanted to dance by myself in a dark room
> filled with the wingless bodies of bees—
>
> to make of this our own Old Testament
> with all the same beheaded kings
> pointing at all the same beheaded prophets.
>
> The same Christ running through every door
> like a man who forgot his child in the car.

But the lights were too bright.
I couldn't hear him because I wasn't on stage.

> I could have been anyone's idea of pity.

How quiet our prophets.
> Let my bare back remind him of every river he's swam in.

Miel and *miel.*

> I pulled the bees off the string
> and cupped them in my palm.

I told him my Spanish name.

There was nothing dry on my body—
The lamps falling over in the dark of me.

Marlanda Dekine

I Am Bound for de Kingdom

My granddaddy Silas was born on the Nightingale plantation
in Plantersville, South Carolina, on riverbanks that loved
three generations of my kin, captured
in a green-tinted photograph, hanging in my daddy's den.

Tonight, my eyes will take each old-world bird from the cropped space,
send them home with their songs and favorite foods.

>   *Look out for me I'm a-coming too*

with rice, okra, hard-boiled eggs, and Lord Calvert.
My daddy says if I get out of my car on Nightingale land,
the folks who own it might shoot. My daddy says,
"Never leave the driveway."

>   *Glory into my soul*

I watch all of my ascendants. Their faces reflecting me
in that photograph. Their eyes are dead
black-eyed Susans.

V
We Shift / We Wield / We Bury

Iliana Rocha

Truck Stop

Like

that afternoon when my basset hound went
missing, Daisy escaped what we all wanted to—
dull end of my father's boot,
lethal floral disc.
I saw her imprint on Highway 59,
careless work of a Chevy's tire,
in the time before I learned what it meant
to care. Blood had reached its claws
& tore through her ribs. As I drove to my first
job, I found her, down the road
from where railroad workers placed orders
for chicken fried steak & okra, gravy smothering
the food with something like glory.
With his numb arm, Johnny scooting
wet dollar bills & change, cloudy
by the intimate exchange of many, many hands,
across the green counter:
I don't know why I eat this shit.

Jean relived her divorce out on her crotch,
scratching the hell
out of its wilderness, while Peggy
lost a Band-Aid somewhere in the lettuce.
When I dropped the order of onion
rings soured by their buttermilk
& flour, the slippery
floors gave them right back. *Here ya*
go! Fresh outta the fryer.
Leslie hid in the trash can so her boyfriend
couldn't find her. I asked the bump in the middle
of Jean's forehead if life would lead me away
from this, from Peggy's swirl of bouffant
& ash the same off-white,

that phone perpetually
ringing inside me: *Hi, yes, I'll take a #1 Combo with a Coke . . .*

In the most humid months, changing the sign
to promote the steak finger basket
for $3.99, mosquitoes took
their aggression out
on me, & all kinds of aggression persisted,
& Peggy's husband continued
calling every thirty minutes, & marriages
were consummated & continued to fail, & I fucked
up another order, & my mouth was still
healing, but nothing else died.

Keith S. Wilson

the fifth note

                    we are young and nothing
has consequence or if you ask

we say nothing, know
only the moment to moment matters

since any tragedy is, to us, a drivable road (joy
is hourly) and so, so

what. to stitches sewn. and boyish jokes, which—
brushing the webs away in old trucks—keep us

in stitches. and we unload.
so what

that the nerves won't reconnect or grow
            (spider legs are those

keeping flies and diamonds of water), and won't
he learn to favor other fingers? and isn't it kind of wild

to be left-handed? romantic
even? aren't all of us half

human half furnace,
                            our insides mean and red,

and didn't he stoop low to lift the case of orange soda
by himself, until some of us, but mostly him, spills

like so across the concrete glistening?
from here

we're split
in two: they'll transport

him, his torn
hand,

to a doctor so long as first he signs a form releasing
the burden of the store (they hold the paper like gossamer

wings or silk or thread
so they'll remain clean) and back in the back,

on the line, which the rest of us never leave,
they talk us through it: the bleach, the stringy legs

of a blue mop to soak the blood and so

tonight some of us will go home having lifted
a purple spider, so what,

so and so will cover this
shift, we will cover that—how even would they know

as we know how inarticulate
we can be when we are not bragging,

with our hands, our hungry buckets of blood and water
(his stitches gleam so much like spider legs. or seem)

Layli Long Soldier

38

Here, the sentence will be respected.

I will compose each sentence with care, by minding what the rules of writing dictate.

For example, all sentences will begin with capital letters.

Likewise, the history of the sentence will be honored by ending each one with appropriate punctuation such as a period or question mark, thus bringing the idea to (momentary) completion.

You may like to know, I do not consider this a "creative piece."

I do not regard this as a poem of great imagination or a work of fiction.

Also, historical events will not be dramatized for an "interesting" read.

Therefore, I feel most responsible to the orderly sentence; conveyor of thought.

That said, I will begin.

You may or may not have heard about the Dakota 38.

If this is the first time you've heard of it, you might wonder, "What is the Dakota 38?"

The Dakota 38 refers to thirty-eight Dakota men who were executed by hanging, under orders from President Abraham Lincoln.

To date, this is the largest "legal" mass execution in US history.

The hanging took place on December 26, 1862—the day after Christmas.

This was the *same week* that President Lincoln signed the Emancipation Proclamation.

In the preceding sentence, I italicize "same week" for emphasis.

There was a movie titled *Lincoln* about the presidency of Abraham Lincoln.

The signing of the Emancipation Proclamation was included in the film *Lincoln;* the hanging of the Dakota 38 was not.

In any case, you might be asking, "Why were thirty-eight Dakota men hung?"

As a side note, the past tense of hang is *hung,* but when referring to the capital punishment of hanging, the correct past tense is *hanged.*

So it's possible that you're asking, "Why were thirty-eight Dakota men hanged?"

They were hanged for the Sioux Uprising.

I want to tell you about the Sioux Uprising, but I don't know where to begin.

I may jump around and details will not unfold in chronological order.

Keep in mind, I am not a historian.

So I will recount facts as best as I can, given limited resources and understanding.

Before Minnesota was a state, the Minnesota region, generally speaking, was the traditional homeland for Dakota, Anishinaabeg, and Ho-Chunk people.

During the 1800s, when the US expanded territory, they "purchased" land from the Dakota people as well as the other tribes.

But another way to understand that sort of "purchase" is: Dakota leaders ceded land to the US government in exchange for money or goods, but most importantly, the safety of their people.

Some say that Dakota leaders did not understand the terms they were entering, or they never would have agreed.

Even others call the entire negotiation "trickery."

But to make whatever-it-was official and binding, the US government drew up an initial treaty.

This treaty was later replaced by another (more convenient) treaty, and then another.

I've had difficulty unraveling the terms of these treaties, given the legal speak and congressional language.

As treaties were abrogated (broken) and new treaties were drafted, one after another, the new treaties often referenced old defunct treaties, and it is a muddy, switchback trail to follow.

Although I often feel lost on this trail, I know I am not alone.

However, as best as I can put the facts together, in 1851, Dakota territory was contained to a twelve-mile by one-hundred-fifty-mile-long strip along the Minnesota River.

But just seven years later, in 1858, the northern portion was ceded (taken) and the southern portion was (conveniently) allotted, which reduced Dakota land to a stark ten-mile tract.

These amended and broken treaties are often referred to as the Minnesota Treaties.

The word *Minnesota* comes from *mni,* which means water, and *sota,* which means turbid.

Synonyms for turbid include muddy, unclear, cloudy, confused, and smoky.

Everything is in the language we use.

For example, a treaty is, essentially, a contract between two sovereign nations.

The US treaties with the Dakota Nation were legal contracts that promised money.

It could be said, this money was payment for the land the Dakota ceded; for living within assigned boundaries (a reservation); and for relinquishing rights to their vast hunting territory which, in turn, made Dakota people dependent on other means to survive: money.

The previous sentence is circular, akin to so many aspects of history.

As you may have guessed by now, the money promised in the turbid treaties did not make it into the hands of Dakota people.

In addition, local government traders would not offer credit to "Indians" to purchase food or goods.

Without money, store credit, or rights to hunt beyond their ten-mile tract of land, Dakota people began to starve.

The Dakota people were starving.

The Dakota people starved.

In the preceding sentence, the word "starved" does not need italics for emphasis.

One should read "The Dakota people starved" as a straightforward and plainly stated fact.

As a result—and without other options but to continue to starve—Dakota people retaliated.

Dakota warriors organized, struck out, and killed settlers and traders.

This revolt is called the Sioux Uprising.

Eventually, the US Cavalry came to Mnisota to confront the Uprising.

More than one thousand Dakota people were sent to prison.

As already mentioned, thirty-eight Dakota men were subsequently hanged.

After the hanging, those one thousand Dakota prisoners were released.

However, as further consequence, what remained of Dakota territory in Mnisota was dissolved (stolen).

The Dakota people had no land to return to.

This means they were exiled.

Homeless, the Dakota people of Mnisota were relocated (forced) onto reservations in South Dakota and Nebraska.

Now, every year, a group called the Dakota 38 + 2 Riders conduct a memorial horse ride from Lower Brule, South Dakota, to Mankato, Mnisota.

The Memorial Riders travel 325 miles on horseback for eighteen days, sometimes through sub-zero blizzards.

They conclude their journey on December 26, the day of the hanging.

Memorials help focus our memory on particular people or events.

Often, memorials come in the forms of plaques, statues, or gravestones.

The memorial for the Dakota 38 is not an object inscribed with words, but an *act*.

Yet, I started this piece because I was interested in writing about grasses.

So, there is one other event to include, although it's not in chronological order and we must backtrack a little.

When the Dakota people were starving, as you may remember, government traders would not extend store credit to "Indians."

One trader named Andrew Myrick is famous for his refusal to provide credit to Dakota people by saying, "If they are hungry, let them eat grass."

There are variations of Myrick's words, but they are all something to that effect.

When settlers and traders were killed during the Sioux Uprising, one of the first to be executed by the Dakota was Andrew Myrick.

When Myrick's body was found,

>   his mouth was stuffed with grass.

I am inclined to call this act by the Dakota warriors a poem.

There's irony in their poem.

There was no text.

"Real" poems do not "really" require words.

I have italicized the previous sentence to indicate inner dialogue, a revealing moment.

But, on second thought, the words "Let them eat grass" click the gears of the poem into place.

So, we could also say, language and word choice are crucial to the poem's work.

Things are circling back again.

Sometimes, when in a circle, if I wish to exit, I must leap.

And let the body   swing.

From the platform.

                    Out

                                        to the grasses.

Justin Bigos

Thumbprint

Call it a delayed reaction,
but this morning, opening a bill
with my thumb and paper-cutting
the flesh right beneath the nail,
I cursed, out loud, the motherfuckers
who had sent it to me—again,
I knew, for I have not paid a single
bill for anything in months. This one,
so intact, so smug in its heft
in my hand, so perfectly off-
white, acid-free, and recyclable,
was not for water or for trash,
not for the minimum interest
due on the plastic card I used
to get my toddler daughter shoes,
not for the half a tank of oil
I could afford last winter—no,
this envelope was from that doctor
in Pittsburgh, over twenty years
ago, on the night I fell down
the oily stairs of a Greek diner,
from the top step to the bottom,
the basement where I washed dishes,
bowls, soup spoons, coffee cups, and knives
for minimum wage, that basement
where I stood back up, bloodied, rapt
with a kind of pain that stewarded
my body through the shift, it's hard
to explain that part but easier
to say: otherwise I'd lose my job.
That doctor I never went to
was now impossibly billing me
for surgery, or just some pain
meds and *a good night's sleep and rest,*

167

that doctor I never went to
because—well, you know by now
what I'm talking about or you don't.
I'm tired of explaining these things.
We all are. And we have a right
to get defensive. To react
when we react. Tearing that paper
open now, tearing it to pieces,
in our plaid bathrobe and slippers,
bleeding from a throbbing red thumb
all over our debts, the kitchen kettle—
yes, there it is—singing in this dark.

Allison Pitinii Davis

The Neighborhood Girls Ask Their Manager for a Raise

—Dairy Queen in Youngstown, Ohio

We're through the way our ponytails
        poke through our visors. We're too old for this,
yet here we are, groveling

        like our daddies did. Raise your eyebrows,
raise your questions: *What of tips?*
        What of payroll? What of under-the-counter

acrobatics? Over-under,
        under-over—when a gym teacher blows a whistle,
who winds up with the money,

        honey? We want the question
on the table. We want it bolted down
        all creature-

feature: a living wage
        for your living dead. Bet your bottom dollar, your B-movie
madness—your hickies-in-a-parked-

        Impala—and we'll raise you your nostalgia. Jerk
your Cold Wars off
        the big screen. Kiss you while the car

is moving. Our blood—it isn't ketchup
        bottles we refill by the hour. We want to talk
tomorrow morning before we head

into the bathroom
to scrub another Saturday off
      our fangs. Ask the floss our canines' curves, curve

this thought around
      your head: if we could afford to quit,
we would.

Craig Santos Perez

A Whole Foods in Hawai'i

I dreamed of you tonight, Wayne Kaumualii Westlake, as I walked down on the sidewalk under plumeria trees with a vog headache looking at the Māhealani moon.

In my need fo' grindz, and hungry fo' modernity, I stumbled into the gentrified lights of Whole Foods, dreaming of your manifestos!

What pineapples and what papayas! Busloads of tourists shopping at night! Bulk aisle full of hippies! Millennials in the kale! Settlers in the Kona coffee! And you, Richard Hamasaki, what were you doing kissing the ripe mangos?

I saw you, Wayne Kaumualii Westlake, broomless, ghostly janitor, sampling the poke in the seafood section and eyeing the smoked fish.

I heard you ask questions of each: Who butchered the mahimahi? What price opah belly? Are you my 'aumakua?

I wandered in and out of the canned goods aisle following you, and followed in my imagination by Sir Spamalot.

In our bourgeois fancy we strolled through the cooked foods section tasting hand-churned cheese, possessing every imported delicacy, and whispering to the cashier, "Go fuck yourself."

Where are we going, Wayne Kaumualii Westlake? The doors of perception close in an hour. Which way does your pakalōlō point tonight?

(I touch your book and dream of our huaka'i in Whole Foods and feel dādā.)

Will we sail all night through Honolulu streets? The coconut trees no have nuts, tarps up for the homeless, we'll both be lonely.

Will we cruise witnessing the ruined empire of America, past pink mopeds in driveways, home to our overpriced apartments?

Ah, dear uncle, Buddhahead, ghostly poetry teacher, what Hawai'i did you have when The Bus quit turning its wheels and you arrived in Waikīkī and stood watching the canoes disappear on the murky waters of the Ala Wai?

Su Hwang

Recyclables

Scavenging: like a gaze of raccoons, they

       Scurry at high noon rummaging

Through black & blue bins—chinks

       Of glass & aluminum distress

The scene lunching on American Express

       corporate accounts. Fingers snapped

At busboys to fetch the manager: *Why can't you*

       Call the police? Those people are ruining

Our ambiance! God forbid bottom feeders

       Seek a share of the light. Synergy

Kombucha, Pacifico, Poland Spring,

       Budweiser, Gatorade, 7-Up:

Crushed under mallet feet by partially

       Masked effigies in pruned polyester

Garb & straw hats. Mute. They hew for

       Pennies with gloved hands slinging

Ballooned satchels of sticky loot over

      Scoliotic backs, exhumed into

Shopping carts that shrill with each haul:

      Wheel askew, bristling against asphalt.

Diane Gilliam

In Line

Last checkout lane at the grocery store, a half-full cart
parked about four feet from the end of the line. No one's there
so I can't tell if it's in line and since I read somewhere
that first-come-first-served is basic to democracy and this is why
people get so bent out of shape about cutting in line,
just in case, I hover back behind.

Then here she comes, from the display of water softener salt pellets
off to the side, forty-pound bags mounded up on a pallet. *Are you in line?*
I ask and she tells me to go ahead, but I'm not in a hurry and not of a mind
to cut in line. By her face I guess she's got eight or ten years on me
though she's dressed much the same: not-tight jeans, tennis shoes,
an ordinary shirt with rolled-up sleeves.

She tilts her head toward the pile of bags—*I used to lift forty pounds*
like it was nothing. We talk about our backs, feet, how a butternut squash
costs more than a steak, and when we get close to our turns, she heads back
to the piled-up bags of salt. I follow, a two-woman carry in mind,
but she says she can do it. A man now in line behind me hurries over, takes
the bag from her without asking, and sets it in the empty end of her cart.

She unloads her groceries, one-handed, one can or box or bag at a time.
Factory line, thirty years, she says. *Wrecked my hands, too.* Knuckles all knotted up,
her fingers a system of strings and pulleys. *I'm only sixty-four.*
How are you today? the young woman at the register asks her.
That's on special, the woman points to the bag. *7.99, regular 14.98.*
She points to the pallet. *Go look at the sticker yourself.*

The computer will know, the cashier says. But no. *Go look at it yourself.*
The woman goes over, squats down and points to the tiny sticker barely visible
on the edge of the pallet, presses her fingertips against the floor to help herself back up.
The cashier doesn't move. *Go look,* she tells her again. Then to me, *They think*
you're lying, they don't see it with their own eyes. The bag boy goes, looks, nods
to the cashier, who scans the bag and the rest of her order. *No* to help out to her car.

On my way out, I push my cart past the woman, stopped a few feet
down from the end of our line, forearms resting on the handle of her cart,
the receipt held up between her fingers, glasses down on her nose,
checking it out with her own two eyes. She doesn't look at me.
She knows what things cost: backs, hands, feet. Too much.
Count on it—always, too much.

Martín Espada

Alabanza
In Praise of Local 100

*For the 43 members of Hotel Employees and Restaurant Employees
Local 100, working at the Windows on the World restaurant, who
lost their lives in the attack on the World Trade Center*

Alabanza. Praise the cook with a shaven head
and a tattoo on his shoulder that said *Oye,*
a blue-eyed Puerto Rican with people from Fajardo,
the harbor of pirates centuries ago.
Praise the lighthouse in Fajardo, candle
glimmering white to worship the dark saint of the sea.
Alabanza. Praise the cook's yellow Pirates cap
worn in the name of Roberto Clemente, his plane
that flamed into the ocean loaded with cans for Nicaragua,
for all the mouths chewing the ash of earthquakes.
Alabanza. Praise the kitchen radio, dial clicked
even before the dial on the oven, so that music and Spanish
rose before bread. Praise the bread. *Alabanza.*

Praise Manhattan from a hundred and seven flights up,
like Atlantis glimpsed through the windows of an ancient aquarium.
Praise the great windows where immigrants from the kitchen
could squint and almost see their world, hear the chant of nations:
Ecuador, México, República Dominicana,
Haiti, Yemen, Ghana, Bangladesh.
Alabanza. Praise the kitchen in the morning,
where the gas burned blue on every stove
and exhaust fans fired their diminutive propellers,
hands cracked eggs with quick thumbs
or sliced open cartons to build an altar of cans.
Alabanza. Praise the busboy's music, the *chime-chime*
of his dishes and silverware in the tub.

Alabanza. Praise the dish-dog, the dishwasher
who worked that morning because another dishwasher
could not stop coughing, or because he needed overtime
to pile the sacks of rice and beans for a family
floating away on some Caribbean island plagued by frogs.
Alabanza. Praise the waitress who heard the radio in the kitchen
and sang to herself about a man gone. *Alabanza.*

After the thunder wilder than thunder,
after the shudder deep in the glass of the great windows,
after the radio stopped singing like a tree full of terrified frogs,
after night burst the dam of day and flooded the kitchen,
for a time the stoves glowed in darkness like the lighthouse in Fajardo,
like a cook's soul. Soul I say, even if the dead cannot tell us
about the bristles of God's beard because God has no face,
soul I say, to name the smoke-beings flung in constellations
across the night sky of this city and cities to come.
Alabanza I say, even if God has no face.

Alabanza. When the war began, from Manhattan and Kabul
two constellations of smoke rose and drifted to each other,
mingling in icy air, and one said with an Afghan tongue:
Teach me to dance. We have no music here.
And the other said with a Spanish tongue:
I will teach you. Music is all we have.

Lauren Whitehead

It Was Already Dangerous

Working the 2–12 shift Driving home in the shiny dark
under the sleepless moon Curling his car around
suburban back roads Almost every day, pushing
drowsily his nice-enough-to-not-get-pulled-over SUV
Iced coffee sugared and milked into cake It was
already dangerous, diabetic as he is, for him to be
smoking all these cigarettes in the empty parking lot,
laughing and missing all these meals, even
while working the 2–12 a.m. shift at the high-end grocery
where the cured meats have their own specified domain
Hanging hocks of pork sliced thin by a woman
in starched whites and a paper hat The grocery
where you build your own six-pack and also where
my dad manages young undereducated smokers
in the business of facing groceries as they come
out of the box You probably haven't wondered
whose hands make known the difference between
scented and unscented garbage bags, which hands
attend the 200-plus flavors of tea in aisle three
of your local You probably pass, unasking,
by the perfected symmetry of toothpastes
and soaps neatly packed, straight-backed like soldiers
But it's my dad, working the near-night shift,
stacking organic frozen pizzas in the cooler, label out
so you don't mistake your vegan for your four-cheese
He is a connoisseur of cabbage, a kale-fluffing man
who knows each condiment by its color-coded brand
And it was already laborious, throwing box after box
off a forklift, hauling pallets of pesto and pasta sauce
It was already heavy but now also all the extra loads
of alcohol, ammonia, bleach, dual-action disinfectant
wipes & toilet paper all the near night, canned meats
and hard cheese and frozen everything He's already 63,
the ideal vintage for an otherwise indiscriminate virus

which lives for days maybe on hard surfaces like
linoleum grocery floors or metal grocery racks or
aluminum soup cans or lipstick-stained wineglasses
haphazardly left on shelves all over his high-end market
by tipsy white women who don't believe in crisis
until it hits their homes It was already hard not to bring
his work home But now it's more dangerous,
this already thankless and unseen and ignorable work
It was too much even before all this impatience,
all this insistence, even before all this aggressive fear
made him miserable, visible, vulnerable, essential

Julie Marie Wade

Food Giant

It was a nice place, as grocery stores go, and I liked the tall windows at the storefront where they painted turkeys for Thanksgiving and snowmen and holly trees in time for Christmas. It was a nice place, so I almost didn't mind accompanying my mother, especially after we got a VCR. Food Giant was the first to rent videos—99 cents for 48 hours—and they sent the tape home in its original cover.

The only way to tell the year is to think back to the movie poster on prominent display—*Cocktail* with Tom Cruise, with a note beneath it, *Coming Soon!* And we were coming soon, and often, and again, pushing our squeaky cart with the crooked wheels, scanning the aisles for canned peas and powdered potatoes. My mother likes Food Giant because it's cheap; I like Food Giant because it's the next best thing to cinema, now that we have a VCR.

But then winter turns the parking lot to slush, breath into thick white clouds—so thick they pass for smoke if you put two fingers together and pretend to drag. My mother says only low-class people smoke cigarettes, then slaps my hand. "We are higher class than that. Stop pantomiming!" she scolds.

Today there are men and women in January coats. They are blocking the doors, shoveling away a light crust of snow, and shouting about oppressive conditions. Some of them I recognize from the checkout line. They have signs they are waving like swords. I stop, but my mother pulls me forward. A woman is yelling her name—*Mrs. Wade! Mrs. Wade!*—but she doesn't respond. The bargains will be better now, now that we are the only customers in the whole wide store, now that the man in suit and tie thanks us and packs our bags. "We haven't had royal treatment like this since Sears." My mother folds up her checkbook and smiles.

Later, I am crying because someone called us traitors, then someone else threw a hard clump of ice against our car. "It isn't a nice place," I say. "It isn't a nice place at all anymore." But my father says I am looking at it all wrong and makes a joke about their little "union sympathizer." He takes me to my grandmother's house, where I am plied with oatmeal cookies and a tall glass of milk, things she has purchased at Food Giant.

"It takes a lot of courage to cross a picket line," Grandma lauds. "We have to support the managers. Why, your father is a manager, and you would want people to support him, too, wouldn't you?"

I look from one to the other: their bright faces, their shining eyes. My father is a manager, like the lonely man with the gold badge who shook my mother's hand and told her he appreciates her business.

"But what about the people outside?" I ask, thinking of the ice rain and the rock salt, strained faces puffing into numb hands.

"They want too much," my father sighs. "It's like they're asking for second helpings."

Which we knew was a sin—my mother had told us. *Greed and gluttony go hand in hand.*

At my desk in dark crayon, I sketch out a letter to Food Giant Management. I write with the full force of misguided righteousness, then illustrate with green trees and golden flowers:

Dear Managers,

Thank you for keeping your store open for us. Thank you for working so hard when others have stopped trying and asked for too much. We are proud to shop here.

Sincerely,

Julie Marie Wade (on behalf of the Wade family)

My mother, beaming, pulls me through the strings of obscenities, the cat's cradle of dirty stares and spit. She marches up to the manager and hands him my letter. "You wrote this?" he asks. "All by yourself?"

I nod, and he shakes my hand with gusto, then reaches for the masking tape. My letter looms large and colorful on the wall, beside the movie posters and the classifieds. "For morale," he says. "To boost morale."

Tom Cruise is still *Coming Soon*, but I have arrived—my new life as an activist, my new vocation as a booster of morale. Soon, it will be my name encased in pink neon, my hair slicked smooth as a movie star's. *Local girl saves Food Giant after workers walk out! Second-grader becomes youngest grocery store manager in history!* Oh, for the big picture that is missing here, for the shame that is soon to follow. Oh, for the girl I once was—pusher of the cart, clutcher of the coupons—shadowing her mother down the lonely aisles.

Bill King

For God So Loved the World He Gave Us Vision

Outside, that is, on TV, the President bellows beside
a helicopter about China and the farmers of America
who are so great they will chop plants into the dirt
instead of harvesting the beans.

Because what farm girl does not dream of becoming
"permanently entwined with both politics and export
markets," with synthetic fertilizers and robots that run
at night when "traditional hand laborers" cannot?

She must know that we no longer have need of humanity—
domestic or imported—or deer that bed down in the fields,
or bees that linger in the golden hem between the fence
and the road each fall.

For God so loved the world he gave us Vision
Technology and rich men with silver tongues
that we may open our eyes to enter
the second time into our mother's womb

and be born again. So let it be known that here
cows breaketh no wind, brook trout sitteth
under the shadow of every stone, and wind bloweth
no hurricanes to destroy the sinners of the world,

who, safe again, may leave their office parks to visit
the coast, pop a beer, and stare out from their beach chairs
at dolphins, and beyond that, the masthead lights
of shrimp boats, bobbing at the end of the world.

Edgar Kunz

Model

In a button-up and jeans I pretend
to pump unleaded into a rented Civic.

In a peacoat and slacks I pretend
to pump premium into a rented Benz.

Inside, I stock the already-stocked
shelves: Sun Chips and Snickers,

jumbo packs of bottled water, Powerade,
Coke. I wear an XXL polo with the excess

safety-pinned behind me, JASON stitched
in thick gold thread above my pocket.

I smile. I laugh without sound.
When this is over, I will be paid

in gas station gift cards to fill up
the car I borrowed to get here.

Meanwhile, customers come and go:
quart of milk, quarter tank, pack of smokes.

Now and then we have to ask the actual
Jason to please stay out of the shot.

VI

This Is My One and Only Life

Victoria Chang

From *Obit*

Memory—died on February 12, 2015. It was a
routine. We'd arrive, the children would give
my mother a hug, leave the room to watch TV,
and I would sit on a small stool ten feet away
from the La-Z-Boy chair I had given her. The
oxygen machine tired and gurgling, my father
pacing in the other room. *Alibaba,* my mother
said. *What?* I asked. *Alibaba,* she repeated, *I
should buy some.* Again and again she asked me
over several weeks as if for the first time. I can
still hear her voice, the shrill accented chorus
of the *A,* the *li,* then *baba,* the same phrase for
father in Chinese. Even as she was dying, she
thought the path to God was money. I wonder
if she heard coins in her dreams, if when God
touched her forehead, His fingertips felt like
gold. I bought her the Alibaba shares in March,
and it's up 40.64%.

Levi Romero

Most Skin Hit Road

the visiting community-activist contingency
comes into her home as invited guests
politely invading her life with
gift baskets of hugs, laughter, and
you're looking great! salutations

their warm blessings filling the room
with wide-open arm offerings of good conversation
and quick-comeback humorous anecdotes
to transport her past nagging thoughts

of next month's mortgage
the leaking faucets
the molding wallboard
the house too big
left over from a bad divorce

leaving her with the two children
to carry on with the domesticities
of this place stayed at too long
longer than what was planned
longer than what was wished for
longer than what *until I'm done with school* might've meant

what would make a man
pick up his life
his personal possessions
what he deems as his most precious belongings
and leave his small children

his name and the shape of their eyes
the blood that runs through their veins
their tender skin, their soft complexion
the color of his own mother's

the resonance of his grandfather's laughter
and musical quality in their voice and pronunciations

more than mere traces of himself
upon their temperament, the slow or fast to decision
the methodical calculation
his impulsive nature and neurotic tendency
for quick resolution

these being his traits
stepping back to check the doorknob
in his final leaving
his girlfriend awaiting his arrival
two states away with tomorrow night's
dinner reservations

we stand in the kitchen
fondling for conversation and dialogue
dipping for some topic interesting enough
to make ourselves appear intelligent, compassionate
and genuinely concerned about world issues
and the plight of all humankind
la frontera, las desaparecidas, los braceros, las maliquidoras
that war, this war, that president, *that president!*

she, an attractive woman, still young
speaking fluently in two languages
her eyes dark and warm as the border sundown
photos taken at different stages of motherhood
on the refrigerator door
the magnet poetry scattered and nonsensical
"most skin hit road"

outside the humidity is heavy as a street blanket
shards of broken glass
on the front porch steps
Juárez's flickering lights in the distance
El Paso trains whistling by
her memories of Laredo

my attention nailed now
to the broken rosary necklace
hanging from a porch column

our own histories
who we are
where we come from

could be reinvented
in the next sentence uttered
the next clever line spoken
the next interjection of humor and
sincere display of pleasantries
masking over the face of a new persona

any further answers to all possible questions
made more believable
than the reality of our own true selves
our own leaking faucets, ragged lawns
oil-stained driveways, two nights of dinner dishes
and yesterday morning's half-filled cereal bowls
on the counter

who has time for the trivial things
when we spend our clichéd lives
adorned with momentary lapses of reason
and an existence busied
by just trying to make tattered ends meet

Phillip B. Williams

January 1, 2018

On Fortune.com, an article about slavery
in Libya prefaced by a Dove commercial:
"I don't want there to be white marks,"
a potential buyer says, inspecting a shirt
while a lively tune plays in the background.
The ad is for an invisible dry spray. I laugh
without meaning to as dozens of migrants'
black faces interrupt the once white screen.
Soap-white words annotate the visual: "sold
in slave markets"—but I am still
thinking of antiperspirants, about the possible
scent of an unseeable product. I am still
laughing. I remain in laughter.
It is my latest state of being, of matter.

Nikky Finney

At War with Ourselves
The Battle of and for the Black Face Boy

On the occasion of the public slaughter of Tamir Rice, by a man sworn to protect and serve who refused to see a Black boy at play

Boys needed to turn swamp and forest into gold!

In 1851 he is stopped and frisked, then packed down
in the ice of iron at the bottom of the *Jesus*, sixteen
hours a day on his back for one hundred ninety-two
days, he has three square feet of space and ten vertical
inches of air, the cat-o'-nine-tails whips away, the jaws
of the speculum oris feed him horse pea mush, by
Amazing Grace, he is alive. Sharks follow the boat,
one hundred times as many black face boys thrown
over as will eventually make the passage. The new world's
leading boy is disposable and in great supply,

Open wide, black face boy, open wide, our brave new world will make great use of you,

Once onshore he is barely breathing. They stand him up
in a vat of palm oil, his black face will be oiled, rubbed,
and watched for hundreds of years. He leaves behind
what privacy is. It is illegal for him to be outside, alone.
A pass or a civil war will be required. On slave row he
is given his three square feet of space and his ten vertical
inches of air, he dreams of the free hips of Black women
that he will never see again, watches how these plantation
men and women walk and move in long ruffled skirts
and top hats, hiding the body whole, keeping secrets,

The beautiful women hauled there with him are opened
wide, the devil is beaten out of his father, his sisters are
blown into the air, like dandelion seed, pussy willows,

weeping willows, black-eyed Susan willows, will grow
dangerously and furiously across the mantle of the land,

Black boy rubbed back alive, rubbed up for luck, rubbed on for sale and battle,

It is the age of cotton futures and iron collars, his master's
initials have been tattooed on his forehead, he hears them
talking through their sweet tea liquor, whispering, *Secession,*
eleven states vote No to the Union and Yes to keeping slaves,
in their fields and beds, Generals Lee, Beauregard, Stonewall
Jackson, Thomas Hunt Morgan, the Confederacy is born!

Slavery now! Slavery tomorrow! Slavery next week! Slavery always! Slavery forever!

The age of enlightenment is over. It is the time of Civil
War Pell-Mell. The battle of Fort Sumter and the delicate
dance of the cakewalk collide. Charleston's cannonballs,
African banjos, and English lutes break the air of one
accord. The age of cotton and cake dance and the birth
of photography take the floor, people curtsy and bow,
then shoot each other in the face. They argue over who
is and is not free. The plentiful black face boy is moved
even more center stage,

Nothing about black face boys is disinteresting to the Confederacy or the Republic,

A joint announcement is made: blackface on a Black boy
henceforth and forever more shall be used to sell tobacco
then toothpaste, break the Union, save the Union, ink
amendments using the Siamese twins *Freedom* and *Equality.*
On parchment after parchment, from South to North, they
agree he will never be much to crow about but they never
take their eyes off him. Everywhere he tries to move the
music of his walk brings down the cannon's fire. They will
forever listen out for him. He is not, nor will ever be, as the
future will soon report, *Forever Free.* What they can sell of
him will be well marked, but nothing will be labeled *leading*
or *man,*

Black face boy, the world is changing fast and we have a great and growing need for you.

His black is the real thing. The kind that won't wash off,
on or off the minstrel stage of war. He wants to stay black

and alive and with the living. He wants to move his black
body into the great fight for freedom, the fight to belong.
He wants to belong to his first life and to the one coming
fast ahead. He knows how to imagine a better life without
a pass, knows he has to keep moving even when he is laid
down in his Black boy hole each night,

Stripped of culture, hulled of history, shucked of language,
religion, he begins to make himself all over again from
scratch, from black and blue memory, he takes flour
from the cotton boll, milk from cow teats, leftover iron
from the hold of the *Jesus*, eggs and gristle from beneath
warm feathers in the coop necessary for flight. The wish-
bone of a frying chicken is pushed down inside his woolly
hair for luck. There has never been one who had to make
his self all over again. For this he should be called Sweet
Son of the New Republic, Sweet Evening Prancing Star
Gazelle, Mr. Boy Liberty, Titanic Sweet Man to Be,
Son of Mr. Swagger and Mr. Dash, the country's new
heartthrob,

Come forward {Nigger} and save your country! The recruitment poster sings out!

The war blooms and black face boys are renamed
Contraband and *The Great Available.* The tall bearded
statesman from Kentucky lines them up on land and sea
but everyone North and South fears replacing the hoe
in his black hand with a musket. Ball's Bluff, the battles
of Whereas and Heretofore are coming, the age of iron
off the neck and in the powder barrel. The black face
boy will step out and fight his way to freedom but he
wonders will history ever truly *carte-de-visite* his courage,

General Lee paints graffiti on a recruitment poster: YOU ARE THE GREAT
DISPOSABLE!

The patent-pending president invents a hoisting machine.
He is fascinated with gadgetry, incendiary weapons, has
a penchant for metaphor and ironclad war ships, aerial
reconnaissance. He fights with breech-loading cannons
and places his black face boys squarely on the flaming
checkerboard of the Republic, hoisting them up and
down, when and where needed,

Repeat after me: We are engaged in a great Civil War. Say it again! Again!

After Big Bethel, and Hoke's Run, Wilmington, Bull
Run, and Camp Wildcat in Kentucky, the horrors of
Andersonville Prison, the massacre at Fort Pillow, six
hundred sets of black arms at rest and high in the
surrendering air are shot down, the battle of and for the
black face boy moves into the heart of history. Feuding
brothers of the new nation believe they fight for honor
and their way of life. Suffering and pride turn everything
red, white, and blue. Back and forth, they win, they lose,
blame each other, whole families burn whole families
down. Four years of muck and misery,

The black face boy is why we are here, the cause of all our trouble,

June 20, 1864, Private William Johnson who walked away
without a pass is now walked to his tree, on an elevation
in plain sight of enemy Confederate troops, the Union
stops the war to hang him by his black face neck. After
all it is a citizens' war, a war of understanding, brother
to brother let us put our great disagreements on hold and
greatly agree on this. A point must be made: Every man
is not equal. Every man does not get to walk his own way.
A twin noose of blue and gray is slipped around his neck.

*Give me your hand, sweet Lord, and help me sail away, help me move my feet off
this bloody land!*

On Navy ships a black face boy is called a *hand*.
The first he hears of this he touches his fingers in the
dark of a sea lit only by moon. Denmark Vesey is standing
starboard holding David Walker's *Appeal*. Out on the
open water eighteen thousand black face boys, and eleven
black face girls, sign up and sail, to fight for freedom.
On deck they learn to walk again without a pass. From port
to port they close their eyes and feel their bodies slipping
away from chains and cotton toward a horizon waiting with
moving picture dreams.

They walk the wet planks in Navy peacoats, flat Navy caps
with red flared scarves stained with teardrops made of
dried whale blood. Many are the formerly enslaved, but
four hundred have whaling tattoos from another time.

From the age of whale blood and black face boys, their
fathers, maritime men, long before this uncivil war, fought
whales for their lamp oil, not Confederates for their cotton,
John Robert Bond, African and Irish, of Liverpool, enlists
in 1863, *to help free the slaves.*

Black faces wearing the knot of the Navy and not the
knot of a noose. Men who had never lain on their backs
chained in the ice of iron, for sixteen hours, one hundred
ninety-two days, now reaching for those who had. Back
on the high seas blue-black literate sailors read from
Philadelphia newspapers to the newly freed black face
boys who could not, whispering into their ear, *Oh yes,
oh yes, one day you will read with me and belong.*

Black face men oiled with whale blood fighting for the Union. Aye, sir!

It is the age of the final count. Under the silk of Alabama
fields, beside the charcoal of Tennessee streams, in the
pushback of Maryland sand, inside the Potomac and the
long brown thigh of the Mississippi, seven hundred fifty
thousand bodies of brothers and ex-slaves lie side by side,
five hundred thousand more hacked by war, now bandaged
wandering hospitals and field stations. There: nineteen black
boy legs lie cut away atop a pile of all-white arms, one teal
blue eye in a jar stares back across at a blind Black boy sitting
alone on the floor, with nowhere else to go or be,

We need you black face boy in war and in peace,

It is the age of electricity and raising the white flag.
General Lee takes out his pen at Appomattox and signs
away the old South's old way of life. The new artificial
light fools the Republic into thinking they have left the
darkness behind. They have not. But there is moonlight
on Black Mary out on the prairie riding her stagecoach,
delivering mail for the country and the nuns, a shotgun
is between her legs and a pipe rocks between her lips.
Soon it will be the age of moving pictures and television
and after that the battle of the newest twins colored
and white atop every Southern water fountain. Black
face boys and girls will march and sing to the drumming
sound of water hoses while walking the Edmund Pettus
Bridge, desiring adoption of the Republic's illegitimate
cousins *Freedom* and *Equality,*

A black face boy will take his last walk on the balcony
of the Lorraine Motel. Two more will step up to the
winner's block in their rightful place, their black gloved
fists rising publicly in private over Mexico City like the
wings of a black eagle in flight. It is the age of plastic
and global warming. The waters of the world are beginning
to churn. Arctic ice will soon have nowhere to go but up.
Dynamite and hate rise with them. Four little girls from
Birmingham will soon watch over the world in their
flaming Sunday school dresses. Black face boys have been
walking from Virginia and Kentucky to the U.S. Patent
Office for one hundred years without notice or applause,
their calculations, clocks, and inventions steadily pushing
the world ahead,

He is still the cause of all our trouble. Still never to be trusted, never innocent.

It is the age of fear and gun shows. The Republic is
deeply worried about the gates of the City. It used to
be clear who could walk in and who could not, who
could stay and work without a pass, who could vote
and who could be president. It used to be easy to tell
who was who. Black face boys know they are the sons
of men just like every other son. They are sons who
want what all sons want, the freedom to invent, the
freedom to be himself, the freedom to have nothing
to prove, the freedom to play more than basketball,
the freedom to not hide his heart or his walk, or his
ways, the freedom to move more than three square
feet of space before being stopped and measured out
his requisite ten inches of black boy air.

What is that in his hands? Why are his arms so long? Why is he still here?

We are in the eighth age of extinction. Scientists are bringing
the woolly mammoth back because every elephant is gone.
The prison-industrial cities rise on the horizon like the new
peculiar. Modern black face boys lie side by side, eighteen
hours a day on concrete like human forks and spoons, living
out their lives in the new ice of new iron. It is the age of not
enough black face boy poets and fresco painters, the age of
electric cars running underground and Aryan robots shooting
black face boys as they sit one car over, their music still too
loud, and shot again if they dare knock on the door of the
Republic, needing help, a dead battery in their arms,

Through the peephole the Republic peeps: dark woolly
hair, woolly dark eyes. All they see is rape and desertion.
Is that a loaded musket between his legs? Flashbacks of
Sherman's triumphant March to the Sea, the bloody
human trenches of Antietam, twenty-three thousand dead
in twelve hours, and Gettysburg's fifty-one thousand,
all because of him,

We stopped the war to hang his grandfather just to make our point. What's his point?

His point is this: It's the age of Wall Street. The Republic
strikes up the band, needing to sell something for
nothing. That's what profit is. The Republic focuses
on the music and muscle of the sons of the first black
face boy. Quickly they separate those who can run and
jump and entertain from those whose poor black faces
must stick to selling toothpaste on the corner.

Look away now, look away. Look away, look away, look away, Dixieland,

It is the age of surrender. The black face boy, still in
great supply, is made into the Republic's new money.
Heads, he stays and entertains us. Tails, he goes to
jail. The black face boys on the corner decide to get
busy reinventing, like their fathers they can only use
their minds and hearts as tools, any materials needed
must be already on their backs, so they loosen and
lower their pants beyond the Republic's legal hip line,
cinching the sailcloth waistband in their left hand
and pushing their Black boy legs out in front, like a
pod of whales moving through any future battlefields.
Singularly, they march in silent refusal of the three
square feet of space and ten vertical inches of air.
This modern, still disposable, black face boy does
not require annual reenactments of cannon fire,
suffering, hangings, or death by neglect to know
what in a democracy is beloved, the freedom to move
free. The black face boy has invented his own way
to get there. The black face boy has reinvented walking.

Bryan Borland

American Interrogation

Each night the moon is larger
the quarterly profits grow   we make
more money than ever before   pay less in taxes
talk of buying new shoes   another jacket
we want to ask the woman who wears a blanket her name
a food she loves   *mashed potatoes and gravy*
we want to make her a plate   we will do this   promise
ourselves   we will do this
the later it gets   how careless movements sting
the cigarettes on the ground   the bodies of bees
the people in our lives
who say things so casually   *do as we do here*
you must protect your own   you must learn the language
[you must
love the ruin]
this is America
          this is America:
flood waters on choking farmland
across industry of incarceration   across industry of illness
whale whose insides are more plastic than whale
          [and you will never forget this]
never forget
the questions begging answers
as if someone were starving
what are we made of
and when did it happen
and where were we when it did

Christopher Soto

Job Opening For Border Patrol Agents

Requirements
- U.S. citizenship
- One year military or police experience
- Ability to read & speak Spanglish

Education
- No college degree required

Duties
- Jugs of rosewater slashed open // Slit in the shape of a frown
- Mexican teenager // Unarmed but shot
- Neon burial grounds // Tumbled through the border
- Money stolen // Medications confiscated // Children crammed into Overcrowded cells
- Toilet paper // Placed on the floor for warmth // One barrier before the Cold cement
- Drugs smuggled by border agents
- Checkpoints opened during the hurricane // Migrants couldn't seek safety Without being detained
- Surveillance cameras shook through // Skinhead passports
- Border communities petroleum // Patrolled desires
- Believed you were good // For doing your job // Even when your job means Harming other people

Salary
- $40K & raise every year // Plus overtime

Benefits
- Infrared scopes for night operations
- Half price on used lungs
- Required to carry a firearm

- Equipped with off-road vehicles // Horses // Watercrafts // Motorcycles // & ATVs
- Stood before the mirror // Throwing rocks

How To Apply
- Send in your name // We promise insomniacs have the best day dreams
- Full-time // Latinos preferred

Patrick Rosal

Pride Fight

The 600-lb. man and the 150-lb. man square off.
And people have paid to see these two
nudge each other, blow by bloody blow
(or by submission), as close as possible to death's
front porch, without sending the other man
through that last gray door.

We're yelling *Fuck him up! Oh Shit! Get out
the way! Smash him!* Though I don't know
who I'm rooting for. I'm an American.

I could want the pale runt
to wreck the dark hulk to his knees
or cheer the giant as the pipsqueak
darts around the ring to dodge his lumbering foe.
The big man is casual,
swipes a paw at the air and misses
when the little man scuttles by,
and this goes on for some time,
the crowd jeering no one in particular.

We know, deep in our bodies, just about anything
is grotesque if you make it large enough. Science says,
in nature, all forms fail when you multiply them by scale.

And in this near-death match, I wonder
if what we're yelling at isn't a behemoth's
bullrush toward this sack of taut
scrawn, the farthest margins
of all the gruesome multitudes each of us contains—
on one end, all that is puny, a fragile
and fleeting thrash of flesh,
on the other, everything humongous and terrible

(as if we could measure every catastrophe and rapture
according to this exponential order).

Dear reader, perhaps, if you're like me,
you're asking, *Yes, yes,*
but who wins? and I'll tell you: it is the big man
who catches the little man charging in.

The big man falls, full weight,
and smothers his rival, whose face is smooshed
against a massive calf. Though the little man flaps
and squirms, turns red, he manages
from the bottom, with both *his* legs,
to take hold of the big man's leg. The smaller man,
struggling, tucks the one enormous foot in his armpit,
and, with the might of every buck and a half of muscle
in his body, arches his back and, vise-like, squeezes.

If we thought the big man had but one
stoic face for the world,
he shows us at least one other,
and it is pain.

The big man, sweaty and exhausted,
his ankle about to snap,
taps out.
No one in or out of the ring
exults. We are the ones
who can't move.
We fall into a moment of precise silence,
as if we can't believe our eyes,
as if we've just witnessed two men become
exactly the size of ourselves.

Ross Gay

Bull Dragged from Arena

which we only barely noticed
for the toreador's gilded strut
beneath the stadium's swoon, hat
in hand, the occasional rose twisting
through the air to his feet, dragged
limp and drooling by horses
adorned with ribbons
and bells.

Adrian Matejka

Somebody Else Sold the World

Hunger is an antagonist.
—Ben Okri

Outside, the antagonists
are wet with flag colors
& sycophancy & I'm alone

in the front room again
like it's 1982 again when
the power got cut off

& the neighbors brawled
like sullen countries over
the demarcation of kitchen

table & china hutch. Another
revolution breaking in half,
another slim-ringed alliance

snapped under the weight
of lost referendums. Where did
their long-stemmed love go?

Even now, I'm sitting in
the window seat in the year
of cottonmouth & disaffection

as white people goose-step
masklessly & the antagonists
imagine new ways to dismantle

poor people. Sitting, running,
dreaming, coughing, seeming:
cuffs for all of them. Bullets,

too, glinting in perpetual
velocity. To be poor is to always
be blamed for your already

busted happenstance. There's
no changing that American
tradition now, not even during

a pandemic. Meanwhile,
the antagonists boat out
to their islands of isolation

& repose. Anything they need
is essential, while the rest of us
stay in place like furniture.

Jacob Shores-Argüello

Behind You

12. Behind You

11. Because some jobs you just can't leave

1. Ten years since
I've worked
in a restaurant for ten years.

10. Because rent.
   Because of running out of time.
        Because of
making
due.

2. Dish pits, bus tubs and prep.
        Kitchens sparkling
with char and sweat.

9. *Behind you.*
Restaurants, the architecture
   of my
   anxieties.

3. After work
   we'd drink a beer
for every table we'd served
   and we'd
   sink,
        sink.

8. *Behind you,* I'll say,
   running my
        trays.

4. *Well at least you don't
   have to take
   your job home with you,*
a friend said.

7. I don't know what you see
   when you die
in your sleep. But I think I'll be
in a crowded kitchen,
   trying to get through.

5. But it's been 10 years,
and in my dreams I'm still
clocking in late
   for dinner shifts.

6. For slow Mondays where you owe
   the restaurant
      more than you make.
   For $2 and a quarter an hour.

Dorianne Laux

Waitress

When I was young and had to rise at 5 a.m.
I did not look at the lamplight slicing
through the blinds and say: Once again
I have survived the night. I did not raise
my two hands to my face and whisper:
This is the miracle of my flesh. I walked
toward the cold water waiting to be released
and turned the tap so I could listen to it
thrash through the rusted pipes.
I cupped my palms and thought of nothing.

I dressed in my blue uniform and went to work.
I served the public, looked down on its
balding skulls, the knitted shawls draped
over its cancerous shoulders, and took its orders,
wrote *up* or *easy* or *scrambled* or *poached*
in the yellow pad's margins and stabbed it through
the tip of the fry cook's deadly planchette.

Those days I barely had a pulse. The manager
had vodka for breakfast, the busboys hid behind
the bleach boxes from the immigration cops,
and the head waitress took ten percent
of our tips and stuffed them in her pocket
with her cigarettes and lipstick. My feet
hurt. I balanced the meatloaf-laden trays.
Even the tips of my fingers ached.

I thought of nothing except sleep, a TV set's
flickering cathode gleam washing over me,
baptizing my greasy body in its watery light.
And money, slipping the tassel of my coin purse
aside, opening the silver clasp, staring deep
into that dark sacrificial abyss.

What can I say about that time, those years
I leaned over the rickety balcony on my break
smoking my last saved butt?
It was sheer bad luck when I picked up
the glass coffee pot and spun around
to pour another cup. All I could think
as it shattered was how it was the same size
and shape as the customer's head. And this is why
I don't believe in accidents, the grainy dregs
running like sludge down his thin tie
and pin-stripe shirt like they were channels
riven for just this purpose.

It wasn't my fault. I know that. But what, really,
was the hurry? I dabbed at his belly with a napkin.
He didn't have a cut on him (physics) and only
his earlobe was burned. But my last day there
was the first day I looked up as I walked, the trees
shimmering green lanterns under the Prussian blue
particulate sky, sun streaming between my fingers
as I waved at the bus, running, breathing hard, thinking:
This is the grand phenomenon of my body. This thirst
is mine. This is my one and only life.

Silas House

A Crowded Table

I first knew the truth about our neighbor Michael when he was nearly beaten to death. He was thrown over a cliff behind our trailer and his cries for help awoke me in the blue hour, when the sun had not risen but the birds had started morning prayers.

After I woke everyone, we stood on the high bank together until they, too, heard his guttural moans. My father hustled down to pull Michael up through the tangled briars toward where we had all gathered—my mother, along with my aunt and first cousin, Ann, who lived in a trailer right next to ours.

Michael leaned, weak and addled, against my father as they struggled to us, his head down. Then the teenager raised his face and all of us could see his two blackened eyes, the deep gash across his right cheekbone, his badly busted lip. But we could not see the bruises beneath his shirt where they had kicked and punched him while they called him a faggot. When Michael saw Ann, his best friend since childhood, he collapsed in tears. My father turned away, ashamed to see the young man weep.

My mother and aunt went into action. "I'll make some biscuits," my mother said, cinching the belt around her housecoat. My aunt took a hard draw on her Winston Light and marched inside to start sausage for the gravy. After my father had done his best first aid on Michael, we sat at the round table in the small kitchen of my aunt's trailer and ate together. Cathead biscuits, gravy, and sausage, fried eggs, fried apples, and fried potatoes. My aunt and mother, true to our culture in southeastern Kentucky, never cooked a small meal. The silver sound of forks replaced the raucous conversation that usually sang out at our table.

That night at supper, I realized that my parents knew why Michael had been beaten. Because, my father said, he was "a Queer," "a sissy." My parents had most of it figured out, and Ann would fill in the details later: The boys had come up on Michael when he was walking home. They had beaten him mercilessly and then thrown him over the bank right behind his best friend's home. My mother said that she loved Michael and hated to see him treated like that, but he needed to learn "to act like the other boys." They likely figured their six-year-old wouldn't know what any of this meant. But I did. In just a few years, these words and phrases would come to identify me.

By the time I was ten, my father, uncles, cousins, and classmates regularly called me a sissy, too. Even my phys-ed teacher—a miserable, track-suited woman whom I now suspect was closeted herself—called me this height-of-all-insults in front of the entire class. What could be worse than for a boy to act like a girl? I walked like a sissy, threw a ball like a sissy, sat like a sissy. I liked to read, which was sissified. I loved to dance and refused to squirrel hunt. I wanted to be in the kitchen, washing dishes and helping my mother and aunt cook. All sissified. That word was a brand that burned deep into my skin.

The first person to release me from all this was my aunt, Sis. She was also a grand-mother, a second mother, a protector who spoiled me. She let me cry when I needed to. Sis was a melancholy person who had a good cry every few days and swore by them. "I've got them old blues again," she'd say, dotting a pink Kleenex to her eyes. "Hand me my cigarettes."

When I asked to help in the kitchen, Sis didn't turn me away. She taught me to fry eggs, string green beans, peel potatoes. "Always eat one raw slice for luck," she said.

Sis showed me how to fix the two most important things of all: biscuits and corn-bread. She told me that bacon grease and buttermilk make just about everything better. Sis and I would sometimes sing and dance to records in the kitchen. She'd shuffle her feet to Bob Seger or Prince or Loretta Lynn as she peeled potatoes, a cigarette clenched between her teeth. One time I noticed there were tears in her eyes as we danced. She turned away so I couldn't see. Perhaps she had already figured out how much I was like Michael and how, someday, I might face the same violence for simply being who I am.

Recently the Highwomen put out a song called "Crowded Table." The chorus goes, in part, "I want a house with a crowded table / And a place by the fire for everyone."

My family always believed in the concept of the crowded table.

Won't you eat with us?
The more the merrier.
Now hush, there's plenty.
Y'all come on and eat.
Say the blessing.

Throughout my childhood, especially in summertime, we were always getting together to eat at our house or my aunt's, the two centers of activity in our large family.

White half-runners cooked with salt pork and new potatoes, freshly pulled green onions, tomatoes so red and ripe the sight of them made my mouth water, peeled slices of cucumber, corn on the cob (called "rosheneers" in my family—a distortion of the words "roasting ears"), cabbage fried in a cast-iron skillet with lard, salt, a lot of pepper.

And cornbread. Always cornbread, the queen of every meal.

For dessert, blackberry dumplings or banana pudding or cherry cobbler. Perhaps a Better than Church cake, pineapple upside-down cake, or Pig-Eatin' cake. Sometimes there was cold watermelon or cantaloupe ("mush-melon," in my family's parlance), always raised in my daddy's garden and heavily salted.

Friends attended these feasts as well as family. They were usually folks who did not have much family to speak of, or had been turned away by their own. People like Michael, whose father never stopped taunting him for how sissified he was.

To hear my family's pedigree—poor to working class, Appalachian, white, evangel-ical, all self-identifying hillbillies, some self-identifying rednecks, most staunch Repub-licans—a lot of people would be surprised to see who gathered at their tables. People of different orientations, gender identities, races, ethnicities, cultures, beliefs, and sensibilities have marveled at the crispness of my aunt's fried chicken, the miraculous density found in my mother's chicken-and-dumplings, the balance of crunch and softness that distinguishes her buttermilk biscuits.

But here is the part I have dreaded telling you.

While my parents and my aunt always welcomed guests to the table, I am sure they would not have readily set a place for Michael if he had insisted on bringing a boyfriend. They would not have been so keen on pulling out extra chairs for the many people of different religions and cultures who have joined us if those folks had talked too much about worshipping different gods or no gods at all. Any conversation about Black lives mattering or a grandchild complaining about deadnaming—the hurtful act of calling a Trans person by their former name—would have been shut down immediately. They were always fine with people joining in, so long as those people were quietly different.

Throughout my childhood, I witnessed tremendous homophobia from both of my parents. My aunt Sis, so open-minded and loving to me, was quick to allow casual racism to rear its head in disgusting language. This habit led to the only true arguments she and I ever had. Many of my cousins who have welcomed so many different kinds of people into our family gatherings are vehemently anti-immigrant and proud to openly condemn anyone who protests, whether it be for women's rights or racial equality. The sharpest blade of my life has been this dilemma: How to reconcile the fact that people I love, and who love me, possess such hatefulness, often defended by Scripture.

I still don't have the answer, but I do have hope. Here's why.

There is no monolithic Southern family. Mine is the one I know best, and I have witnessed great change occur within us. My parents, who once chatted at suppertime about rounding up and forcing all gay folks onto an island, now welcome my husband and me to their table as a couple. They buy us joint Christmas presents, go on vacation with us, and refer to us as a coupled entity: y'all. They support and adore our son, their grandchild who has transitioned to male over the last couple of years. Sometimes when we are at the lake or dining together in a restaurant, I stop to marvel that we are all out together, my parents laughing and unafraid of how people might see us.

Over the past decade, my parents reluctantly began an anguished self-examination. They started to listen. They laid down their pride. This is the way forward for the South, for all of us. To listen. To possess humility. To look at ourselves. And ultimately to change. The future I imagine includes everyone who is willing to love. To gather all at a crowded table. And it includes letting the hate-filled ones know that they will always be welcome—but only if they get themselves sorted.

I can go on loving them, but it will be a quiet love—because there is a thin line between grace and enabling. I can sit at a table with those whose opinions differ from mine. I will sit at the table with anyone who is willing to be open-hearted. But I will no longer subject myself to filling my plate beside those who actively endanger the lives of others, who vote to take rights away from women and LGBTQ people, who refuse to admit that they, too, must work to help heal the wound of racism in our country. I can no longer pour glasses of sweet tea for those who believe the environment doesn't matter, that immigrant lives are inferior, who wrongly insist there is already justice for all.

Over the past few years I have had to disrupt too many family gatherings by calling out my cousins or others. When they spout their disgust for differences, I'm considered the bad guy for defending myself and others. They lean into each other, laughing, and tell me I'm too serious, that I've allowed politics to divide our family. Once again, I'm just the sissy who thinks too much. Once again, I'm left to simply be thankful that at least my parents have been willing to do the work of self-examination.

Earlier this year, I saw Michael for the first time in decades. He had moved to Florida when I was a teenager. A cousin of mine passed away, and Michael came back home to pay his respects. Not much has changed for him. He never really came out and has never had a public gay relationship. Sometimes a place and a people do damage that can't be repaired. Michael has moved through his entire life afraid that if he isn't quiet about who he is, then he'll be beaten again. Negating and shunning have left their scars, too.

After the funeral we went back to a family member's house, where a local church had prepared a feast for the mourners. Michael and I piled our plates with ham, fried corn, hashbrown casserole, sweet potato casserole, and macaroni salad. We sat together at one of the long tables on the porch. I asked if he ever missed home. "I never thought I would," he said. "I thought I'd never look back. But I have, every day." All these years later, and he still wanted to be accepted in the South where he had grown up. I do, too, but so far, I've only found that acceptance at my parents' table. There's a small county-issued sign where I grew up: Hometown of Silas House, Author. A few years ago someone spray-painted FAG across it. My father took down the sign, scrubbed the paint away, and put it back up. There are few things that have broken my heart more than this image of him.

My mother came to sit with us. She ran her hand down Michael's arm, and there was an apology on her face. Before long, my husband and my father joined us. And we ate together.

I believe in forgiveness and giving grace. I do not believe in offering myself up for a beating, whether physical or spiritual. To set a welcoming table in a truly New South, we must actively work to nurture others and aim toward justice together, for everyone who is being oppressed and belittled. We must listen. The South of my dreams is a crowded table of many different colors and accents. Stacked on the table are platters full of the food I grew up with and delicacies I have never known before. My husband and I will be treated like everyone else. My cousins will be there. Their hearts and minds will have opened up to new songs and new dances. Everyone won't think the same way, but they will all bring love, first and foremost. That's the table where I want to break cornbread together.

Bless this food.
Love your neighbor.
Amen.
Pass the butter.

Alice Driver

Que me manden a matar/
If They Send Someone to Kill Me

Yo pienso que tengo todo el derecho
porque mi esposo,
él, él entró bien a trabajar allí.
— Angelina Pacheco

Angelina, recently widowed, didn't know the name of her lawyer. *Yo de abogado ni nada.* It was early June 2021, and she was making fish pupusas as her son Juan Alberto, twenty-seven and undocumented, watched. When I drove the mountain roads from Oark to Springdale, Arkansas, that Sunday afternoon—roughly sixty miles that takes an hour and a half—I did not know if Angelina would be home. She often didn't have money to cover her phone bill, so the only way to talk to her was to show up at her house. To arrive at her house, I had to drive down Don Tyson Parkway, past churches, schools, libraries, and NGOs funded by Tyson Foods.

When I parked, I saw her husband Plácido's green car in the driveway, abandoned since his death because Angelina didn't know how to drive. As I walked up to the door, stray cats ran out of the rosebushes to greet me, and I spied a pile of kittens, eyes still closed, in the shade of the bushes. I knocked several times, put my ear up to the door, and then sat on the stoop with the cats. Minutes passed, and then the door slowly opened and Juan Alberto, face weary with sleep, peered out.

Angelina and Juan Alberto talked about the anniversary of Plácido's death, which they wanted to honor on July 2—the day he died of COVID-19. Juan Alberto shared his last memory of his father, Plácido, which involved plans to plant tomatoes. He opened the back door and pointed to where the tomatoes grew after his father's death. Juan Alberto remembered the moment his father, after testing positive for COVID-19, predicted his own death: *Ya no me van a volver a ver, ay, cuidas a tu mamá.* Back in the kitchen, Angelina said she knew the lawyer wasn't in Arkansas because no Arkansas lawyer would sue Tyson, a company that, in all but name, runs the state financially and politically. *Allí se infectó en la Tyson.* Angelina said she thought the lawyer lived in Texas. Somewhere in her house—a small, crumbling brick structure—she had the contract. *Ay, es duro quedarte uno solo.*

She looked at a calendar on the wall as she formed the pupusa dough and saw that July 2 fell on a Friday. Instead of visiting her husband's grave or holding a mass in his honor at church, she would be at work processing chicken at Simmons Foods in Siloam Springs. She pulled up her skirt and showed me her swollen leg. She didn't know what was wrong but said she would continue to work until she could go to the doctor and find out.

She covered the pupusas and walked out of the kitchen, down the dark hallway, and into the bedroom she had shared with Plácido. She emerged with a large plastic Ziploc bag full of papers. She can't read, so she handed it to me. Among the documents I found a contract in Spanish with the name Dicello Levitz Gutzler listed at the top. According to the address on the contract, the law office was in Ohio. I relayed that information to Angelina. She doesn't speak English, so it was good that the legal team had provided her with a copy of the contract in Spanish. However, she is also illiterate, which is why she couldn't consult the contract to find the name and location of the law office representing her as the lead plaintiff in a class-action lawsuit against Tyson Foods. The first paragraph of the document explained that the law firm was bringing a class-action lawsuit against Tyson Foods "based on Tyson poorly managing the response to the COVID-19 pandemic." Los de Tyson bien saben ellos que mi esposo allí se enfermó.

Angelina talked about Plácido as she took pieces of a whole fish she had cut up, including the head, and put them in the pupusas. "My husband began work there healthy. Then his lungs were affected by the ammonia [chemical accident]." She remembered that on most nights after the 2011 accident, he would wake her up and ask her to rub his back. Tearing up, she shared that he had often told her, "I can't take the pain." After the chemical accident, doctors and nurses at Tyson, part of the company's internal medical system, told Plácido that he was healthy. En la noche, cuando venía de trabajar, me decía levántate vieja, ven sobarme la espalda. Ya no aguanto, me decía. Vieras cómo me duele. However, he had trouble breathing, was in constant pain, and developed a cough that got worse year by year.

Angelina explained the evolution of the lawsuit and her initial conversation with Magaly Licolli, cofounder of the workers' rights organization Venceremos. "Magaly came to tell me [about the lawsuit] and to coordinate, but I told her, well, I don't know anything. I don't know any lawyers."

"What Venceremos wants to do is grow the consciousness that there is no need to exploit workers to have profits," Magaly explained. "You know, there is no need to kill workers in order to have profits or earnings." Based on her work organizing poultry processing workers in Arkansas, Magaly knew Plácido's case well.

Angelina often said, "Plácido would be alive if it weren't for Tyson," and she wanted to seek justice for her husband's death. When a representative from the law firm came to Arkansas in the summer of 2021, Angelina met with him. He told her that Plácido's case was the strongest, given that doctors not affiliated with Tyson had documented his condition for years and had mentioned the company's role in his health issues in their medical notes. El caso más fuerte es el suyo y me lo dijo en inglés.

The doctors and nurses who worked for Tyson would play a role in the spread of COVID-19. According to Tyson employees, some of whom recorded their conversations, they were urged to return to work even after testing positive for COVID-19 if they didn't exhibit symptoms. Others reported being denied COVID-19 testing, despite being directly exposed to the virus by coworkers. Tyson has a high degree of control over its workers' lives. They are prevented from seeking outside medical and legal opinions by long work hours, low pay, and the constant threat of being fired. Like Angelina, many of them don't speak English, have little or no education, are illiterate, are undocumented, or have an unclear legal status. Despite Plácido's ongoing medical issues, Angelina said the medical staff at Tyson nunca le dieron una contestación que era lo que tenía. These workers rarely question their employer, even when their lives hang in the balance.

As she served the pupusa containing the fish head to her son, "his favorite," she talked about how almost everyone in the family got COVID-19 from Plácido. "You feel miserable, tired," she said, recalling her time in the hospital. "That sickness is very sad."

Before leaving, I asked Angelina if she was afraid to sue Tyson and put her name on the class-action lawsuit. She looked at me and said, "If they send someone to kill me, well, I tell myself that I've already lived long enough." Digo yo, me llega a pasar algo, pienso yo en mi pensamiento, me llega a pasar algo por haciendo esto, digo yo que me manden a matar, a ver qué digo yo en mi pensamiento, pero luego, pues, digo y al cabo ya viví bastante. In a state run by Tyson Foods, where the local media serve as little more than the company's public relations branch, her statement didn't strike me as far-fetched. She knew her opponent and was ready to lay everything on the line for justice.

As I was leaving, Angelina asked if I could call the doctor to find out the time of her appointment, since nobody at the doctor's office spoke Spanish and she and her son didn't speak English. Despite Tyson's employing primarily immigrants and refugees, the state and its residents have done little to provide services in other languages, even one as basic as Spanish. The appointment was scheduled for a Tuesday, and since Juan Alberto had to work and Angelina didn't drive, she had no ride. I told her I could take her to the appointment.

When I arrived at Angelina's house to take her to the doctor, she told me she had some medical documents of Plácido's to share with me. I thought I would drop her off at the clinic, but nobody there spoke Spanish, so I stayed to help Angelina fill out forms. As we waited, Angelina tried to convince me to take her to a casino in Siloam Springs afterward. She and Plácido had gone there together. She said they would never make a living wage processing chicken, but at least at the casino they sometimes won some money.

Angelina remembered that on days when Plácido was in pain and thought everyone else had left the house, he would sit in the bathroom and cry. A veces estaba él llorando solo y el lloraba y pensaba que no había nadie. A veces cuando me iba a trabajar ahí estaba llorando en el baño.

When we returned to her house, Angelina placed a manila envelope containing 385 pages of Plácido's medical records on her kitchen table among the bags of limes and boxes of ripe mangos she had purchased at the Mexican corner store. She thought she might have more medical papers in the bedroom and asked me to follow her as she looked for them. Entering, she pointed to a wooden crate beside the mattress, an altar to honor Plácido. On top of the crate, she had arranged a photo of him with a grandchild, a handful of dried flowers, and three cups that she explained were "coffee, water, and tequila." She smiled as she noted, "Look, he is drinking the coffee!"

Angelina told me about her life. She had been visited by three ghosts, she said, including Plácido. Some nights, she felt her husband beside her in bed. She grew up in rural El Salvador and began working when she was just a child. She didn't attend school, which was typical, she said, "especially [for] women—it is an issue—they never had the opportunity to study." She had twelve siblings and described her childhood as one of "sad poverty." Her father was physically abusive—he hit her—and because of that she left home at thirteen. That year she met a thirty-year-old who got her pregnant. Over time, she would tell me about the other two ghosts who had visited her.

I read through notes from Plácido's doctors that mentioned Tyson. According to Angelina, Plácido had once told his supervisor at Tyson that the venom of the ammonia lived inside of him and was the reason why he was fucked. Yo estoy bien jodido, por ese veneno que está allá adentro. A record dated June 4, 2020, by Dr. Elizabeth Haley noted that Plácido had arrived complaining of shortness of breath. "He has multiple sick contacts at work with COVID-19. He has general malaise. No nausea, vomiting, diarrhea. He works at Tyson Berry Street plant." Plácido's wife, son, and other family members who were familiar with his breathing issues didn't think he had COVID-19, and they had been caring for him and in close contact. On June 6, 2020, Plácido returned to Mercy Hospital. Dr. Samuel Hunter noted that he had a "history of exposure to ammonia fumes" and wrote, "He notably works at Tyson Berry Street Plant. He separates pieces of chicken at work, notes around 6 people have been sick, has had possible COVID exposure." Unlike many workers trapped in Tyson's internal medical system, Plácido visited outside doctors and documented the health issues caused by the Tyson chemical accident and the work environment during the pandemic. Doctors noted that he had potentially been exposed to COVID-19 by coworkers. Although Tyson never officially recognized Plácido's medical condition nor provided workers' compensation for the injuries resulting from the 2011 chemical accident at the Tyson in Springdale, those issues had been documented and would likely come back to haunt the company in court.

Angelina felt at once alone and accompanied as she sought justice for Plácido. Era el espíritu de él porque yo lo siento como un fantasma. He visited her as a spirit, as a ghost, and together, from the world of the living and the world of the dead, they moved forward on the strength of their truth.

VII
Something Necessary to Give

Len Lawson

Work Is

—with respect to Phillip Levine

Work is
standing outside to shake loose the dawn
with brown paper bag of lunch in one hand
and cigarette lamp to light the world in the other
watching both lanes of highway in front of home
for the ride that will carry you into the jaws of the factory

Work is
standing outside on breaks in a chanting circle
heaving plumes of burnt offerings from cigarettes
while you and your cohorts discuss babies and
mamas and baby mamas and baby mamas' mamas
hoping to pry open the jaws of the factory
for overtime to save them all

Work is
the blackened cracked lips
mangled spine
beleaguered eyes you gave
for decades to fill the belly of the factory
The gray hair
creaky joints
hip replacement
The caravan of prescriptions lining your coffee table
from exposure to asbestos
Pill box labeled with days of the week
Days you remember awaking at godly hours to serve
as priests and priestesses to the heavenly host of some
overseas company misspelling your name on pay stubs

Cathleen Chambless

Lyft Asks Drivers to Share an Inspiring New Year's Eve Story, Miami 2019

Wynwood infests Overtown,
pink high heels, Prada bags, Becky's,
tons of *lyke omg selfies!*
I try to explain to teenage passengers,
whose fathers invest in Wynwood,
No, it is not making the neighborhood better.
Meanwhile, Downtown is
a python spewing skyscrapers that
meld and slither over Overtown,
leaving metallic acid and screams,
because building I-95 wasn't enough.
Brickell expands slams symmetry & cement.
This is called New Brickell;
This is Little Havana.
Built of Cuban Linx & roosters' crows
& I love every cock-a-doodle conjuring,
but hate the peeps of rich snowbirds &
snow fledglings attempts
against a sound that can't be put to death.
The Ceiba tree, with iron spikes and hidden jars,
every root groove a portal
cupping dirt that sprouts jade bladed gallo tail feathers.
Botanicas replaced by bars
Nothing is Holy.
Little Haiti demands to exist even if it's called Lemon City now.
The Haitian Cultural Center even has a different name.
Local stores & restaurants soon board up,
fireflies crushed in a hand.
Knowledge means nothing—

A sixty-year-old passenger asks me what I do aside from Lyft,
I'm a college professor.
You must think you're clever, don't you?
Yes, I'm intelligent.
I drop him off at Gold Finger, a gentlemen's club,
he doesn't tip, I pick up
a stripper, an eighteen-year-old, working in
a satin black bunny corset
lace-up pumps hugging her calves,
and she sways with her mascara streams,
pushes forward, crushing embers of her cigarette butt.
New Year's Eve should've been a good night,
But her employers took another cut from her body.
I drive her home to Miramar.
She's asleep next to me in the passenger seat.
Her Baby.
There is a picture of a baby on her phone screen.
On the turnpike over marsh, sawgrass, new
developments for empty space.
No one buzzes her in.
No one answers her phone call.
She climbs a fence
and smashes her body home.

Christian J. Collier

The Man of the Small Hours

He lights a cigarette
after locking the front door, letting the building sleep.

The winter's gossamer palms knead his sweat into a silver ballet of steam above his head.
The deep, slow drag he takes tells me

he has thirsted for this.   Needed it.   Witness is the work of
living to explain the world the shadows watch.

In his low-lit face, I see a father surrounded by hours. Barely living. Barely enough there
in the tautness of his body & wallet

for the three children he hopes to hand tomorrow to. He doesn't know what it is
to part the black veil of his mouth with the gospel of the off day.   He punches in

sick or slanted.   He exists as a near-ghost
in the night with the croak of the bad wheel on the cleaning cart

hovering,   a war drum
before him. His weeks, like his father's, are stained with the not quite. The almost.

One thing always sacrificed.   One bill, at least, always unpaid
at the end of two jobs. I thank the God that holds his bones together

for granting him this intermission
between labor & the long haul home. I ask that He not let the lit square do its rancid
business.

Men like him are a mostly nameless faction.
In the late minutes when the old-timers say only legs & hospitals are open,

they move cities forward
while their families remain plateaued.

Men like him wear the meaning of work
in the dry, blotched shores of their hands.

Yesenia Montilla

300

My brother tells me he has spent over 300 on cigarettes this month alone—for my mom—who when out of them lays in bed with the covers pulled to her chin, all the shades down. He says: *I've asked her repeatedly to just smoke one, whenever she feels she's about to lose it; the way we're going, I don't know if I can keep this up.* I think of all the things 300 could buy: beautiful produce, a new pair of spring kicks, a real beauty routine, movie nights out at the actual movies, nosebleeds at Hamilton, I could take a plane and go see about a boy, I could visit Yemaya, I could drown my sorrows in fancy cocktails and bone marrow. 300 is a fucking clutch amount, you can invest it, save it, spend it, give it away. I tell him something to make him feel better—to make myself feel better too—I imagine where he would be if we multiplied all the 300 dollar months and dumped them in an account. Would he be sipping a beer in Mexico City? Would he be strolling his way through Paris? Would he be eating his way through Shanghai? His whole future, everything he could be suddenly feels a faraway dream. His entire life, his haves and have-nots billowing above our heads in a puff of smoke—

Debora Kuan

The Night after
You Lose Your Job

You know sleep will dart beyond your grasp. Its edges
crude and merciless. You will clutch at straws,
wandering the cold, peopled rooms of
the Internet, desperate for any fix. A
vapor of faith. An amply paid gig, perhaps,
for simply having an earnest heart or
keeping alive the children you successfully
bore. Where, you'd like to know,
on your résumé do you get to insert
their names, or the diaper rash you lovingly cured
with coconut oil, or the white lies you mustered
about the older man in the cream-colored
truck that glorious spring day, who hung his head
out the window and shouted, "Coronavirus!"
while you were chalking unicorns
and seahorses in the drive? Where
do you get to say you clawed through
their night terrors, held them through their sweaty
grunting and writhing, half-certain a demon
had possessed them, and still appeared
lucid for a 9 a.m. meeting, washed, combed, and collared,
speaking the language of offices?

At last, what catches your eye is posted large-
font and purple: a local mother in search
of baby clothes for another mother
in need. Immediately your body is charged,
athletic with purpose, gathering diapers,
clothes, sleep sacks, packing them tightly in bags.
You tie the bags with a ribbon and set them
on the porch for tomorrow. Then you stand

at the door, chest still thumping wildly, as if
you have just won the lottery—

       and so you did, didn't you?
You arrived here, at this night, in one
piece, from a lifetime of luck
and error, with something necessary to give.

Ray McManus

Fuck It

Because you don't care about the job as long as it pays.

Because everyone has to jump in a hole, and everyone has to reach
for a neck to find a plug to drain a pan to scrape out a trap.

Because you think the boss's son doesn't have to jump
in anything because he drives a clean truck.

Because you think one day you will too.

Because you're facedown in a crawl space digging through
another man's shit with gravel pushed against your belly.

Because one day, you'll have time to tamp out
your blessings but they won't be near enough.

Because nothing just falls towards the mouth
the way light cuts the evening as it creeps up the driveway.

Because tiny fingers push down window blinds, and eyes squint
for your shadow's return, eyes that don't know the word *quit*.

Cooper Lee Bombardier

Prayer for the Workingman

Sometimes it is the smallest things that surprise you. The kindness of a teamster, for instance. The hammers are already falling by the time my fog fades, but it is early enough, anyway. Roach coaches pace their street corners as possessively as dealers; broad-shouldered men with hard hats and thermoses tucked under their arms wander slowly away from the 22-line bus stop. Pigeons and seagulls flap silently between Dumpsters, gathering breakfast while most of the city still sleeps.

I think my motorcycle, it knows the way, like that horse in the Robert Frost poem. It carries me to work without me even thinking about it, without so much as a little nudge in its ribs. Next thing you know, I'm at the top of Potrero Hill, the sun scrambles its way on top of Oakland, the container cranes like prehistoric beasts in the surly dawn light. Lucky for me, my baby likes my Carhartt's dirty and my palms calloused, because I'll tell you, when dusk falls and I'm done shouldering my corner of the American dream for another day, I sure as fuck don't feel like a poor man's Paul Newman. Some Casanova with a weary spine. Some days, it's easier to drink the ache out than it is to push it thru the gristmill and hope it oozes out the other end as art.

What you trade for a steady paycheck and worker's pride is the dullness that lack of surprise gives you. Good for the soul, bad for the back, or vice versa. A little security, a little hard work, and a card to punch every day squeezes the spontaneity out from every pore. Sometimes the good, slow, and steady life puts a bullet in creativity's life. You need those broken-open, broken-through moments to step back and see and regurgitate your findings as poetry.

Peace won't be had in this exchange. When art lives inside of you like a parasitic conjoined twin who longs for a life of his own, you won't quell those urges by plunging into labor. Maybe Walt Whitman could do it, but these are different days. It's hard enough to have art, even while you're making it. All you really get when you embark upon work you do not truly love, is knowing that every next day will mirror the last until your back gives out, your knees give out, or your meter expires. Hopefully by then you'll have squirreled away enough cash for a mortgage, your kid's college education, or that brand-new, full-size Ford pickup truck you've yearned for, for years.

One thing I've learned watching my father bust his ass his whole life is that the dream of things is not my dream. I build my family and fortress in intangible brick and mortar of experience. I imagine that I am carrying on the work of my grandfathers, one the forklift driver and union shop steward at a soap factory and the other a long-haul truck driver. The myth of bootstraps is nailed to my psyche. I'm the bastard amalgamation of capability, working-class pride, and queerness. There is so little time to do the work that fixes the world when you are working in the trades. There is so little time to make the art that reflects the world back upon itself so that it can know itself in time.

Blessed are they who can swing a hammer in one hand and a paintbrush in the other. Blessed are they who smooth concrete with one hand and comfort a child or a grandparent or a lonely, lost, or homeless soul with the other. Blessed are they who reach across. Blessed are they who hold up the voices of the unheard and poor and suffering and many.

Katie Condon

Riot

No one tells you labor
begins well before the body
grows big and convulses

—that by the end of it all,
cold baby confused and crying
in the doctor's arms,

you'll have labored seven
thousand hours. In this hour,
beneath the house, a man

installs wiring for the router
and my husband installs stainless
steel appliances in the kitchen.

We have lived in this place
two days. I could get out
of bed and help the men

or I could take to memorizing
the shapes of light dappled
on this wall and practice

calling my idle afternoon
what women have told me
it is: work

on behalf of your fetal
site manager. And yet, the mind
panders to shame, *Take up*

the box cutter, the drill.
At the very least, sort the cutlery.
How lucky the unborn,

that they float inside a prison
of guilt but are, for now,
protected from it. Between

the bouts of hammering
from the crawl space
I have never seen,

I catch bits of the podcast
playing in the kitchen: *equity, workers'*
comp, riot at the union meeting.

MLK said that *a riot*
is the language of the unheard.
The child riots and kicks a rib.

I riot with my guilt, my
heartburn, all my small
aching. Fifteen years ago,

when my parents sent me out
to get a job, I got a job
at a greenhouse. It didn't take long

for a manager to accuse me
of avoiding work when I drew
the hours of each shift out

over the rosebushes
I was asked to prune, cherishing
every useless leaf, every spent bud

before tossing them to compost.
I'd be lying if I told you
that my fascination

with the way the brittle
petals' color becomes more
complex in death

wasn't the origin of why
I took my time. When
did I unlearn the lesson

that there are certain seemingly
trivial things that benefit
from long hours

of being fawned over
and looked at? Even Don West
wrote something like *doing nothing*

is just a way of doing it all
and isn't this what the women mean
when they tell me that most

of the body's work is accounted for
in sleep? I hear in muffled drones
the men negotiate the cost of labor

in the living room. They are
calm, jovial. There is the familiar
camaraderie of shaking hands.

There is no riot
but the riot of my body
willing me to sleep, the riot

of light fatigued and blue
from its daylong shift, the riot
of the cicadas' rattle—

there is the iris, its petals
opening wide around their stamen,
there is the child, finally still,

her fists continuing to form
as if on their own.

Joy Priest

All My Mothers

live in an alley
at the back of a lawmaker's mind.

A mind with no imagination

for our reality, they say. With teeth
rowed like cigarettes, factory still,

my mothers sweat through a week
of soil on their skin,
unconcerned with grace.

One has grace and a gold tooth,
a tiny heart etched in the middle.

One knows a key ingredient of beauty
is sorrow.

Oven burns cross their wrists.
Fingers calloused from hot plates.
My mother's Marcel curl

every Sunday in the alto section,
her tired face holding down the tenor of

a precarious song. I have

many mothers, you see? Some gone on
but still sitting at the bus stop
as their half-life selves

waiting on the city

to carry them to work.
The jealous mourning dove
holding territory above

the shelter taunts my mothers—

one calls him worse-um,
one has no insurance

and a persistent cough, sitting in the back
of a doctor's mind. She says he has

no imagination to offer. No way out of no way.

She hopes that doctor knows there is no way
to distance ourselves
in a one-room house. My mothers think

these well-to-dos ain't too well.

Rebecca Gayle Howell

My Mother Told Us Not to Have Children

She'd say, *Never have a child you don't want.*
Then she'd say, *Of course, I wanted you*

once you were here. She's not cruel. Just practical,
like a kitchen knife. Still, the blade. And care.

When she washed my hair, she hurt. Her nails
rooting my thick curls, the water rushing hard.

It felt like drowning, her tenderness.
As a girl, she'd been the last

of ten to take a bath, which meant she sat
in dirty water alone. Her mother in the yard

bloodletting a chicken. Her brothers and sisters
crickets eating the back forty, gone.

Is grace a resource of the privileged?

In this respect, my people were poor.
We fought to eat and fought each other because

we were tired from fighting. We had no time
to share. Instead our estate was honesty,

which is not tenderness. In that it is
a kind of drowning. But also a kind of air.

Alicia Suskin Ostriker

Mineshaft Dream

I push a button and the cage glides down
to the sub-basement and further
streaked red walls slide past
at least it is warm

the iron grate is painted glossy black
the descent is taking a long time I notice
everything vibrates, there comes

the sound of a stream rushing somewhere
at times a waft of coolness
at intervals tunnels head off
in varying directions

at least there is air
for now
and my lunch in my box
but where are the others

the others where are they
O god where

Ron Houchin

Dream of Death by Factory

Everyone in my family who worked
their lives in steel factories, glass plants
and coal mines died of cancer, bone, lung,
eye malignancies they could only have
gained by laboring in toxic worlds, realms
the wealthy owners of mines and factories
spent only minutes in at a time; places
so foul they forbade their children working
there—but for the rare exception.
The few like me who could afford or finagle
an education and avoid the draft had much
longer, less painful lives. In my dreams
I run the dark streets and alleys claiming
that labor of the body is a killer, unless
you work for yourself in what you love
like I have done. I do this in dreams
because that is where people will listen.

Monica Sok

Factory

We stack wafers the length of our arms,
inspect the chocolate coats in half-hour rotations.
You've eaten Kit Kats before. You've snuck them
from the closet, hidden next to your aunt's sewing kit
and a game called Trouble. But this is not about
taking what you can get without getting caught.
This is about the factory, the chugging machines
cutting candy into four fingers, standing on Line 11
watching the bars go on the conveyor belt.
Then through the plexiglass you see your aunt
going on her lunch break. You are more alert now,
because your aunt is a lifer, of course this is how
she helped you pay for college, your aunt
with no children of her own, who wears her hairnet
while eating her own food, who keeps her safety
helmet on, takes a bath every night to scrub away
the smell of Reese's. Your aunt is a second mother,
more like your real mother. Now you want to tell her
how much you love her, that you heard a man
on the phone at midnight tell her *I love you*,
that you stood behind the door eavesdropping
while she said nothing back. You work overtime
cupping peanut butter cups, a job you didn't want
but the work your aunt has always done to survive,
work passed down to help you save for graduate school
in New York City: the next part of your life.
When it's your last day and you hang up your rubber soles,
turn in the safety glasses, what is the next part
of her life? You've never worked in a factory before,
you may never return there or be a lifer like her,
like your mother and father, your uncles and other aunts,
not because you're smarter or better or luckier than most,
because she doesn't want you there and made sure.

Doug Van Gundy

Lucky

My people crawled up from underground, birthed
into the failing sun of West Virginia and western
Pennsylvania six days a week, eyes blinking, even in dim
winter, adjusting to a light brighter than the one still burning
on their own forehead. Every home in every little town
walking distance from work, every white frame house facing
an undulating brick street, each household centered
on the mine or the mill: coal and glass, coal and steel, coal
shoveled into the furnace, loaded into the stove, ground
into the knees and elbows of sweat-stained work clothes, everything
underlaid by that prehistoric heat. My people came from coal-
country Scotland, trading the pit for the deep mine, that monoculture
for this melting pot, one back-breaking job for another
that was exactly the same. Sometimes somebody died. Sometimes
a broken back or snapped femur was called *lucky*. Saturday nights
they went dancing at the Moose or Elks. Sundays they were starched
Presbyterians, skin scrubbed bathtub pink. Monday morning,
they were back in the earth before daybreak, the lucky
among them resurrected in time for supper.

Jake Skeets

Let There Be Coal

I.

A father hands a sledgehammer to two boys outside Window Rock.
The older goes first, rams a rail spike into the core, it sparks—

> no light comes, just dust cloud,
> glitterblack.

The boys load the coal. Inside them, a generator station opens its eye.
A father slips coal slurry from a Styrofoam cup, careful not to burn.

II.

train
tracks
and
mines
split
Gallop
in two

Men
spit
coal
tracks rise
like a spine
when Drunktown
kneels to the east

III.

Spider Woman cries her stories coiled in warp and wool. The rug now hung
in a San Francisco or Swedish hotel.

We bring in the coal that dyes our hands black not like ash
but like the thing that makes a black sheep black.

IV.

This is a retelling of the creation story where Navajo people journeyed four worlds and God declared, "Let there be coal." Some Navajo people say there are actually five worlds.

Some say six.

A boy busting up coal in Window Rock asks his dad, "When do we leave for the next one?"

His dad sits his coffee down to hit the boy. "Coal doesn't bust itself."

Savannah Sipple

When Those Who Have the Power Start to Lose It, They Panic

They rut young girls.   They come   to play. They carry
their wallets   in front pockets,   checkbooks
in glove boxes.   Money.   No money.   They drink
beer.   They drink bourbon.

[She shouldn't have been drinking.]

                                        They say shit like
boys will be boys   and   *you have to consider his side*
  of the story   they mean his side of the story   is the only one
that matters   *there's two sides*   Girls should live
legs open and   mouths shut.   Go to church and dress up.

[What was she wearing?]

They four-wheel on weekends.   They ride in golf carts,
in Ubers,   on bicycles.   They get elected President.
They want their girls tough enough to ride shotgun, limber
enough to stretch   across backseats,   across laps,
against doors,   in back alleys,   behind Dumpsters.

[She was out too late.]

                                        They want girls
sober enough to see,   drunk enough to see double,   *two sides!*
to moan,   *no* sounds like *yes* to their ears.   *No*
sounds like *yes* to their ears.   *Don't tell me no.*

[She had a mouth on her.]

                                                        unless
we're talking about how twenty minutes might ruin the rest of
their lives, then *No!*—
wait—we don't deserve this.   *There are two sides!*
Listen to me!   They don't fuck up, do they?   They get up,
pay 120 thousand dollars,   walk away.

                    [She shouldn't have even been there.]

Melva Sue Priddy

The Trouble with Young

One fresh heifer never left the dairy barn,
this all new, and she just wanted her calf.
She wouldn't stand for milkers and he wouldn't give in.
He beat her head with a 2×4, killed her,
then cut her throat to bleed out, saved the meat;
three of us, seven, eight and nine, watched, did as told.
We opened the doors, released the other cows.
Once he'd loaded her carcass for the slaughterhouse,
we washed out the blood, we rounded the cows back in,
we finished milking, sanitized.

We always had trouble breaking in heifers,
young and small their first time
into the milking stalls after calf weaning.
He gave them tight quarters, stairs, a sharp turn.
He gave them narrow stalls.
Some kicked and balked after he left,
and he was mad if we called him back again.
The older cows knew what to do. They stood still,
dirty hooves at our shoulders' level.

Within the year, another heifer, fixed
with new mechanical kickers, threw a fit,
pitched herself back and forth, bellowed,
startled the other cows who broke the doors and gates.
They all fled the barn. The heifer bucked across the field
until she broke the kickers. We chased her, wild-eyed,
back in, and he tied her to a tall metal post.
He used the same 2×4 until she fell and hung herself.
Mad we'd needed his help, mad she'd broken the kickers,
mad she'd wasted our time running around, mad because,
god knows, a cow won't give down milk after running around.
And then to fight and hang herself—poor,
the meat, because of her recent calving.

Lyrae Van Clief-Stefanon

Penitential

with drinking
with the middle of June in February
with ice and slick blackened surfaces
with a mistake
with endurance
with Jodeci because you cannot hear
      "Stay" without Jodeci
      "and sober we stayed"
with interest
with departure
with fighting and sex
with modesty
Where are we with modesty?
with scratches
with no hangovers

     with apologies
the body of the bird. arrives
without witness.
with beauty, however.
a kingfisher, markings
beautiful enough to draw
the eye towards ground,
the banal asphalt. what
made you look? you
working out your nerves
before the open trunk where
a new friend has stashed
a bottle of good whiskey
and at the burn. but no
at the lack of burn.
at the good silk down
the throat memory & action
come together. to drink

good whiskey is both to do
& be and remember being
to find dread in the memory.
look at the ground.
there, the dead kingfisher
already an omen, a beautiful
threat. but look closer. see
something besides the way
beauty threatens. the discarded
thought of yourself. see
the bird without your life
shadowing its death. not your
future. failures. but a life,
a bird. a real bird.

Philip Metres

Disparate Impacts
The Testimony of Joseph Gaston

I've moved around
my whole life
      Cincinnati Columbus Nashville Cleveland

    after I got out
    of prison

        I was homeless for just
        over five years

          always in motion

               "Judge Boyko . . . to take senior status"

nobody but nobody
would rent to me
              "I intend to maintain
              pretty much a full docket,
              but maybe a little less to enable me
              to travel and sit on other courts . . ." Boyko said.

        I went to ten different apartments
        their management companies
            all rejected me
        for felony conviction

           it was discrimination

        I got so fed up I asked Legal Aid
        I asked the Urban League
        the Ohio Civil Rights Commission

but no one would
                    represent me

everyone told me it was a useless fight
        told me the judge would rule
                        against
                everyone told me to wait

        so I took three months
        filed my own case

                based on "disparate impact"

                        it was a good
                        lawsuit really beautiful

Plaintiff contends the Defendants engaged in discriminatory housing practices, including refusal to rent, discrimination in rental terms and refusal to make reasonable accommodations in rules, policies and practices, in violation of the Fair Housing Act. He further alleges he has a disability which substantially impairs major life functions, but he does not elaborate on what his disability is. It appears he may be suggesting his prior conviction is a disability.

                every housing discrimination case
                        goes to Judge Boyko

        everyone knows Judge Boyko
                Judge Boyko has performed well
                        for the system

Opinion and Order: Plaintiff's Motion to Proceed In Forma Pauperis (Doc. No. 2) is granted, his Motion for Temporary Restraining Order and Preliminary Injunction (Doc. No. 3) and his Motion for Appointment of Counsel (Doc. No. 4) are denied, and this action is dismissed pursuant to 28 U.S.C. §1915(e). The Court certifies, pursuant to 28 U.S.C. §1915(a)(3), that an appeal from this decision could not be taken in good faith. Judge Christopher A. Boyko on 2/27/2019.(S,SR)

        So I just
        gave up

                        I wore out my eyes
                                I'm nearsighted now, need
                        glasses to read

what I see:
the system is rigged

"It's meaningful, it's rewarding, frustrating at
times, just like anything else," the judge said.
"But overall, I couldn't ask for a better job."

Cuyahoga County is a haven
for housing
discrimination

an incestuous marriage
between the legal system
and the homeless situation

they can't let you
win

representative democracy looks like
a good idea
but you can diminish
the role of the populace

"Division hurts, and it's felt
everywhere, I think," the judge said.

I was homeless for over
five years on a waiting list at Eden
five
years

no one should have to wait five years for housing

some guys tried to jump me
in the shower at 2100 Lakeside
I didn't comply

they threw me out

living in the streets, sleeping
in the woods

raised enough
for a car, started
sleeping there

then in trains and buses

some drivers let you ride all night long

I liked the 22nd
downtown to the airport
and back

it's a long route

other drivers make you get off

it's a hard life

I wouldn't want anyone
to suffer like that

used to shower in the rec center
kept my bag with me

kept my hygiene up

but I never begged
I wasn't brought up
like that

At the naturalization ceremony,
Judge Boyko reads a poetic statement
by Dean Alfange:

"I do not choose to be a common man . . .
I will not trade freedom for beneficence
Nor my dignity for a handout
I will never cower before any master
Nor bend to any threat.
It is my heritage to stand erect."

police spend most their time
harassing homeless people

I got a ticket for sleeping
        for sleeping!

    I looked it up
    there is no law that says
    you can't fall asleep
    in the state of Ohio

I almost died
        got shot at on West 25th
    got blood clots in my legs
        from sleeping upright on buses

it's a hard life

                social justice institutions
                have become part of the system

        everyone is part
            of this system

                        Federal judges often work hard to maintain
                        their judicial independence,
                        as the appointment is a lifetime one

        Judge Boyko will be rewarded well

    I seek no earthly reward
        just change

    I'm in Eden housing on Euclid
    when I got out
    of prison I wanted to leave
        the state
            they said I had to stay:

                it's called "community control"
                    to maintain parole
                they don't want the money
                    leaving the state

    if I live righteously, on the day of judgment
    I will not be wronged

the change I seek in the system
may never become reality
    but I must try

[*the line goes*
    quiet when I ask Joseph
        his dreams]

some day I'd like to be a cook
    or a youth advocate

and I'd like to see the world
    look into
        the Peace Corps

The judge has offer to teach US law
. . . in Ukraine and Saudi Arabia,
and having more flexibility will allow for
that.

Geffrey Davis

What I Mean When I Say *Labor*

I.
Before god, but after the drugs—though maybe
above all else, because even my endless image
of him holding a crack pipe I invented
through the hurt ugliness of his absence—
my father's hands mean work. From the severe

safety of a silence I once put between us,
my own hired soreness became a warm-blooded door
for his difficult return. Thumbs struck while roofing
slammed open a suffering we could curse

together across the bitterness. I did plumbing and
carried him home in palm-ache from hours

of wrenching a way for water to join
and leave a family. The summer I painted
houses, the shadow of my father's strength
rolled beneath my grip like a crooked smile.

By now, any burn in the knuckles or
tenderness to my touch from too much time spent
pulling something broken but necessary
apart for half-answers feels like nothing
other than elegy:—I want another song.

II.
We've sat down, my mother and I, to do the sorry math—
it always comes back a painful miracle: 1990s, mostly

single, four children, minimum wage, *work* the warmest
soundtrack played on repeat, and her presence worn

thin but nothing like a ghost. There were the nights of her
cold crying into each emptiness she could hear

roaming the rooms of the house. There was
hunger and the homeless shelter. And there was

our witnessing a fatigue that framed
the youth and beauty of her face

like a coffin.
                                        Ma,
what I'm trying to say is, I don't know how
to bless a secure music that,
for love, you made from your almost
not being here. I still carry the key
and lock of it. But I also trust my fear
over all your body has carried but might not
recover. Time, for instance, and real rest.
I want a force other than death
between you and retirement. I'm listening for a hymn
or horizon that draws more light than need
toward your tomorrow:—more faith and some
paid-off, open place to prop your incredibly tired feet
above your tired and incredible heart.

Jane Wong

Snow, Rain, Heat, Pandemic, Gloom of Night

The post office doesn't have clocks.

Waiting in line, I can feel everyone's tension and anger stewing, leaking out of their pores like gasoline. The air fills with the soup of impatience.

There are five people ahead of me. I take it all in: the tapping of a high-heeled shoe, the exaggerated checking of a watch, the shifting of packages from one arm to the other. The line moves and a woman steps up to the counter with her face mask on wrong. It flops down below her nose like loose pantyhose. She keeps touching her mask. Not to adjust it to the correct position, just to touch it. Then she slams her pocketbook down on the counter like she's crushing a cockroach and shouts at the clerk: "Do you know how long I've been waiting in this fucking line?"

*

In the anxiety swamp of 2020, in the roiling heat of July, a white woman in a California post office was recorded screaming "Can you just do your job? It's simple" at an Asian American employee, calling them a "chink" multiple times. Realizing she's being recorded by other customers, she says "chink" again—directly at the phone screen recording her. When she says this word in the video, I am transported back to grade school and the corner of a stuffy Jersey classroom where I'm standing with my back against a wall, the pushpins from posters that read "You Matter!" and "Division as Sharing!" digging into my back. A white boy is singing "ching-chong-ching-chong" and pulling at the corners of his eyes. Years later, as a twenty-something, I will run into him when I'm checking out from Lowe's. Years later, he will scan my light fixtures and look up at me, the bags under his blue eyes like crescent moons: "Hey, you look familiar. Did we go to school together?" The light fixtures will clang together, percussive brass jewels, in my shopping bag.

I call my mother at the start of quarantine. She is a USPS clerk and has been sorting mail there for almost 25 years, mostly during night shift. I tell her I'm worried about her working conditions, worried about COVID-19 safety precautions, worried about how much sleep she's getting, worried about her 45-minute commute to the Trenton mail-processing facility, worried she's taking overtime again, and can't she just reduce her hours? Is everyone wearing a mask? Gloves? Enough distance? Enough hand sanitizer?

"Don't worry about me! I worry about you. Teaching on the computer sounds hard," she says. "Did you eat yet?"

I am a professor at a state university in Washington; I am 2,935.4 miles away from my mother in Jersey. I look this up on Google Maps and it would take me 44 hours to drive home. The blue route line on the map kind of looks like a river. As if I could row my way home, paddle myself amid mud and snow and rain and eye-splintering drought to her doorstop where she would be there, hot pot boiling in the kitchen, arms raised, saying, "I just put the fish balls in, so you're just in time."

"I'm going to eat soon," I tell her, staring at my email inbox, which dings like a doorbell every few minutes. There's an overripe banana on the couch where I'm sitting, my back curled like a bridge that's been washed out.

"You better eat now," she says. On her end, I can hear muffled voices in the background of the phone. "What? I'm talking to my daughter. One minute." I look out the window and see my mail carrier, waving hello. I wave back slowly, the phone pressed hot against my ear.

*

The postal service has an unofficial motto: "neither snow nor rain nor heat nor gloom of night stays these couriers from the swift completion of their appointed rounds."

When I'd come back home from college during Thanksgiving break, my mother would take me to the postal facility on Thanksgiving Day to help her hand out meals to her coworkers. She loves feeding people. Before she passed the postal exam and joined the USPS, before she was a single mom, we owned a Chinese American take-out restaurant and were famous for our spareribs. Turkey, corn, mashed potatoes, and always some Toisanese cooking too: garlicky long beans, wood ear mushrooms with pork belly. I'd carry a teeming stack of aluminum food packets and meet all her friends, who were starting their workday at 9:00 p.m. *Nor gloom of night.* The majority of my mother's coworkers are people of color. Our local facility—which would close down years later, leading to significant layoffs—was massive and the floors echoed with the sound of machinery, yelling, and blips of garbled announcements (replete with a thick Jersey accent) via the intercom. "Study hard," one of her friends told me, tearing the meat from a glistening turkey leg, as if saying: *we work this much for kids like you.* "Damn," he says to my mom. "Jin, this is better than my granny's."

My mother regularly works overtime, especially during the holiday season. Or when her boss begs her to help out because so-and-so has called out or there's no way we can get to all this mail so can you please come in? "There's always overtime," she tells me. "If you want to work, the post office will give you work." Her giant work bag is always stuffed with Tupperwares of food, ginger to keep her awake during night shift, Tiger Balm, and Band-Aids. There are always coupons stuffed in there too, 15 percent off at Bed, Bath, and Beyond, etc. When she says she's having "lunch," she's actually eating in the middle of the night. For many years, my mother suffered from bouts of vertigo. Her equilibrium off cycle. Throwing up and falling over. A tea bag spilled open, a rug pulled out from under a spinning world. Her vertigo is better these days. "I'm telling you, yoga helps," she insists, popping another ginger chew. She knows how to find YouTube videos on her phone now. She doesn't like it when I worry. She makes ginger chews herself, drying out ginger along her kitchen windowsill and dusting them with a kiss of sugar. She likes them stronger, spicier. "Zing! You're awake!"

I am the first in my family to go to college. And certainly the first to receive a doctorate. Teaching from home during the pandemic, I sit in the muck of my education.

*

You depend on the postal service. You depend on it for your ballots, your medicine, your legal documents, your stimulus checks, your online purchases, your care packages to keep you tethered across all this foggy distance. *Neither snow nor rain nor heat nor pandemic.*

My mother sends me Asian pears wrapped in scarves, seaweed sesame crackers, and bags of salted pistachios and dried figs from Costco because she worries that I don't eat meals between teaching classes (she's right). I shake with joy when I cut open the cardboard, each morsel packed to the brim of this flat-rate Priority Mail package. I smell the box, as if I could smell her, ginger lingering in each corner.

When it's my turn in line at the post office, I go up to the counter. The clerk is an older Indian American man; he immediately apologizes and doesn't look me in the eye as he moves mail into a slot: "I'm so sorry for the wait. Thank you for your patience."

I smile behind my mask and pass him my envelopes like I'm offering a slice of fruit. "How are you doing today? My mom's a postal worker too." He looks up at me immediately, his eyes crinkling into a smile as the customers behind me sigh and tap and groan and grumble and pout like *is she seriously chit-chatting right now?*

"You know, I'm doing okay," he says, laughing, already reaching for the books of stamps. "Where does your mom work? How's she doing?"

*

Inscribed into white granite at the Smithsonian's National Postal Museum is a poem. The first section reads:

Messenger of Sympathy and Love
Servant of Parted Friends
Consoler of the Lonely
Bond of the Scattered Family
Enlarger of the Common Life.

Nearly a year has passed since the start of quarantine. My mother processes next-day delivery mail and change-of-address mail. So many people who need their mail immediately, so many people who can't afford rent, moving. These days, when I call her and ask her how she's doing, she tells me: "You know, the mail has to get there on time. Sometimes it's like mail over people." I think of how hard she's working, how worn her gloves are, how loud the machinery is, churning around her like the Atlantic Ocean. And I think of all the angry people who don't get their mail on time, who slam their pocketbooks down at the service counter. "There are no islands in the Postal Service. All of our processes are linked. If you do one well, you're going to do well in another, and another, and another," says Deputy Postmaster General Pat Donahoe about the importance of the 24-hour clock. It's not New York City that never sleeps; it's the postal service.

But also, when I call or FaceTime her these days, she tells me about her postal service family. How her close friend Frank just passed away and how they used to joke around about his messy haircut. She's known Frank for 25 years—ever since she started working at the USPS, after our restaurant failed and my gambling father left our family. The camera is shaking on her phone as she wipes away tears. My mother rarely cries and it's hard to watch her like this, in the bloom of grief, and I can't help but cry with her. "I walk by his station and he's not there," she weeps. "Frank, where are you?" Nearly every day, for upwards of 14 hours during overtime, my mother is with her fellow coworkers. This pandemic year, there was more mail than ever. She sends me videos of her coworkers, wearing masks, waving in the break room, strangers yet not strangers. "Everyone, say hi to my daughter!"

What follows is a sweet postal chorus, percussive as they punch in and punch out: "Hi, Jane! Hi Jane! Hi, Jane!"

Janice Lobo Sapigao

my mom makes friends with the nurses

my mom makes friends with the nurses / and together they make a country / she brings them food / and together they are a farm / a restaurant without pricing / a secret menu / i eat with her / at a station labeled "17" or "Room A" depending on the availability / and we are alone / in a sterile hotel without walls but curtains / a luxury without the privilege / each guest is a room open and observable / the nurses / they eat her food in a break room / without us / my mom and her new friends / eat lunch in separation / they are two countries apart / a people, divided / a nation under no god / no mercy / i believe in my mother / the maker of the bombest / adobo and rice / of spaghetti and hot dogs / of vienna sausages / the nurses pledge allegiance / to their patients / their indivisible labor / when we call for someone to come help us / anyone / a nurse comes quickly / comes running / when a machine beeps out of rhythm in our church / nurses, they are the conductors / with answers / priests to a symphony / signing / singing / all the liquids with long names / they call for the gowns / washed and warm / with liberty and phone calls / with medicine everlasting / the diaspora almighty / and on the last day of chemo / the nurses take pictures / & selfies with my mother, / creator of pinakbet and lumpiang shanghai / the nurses are profiled, memorialized, and merry / let her be healed / and if we never come back here / to infusion or oncology / let it be wholly / in the nurses' names / amen

Jennifer Horne

The Horns of Horns Valley Moved from Alabama to Arkansas, Gained an "e," and I Returned Three Generations Later for Graduate School in Creative Writing, of All Things

(In Memoriam, Allan Wade Horne, 1932–2018)

You
    the first of eight
        to graduate
high school
    your four brothers
        and three sisters
starting work early
    working hard
        proud
so proud
    of their
        little brother
a little awed later
    when you'd
        done so well

your mamma
    the seamstress
        at the ladies dress shop

your papa
    the timber cruiser
        in the Ozark hills
would walk miles
    to town
        to find the job
brother Bob
    dropped him in the woods
        he couldn't drive

your mamma
    added the "e"
        when another Horn
in Caddo Gap
    kept getting
        her mail
including
    paychecks
        he cashed

Why didn't I understand?
Why didn't you tell me?

we two little girls
    growing up
        so easy
so comfortable
    in our comfort
        we didn't
we couldn't
    you didn't
        want us to see
how it
    had been
        growing up poor
the stories retold
    as triumphs
        over adversity
when someone
    had a headache
        and no money
for medicine
    deep in the hills
        deep in the Depression

you found aspirin
    by the creek
        still in its cellophane packet

the school
    in Hot Springs
        where you moved
from Caddo Gap
    you were eight
        you had to repeat a grade
but later would say
    it was
        the best thing
that could have happened
    you needed
        the extra year

you moved houses often
    you didn't ever
        say why
you had
    a little boy job
        delivering papers
and you sang
    for change
        at the big hotel

when I wanted
    a paper route
        you said no
I loved you
    I would've
        loved you
if you'd said
    how hard
        it was

Why didn't I understand?
Why didn't you show me?

we drove
    to Caddo Gap
        in your Lincoln

your lawyer car
    your cousin
        was there
on the porch
    of the general store
        as though
he'd been
    waiting
        all these years
you marveled
    at where you'd
        come from

I could see
    the ghost
        of a slim, shirtless boy
overall-clad
    barefoot
        playing in the creek
observing his world
    closely through
        nearsighted eyes
so why
    couldn't I see
        that the story
of picking peaches
    the hated
        itch of fuzz
had a sharp pit
    a hard knot
        of need?

Why didn't I understand?
Why didn't you let me?

Magician-father
    your sleight
        of hand
hid the pain
    that old wound
        of shame
misdirection said
    look over here
        at pride

the client
    you most admired
        had a
6th-grade education
    but I
        didn't see
you wore
    the same bootstraps
        as he
success was
    the measure
        of the man
you were
    always going to find
        the way
things finally
    turned out all right
        in the end
when you praised
    his hard work
        why didn't I understand?

Why didn't I understand? Why
didn't I see?

I'm ashamed
    I didn't hold
        those tales
up to the light
    but like an
        illustrated
Bible story
    I saw them
        with a child's eyes
I have so many years
    to go back and
        reappraise
appreciate each bike
    each Christmas
        each trip to the doctor
your gift
    was our ignorance
        your loss

was our taking
        for granted
                this is
the longest
        thank-you note
                in the world dear
Allan
        Wade
                Horne

Jessica Jacobs

In the Shadow of Babel

A run through Wall Street means passing
the ghost of the Meal Market where grains were sold
beside Native and African captives, means,
even in high summer, alleys shaded to night
and cold as snowmelt streams, making it easy to believe
men-who-would-be-gods once built a tower
to rival the heavens,
              laid the foundation
while seaweed creped the remnants of redwoods
and dolphins rotted in mountain lakes—
the Flood not myth but memory,
their desire to build beyond drowning
sensible. But as one generation built
on the next, citizens were muscled
into one mold, indivisible, indistinguishable
as the clay bricks they passed from hand to hand
in that assembly line to the sky. *And the whole earth*
was of one language: However differently they felt it,
people could only speak their pain the same.

*

But what does such pain mean to me
who runs with no one chasing her, with no one lying
in wait—to a woman running simply
because she wants to?

Yet the past is a tower tall enough to pierce
            time, transmit
all echoes. So tall that, even demolished,
               its shadow casts.

*

To the west, Manifest Destiny of corn-soy-cotton-wheat
displacing all that once grew there with uniform

grids of green and the need for labor to tend them—
the old whisk-away-the-tablecloth trick
done cruelly, so few people left standing.
      Africans branded with their captors' initials,
    then again, with the surnames
of their buyers.
        Native children whitewashed
      by names that meant
nothing, in letters they couldn't read:
Sha-note, "wind blowing through,"
became Charlotte; Lone Bear,
Lon Brown.

To the east, *Blut und Boden, Blood and Soil*: a swastika
crossed by a sword and sheaf of wheat.
      Jews issued IDs stamped with a red *J*
    and new middle names:
Israel for men, *Sarah* for women. Then,
in the camps, shorn to nothing
but numbers.

Fleeing pogroms, vowing to send
for his wife and young son,
at Ellis Island, alone,
      my great-grandfather immigrated
from Kudlanski to Goodman.

*

Like plants smothered by a tarp to cleanse the land
for the one crop deemed desirable.
Like my grandparents' Polish, Yiddish, Hebrew,
and English, like the ancestors no one speaks of
massacred in a Polish synagogue, in a pit in a forest
they were forced to dig themselves—many of them
farmers who knew what it was to dig, who knew
the good that could come from such work.
Like their murders I know only from the archives,
monoglot me, struggling to speak, to listen
to the past.

    Generic American, protected
    by my passing

as not Jewish, not Queer; privileged
to be so often oblivious.

   Though Charlemagne said, *To have another language,*
   is to possess a second soul,

to have the language of your home
is to possess the soul that is your own.

*

As those enslaved were forced to speak
the colonists' language—even that corner
of their minds colonized.
         As *Kill the Indian, Save*
   the Man meant severing
children from their homes, severing their braids,
forcing them into shoes and faith and words
that wouldn't fit.
              As Nazis burned sacred texts,
         trying to bonfire the holy
tongue from Jews' mouths.

              As they were torn
         from their parents
on auction blocks and reservations,
at borders and in selection lines—children,
those words we say to the future.

*

And with no child, with only English,
I feel severed from every time
but the present and question
what now brings me to speak:
                 Because a president
who was and was never my president
praised rabid men chanting, *Blood and soil,*
chanting, *Jews will not replace us,* chanting with
their pink faces flushed and raging
in the flicker of their tiki torches?
                    Because I finally know
the feeling that the country I was born in is mine
but not meant for me? Why
did it take this fear to grow
my voice?

*

Two-thirds of the world
now speaks English, every culture,
bound. Without firebreak,
            a single strain of hatred
        can inflame the world.

Here, murders in synagogues, in the homes of rabbis; beatings
in the streets. On the way to shul, Jews hide
yarmulkes under baseball caps, pry
mezuzahs from their doors.
                Out for a jog, on a walk to the store, in the car
with their kids, in their own damn backyards and beds,
Black men and women, Black children, murdered
by those paid to protect them,
                by those who forced
Water Protectors into dog kennels at Standing Rock
after scrawling arrest numbers on their arms.

*

America—always
    a grander city, always a more
                        towering tower
                built on land stolen
    from those who listened to it
                well enough to know
when dogwood leaves are the size of a squirrel's ear,
sow corn. When lilacs bloom, seed the beans
whose roots will feed the cornstalks that support them.
And once those purples fade, plant squash: a sprawl
of broad green ground cover. Each plant providing
what the other requires.

            At Babel, God said,
Let us navlah *their language—to confound*
but also *to intermingle.*

Let the world tell us
what the world needs and when.

*

While the nights are still cold, my wife and I
join our neighbors to ready the ground
with pickax and spade, to jostle

rocks from their strangle of roots
and turn the dirt with the rich heat of humus
grown from the scraps of our yards and tables;
we water the starts and tuck them gently
in the soil.

And during the summer harvest,
        in this garden open
      to all who want to work there,
    the light so late shadows
grow weary of waiting and slink off
to sleep in corners—with hands heavy
from hauling, lifelines burnished
by soil—we give thanks
for all we'll share, and when the feasting
is through, recite Borei Nefashot:
        a blessing for God
          who *created many souls*
          and their deficiencies.

Complete, we'd have no reason
to speak, to ask, to reach out

our hands. To seek faces and lives
different than our own. Instead,

here we are, together, mouths full
of words for our hunger and need.

Perfectly imperfect, each of us
is a new way of saying.

Jill McDonough

An Hour with an Etruscan Sarcophagus

Not the carved seals or gold libation cups,
mummies, alabaster urns. Two minutes
alone with this Etruscan sarcophagus and I'm
in tears. Nobody saw; I totally got away with it.

Something about the stonecutter's wife, I think—
not the rich couple together in stone forever, not even
the man who carved the jowly face, the woman's hands
on her husband's chest, chest doughy even carved in stone.

But the wife who knows they don't get an Etruscan
sarcophagus, that even though her Etruscan husband
carves them, they can't have this softening
of death, this consolation prize. Last week, midnight

in a friend's kitchen, I burst into tears over what I don't get,
wished aloud I'd gone to Goldman Sachs after college, how
then Josey wouldn't have to work. Rachel put her arms
around me, said *Shh*. Said, *Ah, Jill, you've made all*

the right choices. You've done everything just right.
I'm always wishing for money, for new siding,
just one job, a week off for Josey, off her feet.
But today, fresh from the Etruscan sarcophagi, I'm bigger,

wish for all of us, for you, for the stonecutter's wife,
for your children's children, such a friend in such
a kitchen, such a crying jag, an hour with an Etruscan
sarcophagus to think it all over, write it down.

Rose McLarney

The Way Taken

A waterfall impedes travel, and a mountain slows.
A straight line measure of mileage between points tells
little of how a walker moved on land with such features.

We are unable to fly. What humans can choose is not
to cross streams or ridges in a straight shot, though
the distance would be lesser if swum or clambered.

Usually, we go around, on the route at the hill's feet,
or that keeps our own dry. Follow *least-cost pathways*—
archeologists' term referring to where past pedestrians,

accounting for terrain, are likeliest to have stepped.
What is *cost*? In AD 1000, perhaps the people
who lived here preferred length of effort to force.

Perhaps time rather than exertion was the currency
with which they, with their trails winding slow
and level through the valleys and meadows, paid.
*
What is *we*? Settlers who spoke of taking
the long, crooked road, migrating to the mountains,
are the lineage I can come nearest to claiming.

They picked dirt so rocky it bent tools, wouldn't yield
food. And stayed, as if to choose dramatic scenery
was to set beauty as the highest value. But hard labor

is as central to their story. In which some estimation
of profit led to plowing Native American mounds,
in a few generations wearing them down to half

the height they'd been for a thousand years.
To displacements more terrible still. And to me,
learning to take my first steps on disturbed ground,

then pocketing pottery shards I found. To encounter
again later, opening boxes of childhood collections
and questions about *my* and *first, learn* and *get better.*

*

Here, like anywhere, cheaper has come to mean
the closest spot for constructing the parking lot.
Ease, bulldozers filling streams and wetlands,

laying mounds and mountains low. And, over paved
plateaus spreading out around chain stores, I roll
a rattling cart holding whatever purchase I can afford.

Still, I've spent evenings of late tracing connections
between ancient sites on archeologists' maps of my
home county. Studying their conjectures of the hours

a Mississippian walker would have to have given
to reach each village from the town center.
Figuring to which places it would have cost more

than a day's time to arrive. I picture dwelling
uphill, upriver, where others might tire before
reaching to deliver hard news, at a remove that far.

Heid E. Erdrich

Intimate Detail

Late summer, late afternoon, my work
　　interrupted by bees who claim my tea,
　　even my pen looks flower-good to them.
　　I warn a delivery man that my bees,
　　who all summer have been tame as cows,
　　now grow frantic, aggressive, difficult to shoo
　　from the house. I blame the second blooms
　　come out in hot colors, defiant vibrancy—
　　unexpected from cottage cosmos, nicotiana,
　　and bean vine. But those bees know, I'm told
　　by the interested delivery man, they have only
　　so many days to go. He sighs at sweetness untasted.

Still warm in the day, we inspect the bees.
　　This kind stranger knows them in intimate detail.
　　He can name the ones I think of as *shopping ladies*.
　　Their fur coats ruffed up, yellow packages tucked
　　beneath their wings, so weighted with their finds
　　they ascend in slow circles, sometimes drop, while
　　other bees whirl madly, dance the blossoms, ravish
　　broadly so the whole bed bends and bounces alive.

He asks if I have kids, I say not yet. He has five,
　　all boys. He calls the honeybees his girls although
　　he tells me they're *ungendered workers*
　　who never produce offspring. Some hour drops,
　　the bees shut off. In the long, cool slant of sun,
　　spent flowers fold into cups. He asks me if I've ever
　　seen a *solitary bee* where it sleeps. I say I've not.
　　The nearest bud's a long-throated peach hollyhock.
　　He cradles it in his palm, holds it up so I spy
　　the intimacy of the sleeping bee. Little life safe in a petal,
　　little girl, your few furious buzzings as you stir
　　stay with me all winter, remind me of my work undone.

Joseph Millar

Planet Labor

I should be letting the sunlight
lead me into the darkness today
as my friend likes to say
speaking of jazz
or at least trying to fix the latch
on the front door
beyond which the sprinkler
rains down on the clover
the old man, my neighbor,
planted last year
for his bees, whose honey
I harvested yesterday
in a festival fraught with humming and death
garbed in my white jacket and mask
purchased in Oakland from the Yemeni beekeeper
who lets bees walk on his face and his neck.

Hardest workers on earth
with their gold fur and black leg hairs
packed with pollen, their long proboscises
filling with nectar
flying three miles to the hive.
For the sun has come out
over the hive with its vast female
multiplicity, its center the darkened wax
of the brood and the queen who can live
for up to six years laying thousands
of eggs each day, her sireless drones
mostly useless now, pushed out to the edge
or driven away.

It's a hollow tree or maybe a box
made out of wood and wire
and any good worker can tell you

there's nothing too restful about desire.
If you wanted to sleep
you should have stayed home,
in less than four months
your wings will be gone,
tattered from flying and fanning the air
to cool off the hive
and protect the brood,
they can look for you
lying still on the ground,
your work blooming everywhere.

Mark Wunderlich

Shanty

No one remembers what became of the people
in the house now swaybacked in the marsh—

not the mice whispering and tunneled in the couch,
not the snapping turtle armored on a log

retracting his hard beak into wrinkled folds like foreskin.
Not my mother who visited the shanty once as a nurse,

noting the packed dirt floor, the walls pasted up in newsprint.
They burnt waste oil in a barrel stove they got free from a garage,

dipped their water from a spring now greened with cress.
Ardys Keilholtz knew something of the wife

but couldn't think—*what was she called to home?*
When I was small, I heard roosters crowing from their yard

and think I rode a school bus with the girl,
but now I couldn't say for sure.

Bill Wendt taught me to trap muskrats in that swamp,
staking a Conibear in the muddy muskrat runs with brush.

I pulled their plush-furred bodies from the ice,
sold them for cash money to the fur man in the spring.

How long will I keep telling stories just like this—
dirt floors and traplines and a shack abandoned in a swamp?

The vividness of that world is fading like my father's addled mind.
Poverty is not poetry, this I know. But these pictures

are what's left of childhood and now all my male relatives are gone
though lost and half-remembering—my father—living on.

Kathy Fagan

Omphalos

How many times the blood rush of truck, bus & subway
    has passed below my window.
How often this body, meant to bend & breed—squat like
    my mother's, her mother's & hers—has
paced instead, inside its head, gazing skyward for a noun or phrase to
    shatter the glass of our locked cars & save us,
original cloud
    that might break over all:

raccoon washing its hands like a surgeon in the birdbath,
girl at the drive-through deciding only 42 percent of humanity
    sucks, the rest of them hungry or high,
their wheels aglow like daisies, their wounds debrided, unbridled . . .

Jesus, Mary & Joseph, I have blamed you for everything—
    the decades broken like your rosaries, our few family belongings
missing, glued or taped . . .

            Back home, the air
is scented with Japanese lilac & catalpa's orchid blooms—
    colonized & colonizing:
your body made to carry mine
    dismantled, finally,
    in flame, to this,
of which I am but remnant, a speck
fished from a tear duct with your tongue.

Whose easy laugh is that I'm hearing now?
Whose loneliness, unbroken, goes rolling in the blood?

Abraham Smith

From *Dear Weirdo*

i see just people are museums of their hungers

i just seen the guy with the grenade tattoo over

his adam's apple poopin his hotrod wheel

round for round i want a car shape of a tear

down the neckhole of a gto bear

and yes i am still intent on a resay

one those midlife drunk ascetics

jumpin a yardstick

with a heart problem

me or stick i ain't sayin

pug some mystery in inn

if at all possible make your sunflower

of rebar and of tractor reactor disc bullshit

and of autumn why let me tell it

i to you a dew a spoon

claimin central standard up on a mountain pass

autumn comes

to everybody's pocketos why i read it

just today in these covidian hunker blinds

blam blam the rich shootin us down

like in duckhunt the billionaires

upped their kitty ante 33% in just

march to nov 20/20 roar ro-a-oar

how about that??

foodline stretched along the wide earth

like a weakenin hernia stitch

these ultra of this cornfuck land

hear they gettin injections

of babycalftonguefat in their eyelids sorry porch

for sayin it but the circulars do add up

pile mousy piss brown junk up

in say later november their richy cedar pockets see

gunna get a little ticklish then fell swall away

in my repeater dream anyhay

sneezes jesus with one swift ripping tingle

the streets sudden come alive

i said go out for a pass not for a piss

all hungover eggeye last cube in the tray see

didn't get used so it's swimeye parade mornings

with everybody losing their overdraft balance doin

the natural gas dinosaur dip dip

but who stands up fast on a pill like that??

Richard Hague

Idle Men on Porches

No work in this universe,
it seems.
So what do we talk about all day?
Whose cousin was killed?
Whose wife is long gone?
Whose son hanged himself
in jail?
Whose father is never
mentioned?
Whose cells are broken
with crack?
Whose mouths this morning
fill with curses?
Whose hands crush the bones
of girls?
Whose murmurings encrypt
long days of intoxication?
Whose sentences complicate
our hours of woe?

Strange abundance here:
grief's angry, unnoticed hoard,
health's mass grave,
the bones of broken lives
strewn across our yards,
unused shovels
all around.

Kayleb Rae Candrilli

Ghazal Written For the Lids In Downtown Brooklyn Where I Chose My Name

I grew up poor, no monogrammed bath towels or duffle bags, nowhere to travel but
    into myself.
My mountain had so many small mountains inside of it, and I had breasts. If I had
    to give myself

any name then, it would have been hunter or whittler or fire with only flint. Of
    course, I was stronger
than I should have been. Strength is the nature of a trans boy huddled over
    kindling, lighting themselves

up, into only ever embers. Sometimes I still feel like a woman, and, really, it's not so
    bad if I'm alone.
I don't want to live forever, but I want to live long enough to make people upset. It's
    so easy to lose myself,

whispering sweet incantations for all the gorgeous trans boys left to die in the
    forest. Oh, winter of worship,
I've pretended plenty, and lying to my mother, if only for a few decades, was
    intended as a deeply selfless

thing. I don't remember knowing my name until I knew it—a partner told me to
    keep the Y and that was it—
Kayleb, monogrammed onto a leopard print flat brim. Yes, it's okay to love what
    you love. If I had to ask myself

anything, I'd ask, did this poem touch all it was asked to touch? Did it hold out its
      hand and offer something?
I'd ask, how about the length of my lifeline?
      How long does this new name have?

Eugenia Leigh

What I Learned About Love and Billionaires in 26 Hours

As I left my apartment to satiate my Friday night with a herd of Manhattan strangers, I witnessed this: my roommate, a musician in his early thirties, had invited his mother to eat Thai prawns and panang curry while watching *Psych* together on his laptop in the living room.

I didn't know this existed.

That image provided the context for the next 26 hours.

*

I exited the M train at West 4th Street to have a slice of margherita pizza with a psychology writer who told me he was crafting a book about contemporary love. I asked him if he'd ever been married. No. I asked him if he'd been engaged. Almost. The question cut him up, I could tell.

We hopped uptown to his billionaire buddy's high-rise condo, where the billionaire who made his billions from pharmaceuticals had hosted a dinner before we arrived. I sipped water from a plastic cup served by a hired girl at a long table swinging with strangers and wine. The strangers planned to gather the following week for a party at the UN. One wore a suit that cost five months of my Brooklyn rent. Several owned companies that had recently gone public. Among them were an actress who spoke mostly about the horrible people who'd probe her about her acting, and also a quiet, Canadian-born nonfiction writer whose name sounds like Falcon Madwell, which you'd recognize.

The dinner party split, then five of us, including the writer who brought me and the writer whose name you'd recognize, shuffled to a wine bar in the Village. Then another bar. Then a third. I sipped Perrier at the first. Soda water with a splash of lavender bitters at the second. I didn't drink anything at the last bar, and after what seemed like eons of contributing few words to endlessly meaningless conversations, I said good-bye to the strangers whom I knew I'd likely never see again, and walked away.

Normally, I would have been an effusive extrovert giggling down the sidewalk with my gait tilted with whiskey. I would have slipped new contacts into my smartphone, and I would have posted photos, blasting gorgeous comments on various social media platforms about my delightful new companions and dreamy evening.

But that Friday night, the backdrop to the evening was neither my lack nor my ordinary life. The backdrop was that image of my roommate, at home, loved by and loving his mother whose laughter rang while I shut the front door.

Pitted against that holy image, the evening was mediocre at best.

*

Expression blank, almost rude, I checked out of the conversations all evening. My mind was fixed on my partner David's mom, who'd barely enjoyed one glass of wine her entire life, yet was deteriorating because her liver hosted a swarm of surprise tumors.

I imagined David in Taiwan next to his mother's hospital bed. I imagined his hand caressing hers, limp next to her distended belly. I imagined his worn eyes shot with prayers, then wondered what he was eating. We had been sharing a whiskey root beer float at The Meatball Shop in Williamsburg when he received the call that his mom was dying faster than anticipated.

*

Barely a toe deep into my career, I observed the group of wildly successful New Yorkers, all of them born at least in the decade before mine. They drank expensive pinot noirs and laughed at gossip about other people. They were supposed to be it—the answer I give when people ask me where I see myself ten years from now.

I was in jeans. Plaid boots. My hair was in an unfortunate ponytail and I realized, that evening, that all those quotes and verses and gurus and prophets were right. No amount of money would make us happy. No amount of success would suffice. I didn't see their brand names and name-dropping. Instead, I saw this:

A man I spoke to at the billionaire's apartment had started a company that went public and made him more money than he knew how to manage. His newest project aims to spread happiness. This man babbled in the endearing way children babble when they need you to verbalize your approval.

Every few minutes, the man made self-loathing remarks. He and a woman he'd loved had broken up recently. Here he was, talking about delivering happiness through photographs to Bhutan and Iraq, while occasionally referring to this woman who'd shattered him. She'd deceived him and sliced up his heart—a point he somehow managed to insert into an otherwise entirely unrelated conversation. At one point, he almost cried.

Another man in his mid-thirties later announced he took the hottest girl at his high school to prom. This was important, his tone suggested. Then he said she probably no longer remembered him. As the evening progressed, the quiet writer whose name you'd recognize shifted his awkward body closer to a dancing, laughing neuroscientist and divorcee with twelve years of therapy under her belt. We learned multiple times that her ex was now happily remarried. She didn't notice the quiet, famous writer. He walked home alone.

*

At the end of the night, the guy who introduced me to these strangers told me about the woman he loved—the one he almost married. He told me about her darling daughter, then showed me their pictures. One of the photographs was of a bathroom sign that said "family." He told me that after he maxed out several credit cards with couples counseling sessions, he realized the relationship was unsalvageable. The woman he loved had been scarred so severely as a child that she could never trust him.

It jarred me—how meaningless everything was. The book contracts. The profitable companies. The grants from the government to buy rounds of flavorful poisons for strangers because you want to sleep next to a woman who might one day wear your pajama bottoms as she makes eggs for a child with your frizzy hair while she tells you—really tells you—that she loves you.

The people who schmoozed, spouted their resumés, and showed off their blonde conquests were no different from the orphans I met once in the Philippines. No different from the Brooklyn high school students who wrote poems about the guys who stole their girlfriends. They had everything they could need. Shelter. Food. Clothes. And more of it stored away in countless renovated closets. Yet here they were, hollow for affection.

When I told them David was in Asia, some of them laughed and joked about how this was my opportunity to cheat on him. I scrutinized the way they said these words. How harmless they believed they were. How insignificant love had become in their minds because they were safer that way with love so shriveled, small, and unable to harm them.

I wish we could quantify and visualize our emotional wounds the way our faces shrink, our skin discolors, and our bellies enlarge when the liver explodes and the kidneys power down. I wish an arm would fall off after a divorce. I wish our ribs would shatter or our necks would crack and that we'd stumble around with braces and bandages instead of button-downs and stilettos, pretending to be whole.

*

A few months ago, while David and I hung out with his family in the New Jersey house he grew up in, his nineteen-month-old niece fell down the stairs. David drove his sister, brother-in-law, and niece to the emergency room while I sat around the dining table with the rest of his family, including his mom. We don't know if she was sick at the time.

His mom, the gentlest soul I'd ever encountered, proceeded to tell me the secrets to loving David, a man who is similar to my younger sister—stubborn and porcupine-like around the edges, but deeply compassionate with a sensitive, sensitive heart of gold. I am different. I am compassionate and loving, and openly so. But when you dig deep, there is a black stone in my heart. The stone is hard-pressed to trust people. It walks back and forth with a rifle.

I loved the way his mom laughed. I loved the way nothing flustered her. She could see through people and into their hearts. She could laser through walls and flesh and find the true condition of someone's soul.

*

David called me four times while I was doing the dishes the following Saturday night. When I shut off the water, I heard the phone ringing. Fifth time. I ran to my room and picked up, knowing what I'd hear on the other line. The reception disconnected us, so I grabbed my coat, and in my pajamas, I ran down four flights of stairs and called him back.

*

The writer friend asked if she was dying. I said, "Yes, barring a miracle."

"But you believe in miracles," he said.

I told him I used to be like the woman he loves—the woman who screams, can't trust, then crawls back to say she's sorry. Sometimes, the same spirit who kicks inside the woman he loves still kicks inside me. I told him about David. He told me David sounded like a great guy. He told me he hopes I marry him.

This is a trite thing to admit on the Internet, but I realized that night that I could do without a billion dollars, but I don't know if I could do without love.

*

When she passed away, all of her adult children watched her body deflate. She was young, early sixties, with two granddaughters, one of whom was just born, the other who points at her baby sister's eyes and knows now to say "eyes."

The last time I saw her, she showed me how to make Taiwanese meatballs. She rinsed each palmful of pink meat under cold water before rolling it in her palms. She sent us away with bags of goodies, and even mixed up the packets of flavored hot chocolates so each of us adults could have a personalized variety box to take home.

I won't begin to wonder what kind of grief consumes David. What kind of grief his sister, with her two babies, might know. When he hung up, I stood outside my apartment with the phone to my cheek and wept. I kicked myself for having no good words to say to him. In my room, grief grew into a monster of sobs and I didn't stop it.

Some nights, all you can do is love and love from far away. Some nights, all you can do is weep, on your knees, in your bed, worshipful music blaring through your earphones. I expelled all the sorrow burning in me so I might be strong when I see David in Taiwan next week with nothing to offer him but my wrung-out faith and a few long hugs.

In her book *Phyla of Joy,* poet Karen An-hwei Lee writes, "If you / are a soul in two bodies / life is more complex / and we must labor / twice the field of sorrow."

Some people believe that's the caveat. You get love—something even billionaires can't buy, trade, and sell—but you also get twice the field of sorrow.

Actually, that's the blessing. You have a man you love. If so, then when this man you love wades through his hell, where else would you rather be than next to him, wading also, cracking a joke, holding his hand, and mostly staying silent except to sing a song he knows.

Mikey Swanberg

The Courier

even though the cash isn't yours
it rides in your pocket all day
so that when you hand it over

there is that pang of loss
and then you remember
oh wait   money doesn't mean anything

beneath these dirty rags
I am an ape
this entire city
used to be an onion field

Afaa Michael Weaver

American Income

The survey says all groups can make more money
if they lose weight except Black men . . . men of other colors
and women of all colors have more gold, but Black men
are the summary of weight, a lead thick thing on the scales,
meters spinning until they ring off the end of the numbering
of accumulation, how things grow heavy, fish on the
ends of lines that become whales, then prehistoric sea life
beyond all memories, the billion days of human hands
working, doing all the labor one can imagine, hands
now the population of cactus leaves on a papyrus moon
waiting for the fire, the notes from all their singing gone
up into the salt breath of tears of children that dry, rise
up to be the crystalline canopy of promises, the infinite
gone fishing days with the apologies for not being able to love
anymore, gone down inside Earth somewhere where
women make no demands, have fewer dreams of forever
these feet that marched and ran and got cut off, these hearts
torn out of chests by nameless thieves, this thrashing
until the chaff is gone out and Black men know the gold
of being the dead center of things, where pain is the gateway
to Jerusalems, Bodhi trees, places for meditation and howling
keeping the weeping heads of gods in their eyes.

Gerald Stern

May Frick Be Damned

In Pittsburgh we used to say, "Tomorrow we strike,
go home, make babies," but always with a Polish
accent and the bars were crowded at ten
in the morning. I for one was stopped once
walking on an empty street downtown
with no reason for being there—I had
three dollars in my pocket so I wasn't
guilty of loitering—may Frick be damned
in Hell forever and ever; may money be stuffed
in all his pockets, may an immigrant
set fire to the money; let Wimpy reign,
"Let's you and him kiss," let love take place
in old cars, let them line up at the curb
in Lover's Lane and let the voyeurs go
from car to car with flashlights, I whisper this.

Aracelis Girmay

Santa Ana of Grocery Carts

Santa Ana of grocery carts, truckers,
eggs in the kitchen at 4 a.m., nurses, cleaning ladies,
the saints of ironing, the saints
of tortillas. Santa Ana of cross-guards, tomato pickers,
bakeries of bread in pinks & yellows, sugars.
Santa Ana of Cambodia, Viet Nam, Aztlán
down Bristol & Raitt. Santa Ana.
Boulevards of red lips, beauty salons, boom boxes, drone
of barbershop clippers fading tall Vincent's head, schoolyards,
the workshop architects, mechanics.
Santa Ana of mothers, radiators, trains.
Santa Ana of barbecues.
Santa Ana of Trujillos, Sampsons, & Agustíns,
Zuly & Xochit with their twin lampish skins.
Santa Ana of cholas, bangs, & spray.
Santa Ana of AquaNet, altars,
the glitter & shine
of 99 cent stores, taco trocas, churches, of bells,
hallelujahs & center fields, aprons,
of winds, collard greens, & lemon cake
in Ms. Davenport's kitchen,
sweat, sweat over the stove. Santa Ana
of polka-dots, chicharonnes, Aztecs, African Fields, colombianas,
sun's children, vanished children. Santa Ana of orales.
Santa Ana of hairnets.
Patron saint of kitchens, asphalt, banana trees,
bless us if you are capable of blessing.

When we started, there were cousins & two parents,
now everything lost has been to you.
The house, axed, & opossums
gone. Abrigette & her husband John.

& the schoolyard boys underneath the ground,
undressed so thoroughly by your thousand mouths, Santa Ana,

let that be
enough.

Natalie Diaz

Run'n'Gun

I learned to play ball on the rez, on outdoor courts where the sky was our ceiling. Only a tribal kid's shot has an arc made of sky. We balled in the rez park against a tagged backboard with a chain for a net, where I watched a Hualapai boy from Peach Springs dunk the ball in a pair of flip-flops and slip on the slick concrete to land on his wrist. His radius fractured and ripped up through his skin like a tusk, which didn't stop him from pumping his other still-beautiful arm into the air and yelling, *Yeah, Clyde the Glide, motherfuckers!* before some adult sped him off to the emergency room.

I ran games in the abandoned school yard with an eight-foot fence we had to hop, where I tore so many pairs of shorts on the top spikes, and where when my little brother got snagged trying to climb down, my cousin and I let him hang by the waistband of his underwear for an entire game of eleven. And if that cousin hadn't overdosed on heroin a few years later, he might have proved us right and been the first rez Jump Man.

I got run by my older brother on our slanted driveway, the same brother I write about now, who taught me that there is nothing easy in our desert, who blocked every shot I ever took against him until I was about twelve years old. By then, his addictions had stolen his game, while I found mine.

I learned the game with my brothers and cousins, with my friends and enemies. We had jacked up shoes and mismatched socks. Our knees were scabbed and we licked our lips chapped. We were small, but we learned to play big enough to beat the bigger, older white kids at the rec center on "The Hill," which to get to we crossed underneath the I-40 freeway, across the train tracks, and through a big sandy wash.

We played bigger and bigger until we began winning. And we won by doing what all Indians before us had done against their bigger, whiter opponents—we became coyotes and rivers, and we ran faster than their fancy kicks could, up and down the court, game after game. We became the weather—we blew by them, we rained buckets, we lit up the gym with our moves.

We learned something more important than fist, at least at that age. We learned to make guns of our hands, and we pulled the trigger on jumpers all damn day. And when they talked about the way we played, they called it *Run'n'gun,* and it made them tired before they ever stepped on the court. Just thinking about a pick-up game against us made the white boys from the junior high and high school teams go to sleep. While they slept, we played our dreams.

Roberto Carlos Garcia

This moment / Right now

For Monica Hand

there's a whispered prayer blowing
the crumbs of a season's harvest
off a girl's plate

& a roar breaks from her insides,
the roar a lioness
a beast that knows

& a man kneels somewhere
cupping his tears
    for the loneliness he feels

though he's surrounded by the world,
& a finch in a tree singing
for a lover as the buds on its branch

pop into leaves that will flourish
& welcome the green grasses.
Right now,   a boy is wondering

if people can really dodge bullets
& is he one of them & somewhere nobody bothers
to ask, they simply wait.

Wind spins across the landscape
they say God is twirling his fingers—

The heartbroken hook new bodies,
night after night, drink after drink

& I dance—my feet mashing grapes
for wine & I sing mockingly—
      what is life / what is life?

Laura Eve Engel

Burden of Belonging

—Inauguration Day, January 20, 2017

Today we are grieving our nation's
peaceful transition of power

what we are really saying is we're scared
about how many of us
choose not to recognize
we depend on one another

to stay whole and unhurt

I am responsible for you
here   hold my heart

why am I glad for this burden
of belonging when others
are not

to whom do some of us
not belong
who hurt some of us so

but here they come again
this history of men

who when they were healthy
refused the hearts of their neighbors
until they were weak from it

now their suffering punches up
out of the rich soil

thorny and asserting
you are not suffering I am
suffering

something inside the weed
urges it to need
and kill the garden

to offer and offer itself
until it's choked all
but its own color out

where it was never written
not all suffering is created equal
and not all need

vigilance against the new appearance
of old growth
has never been enough

we must rewrite the ground

Joy Harjo

I Give You Back

I release you, my beautiful and terrible
fear. I release you. You were my beloved
and hated twin, but now, I don't know you
as myself. I release you with all the
pain I would know at the death of
my children.

You are not my blood anymore.

I give you back to the soldiers
who burned down my home, beheaded my children,
raped and sodomized my brothers and sisters.
I give you back to those who stole the
food from our plates when we were starving.

I release you, fear, because you hold
these scenes in front of me and I was born
with eyes that can never close.

I release you
I release you
I release you
I release you

I am not afraid to be angry.
I am not afraid to rejoice.
I am not afraid to be Black.
I am not afraid to be white.
I am not afraid to be hungry.
I am not afraid to be full.
I am not afraid to be hated.
I am not afraid to be loved.

to be loved, to be loved, fear.

Oh, you have choked me, but I gave you the leash.
You have gutted me, but I gave you the knife.
You have devoured me, but I laid myself across the fire.

I take myself back, fear.
You are not my shadow any longer.
I won't hold you in my hands.
You can't live in my eyes, my ears, my voice
my belly, or in my heart my heart
my heart my heart

But come here, fear
I am alive and you are so afraid
                                        of dying.

Jericho Brown

Foreday in the Morning

My mother grew morning glories that spilled onto the walkway toward her porch
Because she was a woman with land who showed as much by giving it color.
She told me I could have whatever I worked for. That means she was an American.
But she'd say it was because she believed
In God. I am ashamed of America
And confounded by God. I thank God for my citizenship in spite
Of the timer set on my life to write
These words: I love my mother. I love Black women
Who plant flowers as sheepish as their sons. By the time the blooms
Unfurl themselves for a few hours of light, the women who tend them
Are already at work. Blue. I'll never know who started the lie that we are lazy,
But I'd love to wake that bastard up
At foreday in the morning, toss him in a truck, and drive him under God
Past every bus stop in America to see all those Black folk
Waiting to go work for whatever they want. A house? A boy
To keep the lawn cut? Some color in the yard? My God, we leave things green.

Darius Simpson

We Don't Die

we second line trumpet step through gridlock traffic.
we home-go in back of Cadillac limousines. we
wake up Sunday best stiff but beaming. we move the sky.
we escape route starlight. we crescent moon conspiracy. we
come alive in the closed palms of midnight. we electrify.
we past due bill but full belly. we fridge empty. we pocket
lint payments. we make ends into extensions. we multiply.
we claim cousins as protection. we so-and-so plus n'em.
we extend family to belong to someone. we siblings
cuz we gotta be. we chicken fry. we greased kitchen. we
hog neck greens. we scrape together recipes from scraps.
we prophecy. we *told you so* even if we never told you nothin.
we omniscient except in our own business. we swallow a
national anthem and spit it out sweet. make it sound like
red velvet ain't just chocolate wit a lil dye. we bend lies.
we amplify. we laugh so hard it hurts. we hurt so quiet we
dance. we stay fly. we float on tracks. we glide across
linoleum like ice. we make it look like butter. we melt
like candle wax in the warmth of Saturday night liquor sweat.
we don't die. we dust that colonies couldn't settle. we saltwater
city built from runaway skeletons. we organize. we Oakland in '66.
we Attica in '71. we Ferguson before and after the camera crews.
we bend but don't break. we break but don't crumble. we won't
die we won't die we won't die we won't die we won't

Notes and Acknowledgments

Rosa Alcalá's "Propriety" first appeared in issue 105 of the *Oxford American.*

Ruth Awad's "My Father Dreams of a New Country" is from *Set to Music a Wildfire*, published by Southern Indiana Review Press, 2017.

Wendell Berry's "Questionnaire" is from *New Collected Poems.* Copyright © 2010 Wendell Berry. Reprinted with the permission of The Permissions Company, LLC, on behalf of Counterpoint Press, counterpointpress.com.

Reginald Dwayne Betts's "In Alabama" is from *FELON: Poems.* Copyright © 2019 Reginald Dwayne Betts. Used by permission of W. W. Norton & Company, Inc.

Cooper Lee Bombardier's "Prayer for the Workingman" is from *Pass with Care: Memoirs.* Reprinted with the permission of Dottir Press.

Julia Bouwsma's "Etymology of Land" is after Kristin Chang's "Etymology of Butch."

Jericho Brown's "Foreday in the Morning" is from *The Tradition.* Copyright © 2019 Jericho Brown. Reprinted with the permission of The Permissions Company, LLC, on behalf of Copper Canyon Press, coppercanyonpress.org.

Marci Calabretta Cancio-Bello's "Poem in Furrows" was previously published in *THRUSH Poetry Journal,* November 2014.

Marcelo Hernandez Castillo's "Wetback" is from *Cenzontle.* Copyright © 2018 Marcelo Hernandez Castillo. Reprinted with the permission of The Permissions Company, LLC, on behalf of BOA Editions Ltd., boaeditions.org.

Victoria Chang's excerpt is from *Obit.* Copyright © 2020 Victoria Chang. Reprinted with the permission of The Permissions Company, LLC, on behalf of Copper Canyon Press, coppercanyonpress.org.

The title of Nandi Comer's "Están Haciendo Trabajos Que Ni Siquiera Los Negros Quieren Hacer" is a quote from former president of Mexico Vicente Fox, reflecting on the state of Mexican immigrants in the United States. It roughly translates: "They are doing the work that even the Blacks don't want to do." "Me tienes aquí trabajando como un Negro" is a common saying that is the rough equivalent of "You have me working like a slave."

Kwame Dawes's "Work" is from *City of Bones: A Testament*. Copyright © 2017 Kwame Dawes. Published 2017 by TriQuarterly Books/Northwestern University Press. All rights reserved.

Marlanda Dekine's "I Am Bound for de Kingdom" appears in *Thresh & Hold*. Copyright © 2022. Used by permission of Hub City Press. All rights reserved.

Natalie Diaz's "Run'n'Gun" is from *Postcolonial Love Poem*. Copyright © 2020 Natalie Diaz. Reprinted with the permission of The Permissions Company, LLC, on behalf of Graywolf Press, Minneapolis, Minnesota, graywolfpress.org.

Laura Eve Engel's "Burden of Belonging" is from *Things That Go*, published by Octopus Books in 2019.

Martín Espada's "Alabanza: In Praise of Local 100" is from *Alabanza: New and Selected Poems 1982–2002*. Copyright © 2003 Martin Espada. Used by permission of W. W. Norton & Company, Inc.

Kathy Fagan's "Omphalos" first appeared in *Tin House* 20, no. 2 (Winter 2018). It also appears in *Bad Hobby*, published by Milkweed, 2022.

Nikky Finney's "At War with Ourselves: The Battle of and for the Black Face Boy" is from *Love Child's Hotbed of Occasional Poetry: Poems and Artifacts*. Copyright © 2020 Nikky Finney. Published 2020 by TriQuarterly Books/Northwestern University Press. All rights reserved.

Roberto Carlos Garcia's "This Moment / Right Now" is from his collection *Elegies* published by Flowersong Press in 2020.

Ross Gay's "Bull Dragged from Arena" is from *Bringing the Shovel Down*. Copyright © 2011 Ross Gay. Reprinted by permission of the University of Pittsburgh Press.

Aracelis Girmay's "Santa Ana of Grocery Carts" is from *Teeth: Poems*. Copyright © 2007 Aracelis Girmay. All rights reserved.

Kevin Goodan's "Untitled" is from *Spot Weather Forecast*, Alice James Books, 2021.

In Pauletta Hansel's "I Confess," the lines "In private, / some Border Patrol agents consider migrant deaths / a laughing matter; others are succumbing to depression, /

anxiety, or substance abuse" are from *The Atlantic,* July 3, 2019. "I Confess" first appeared in *Ratlle,* July 7, 2019, and was published in *Heartbreak Tree* by Madville Publishing in 2022.

Joy Harjo's "I Give You Back" is from *She Had Some Horses.* Copyright © 1983 Joy Harjo. Used by permission of W. W. Norton & Company, Inc.

Allison Adelle Hedge Coke's "Viscera" first appeared in *World Literature Today,* 2020.

Cheryl R. Hopson notes that in "Family Musings, Matriliny, and Legacy," her idea of materiality is built on the work of philosopher Susan Bordo, who writes in *Twilight Zones* (1999) that materiality refers to our inescapable location in time and space, which both shapes and delimits us.

In his book *Legal History of the Color Line: The Rise and Triumph of the One-Drop Rule: The Notion of Invisible Blackness* (2005), Frank M. Sweet establishes that "the 'one-drop rule' (the idea of invisible Blackness) became written into law in many states in 1910 in order to enforce and maintain oppression of Blacks by whites during the Jim Crow Era" (3–4). Another common term was provided by scholar Marvin Harris: the term for "Americans of visible African admixture [who] are considered Black," even if the "admixture is less than 50%," is "Hypodescent" (quoted in *Legal History of the Color Line,* 4).

Scholar Ellis P. Monk Jr. provides that "skin tone is significantly associated with black Americans' educational attainment, household income, occupational status, and even the skin tone and educational attainment of their spouses," and that "skin tone stratification among black Americans persists into the 21st century" and contributes to "ethnoracial inequality in the United States and beyond." Monk adds, "Thus, for black Americans, there are at least two dimensions of inequality: (1) between blacks and non-blacks; and (2) within the black population according to gradations of skin tone" (1313–14).

Randall Horton's ": the making of {#289-128} in five parts" is from *#289-128,* published by the University Press of Kentucky in 2020.

Silas House's "A Crowded Table" first appeared in *Gravy* 77 (Fall 2020), the magazine of the Southern Foodways Alliance.

An earlier version of Jason Kyle Howard's "Mourning Hillary and What Might Have Been" was published in *Salon,* November 15, 2016.

Rebecca Gayle Howell's "My Mother Told Us Not to Have Children" was published in *The Pushcart Prize XXXVIII: Best of the Small Presses 2014 Edition* (Pushcart Press, 2013). The poem also received the *Rattle* Poetry Prize Readers' Choice Award in 2013 and appeared in *Rattle* 42 (Winter 2013).

Luther Hughes's "My Mother, My Mother," from *A Shiver in the Leaves*, copyright 2022, is reprinted here with permission from BOA Editions, Ltd, www.boaeditions.org.

Emily Jalloul's "The Taking Apart" employs information from the Rape, Abuse, and Incest National Network (RAINN). For more information on child abuse, incest, or rape, go to RAINN.org. For immediate help, call 1-800-656-HOPE (4673).

Ashley M. Jones's "Hymn of Our Jesus & the Holy Tow Truck" is from *REPARATIONS NOW!* Copyright © 2021 Ashley M. Jones. Used with permission of Hub City Press. All rights reserved.

Yusef Komunyakaa's "My Father's Love Letters" is from *Pleasure Dome: New and Collected Poems.* Copyright © 2001 Yusef Komunyakaa. Published 2004 by Wesleyan University Press. All rights reserved.

Dorianne Laux's "Waitress" first appeared in *World Literature Today,* November 2013.

Keith Leonard's "Statement of Teaching Philosophy" first appeared in *Waxwing,* Spring 2021.

Layli Long Soldier's "38" is from *Whereas.* Copyright © 2017 Layli Long Soldier. Reprinted with the permission of The Permissions Company, LLC, on behalf of Gray-wolf Press, graywolfpress.org.

George Ella Lyon's "Where I'm From (2018)" appeared in *Cutleaf,* issue 10.

Adrian Matejka's "Somebody Else Sold the World" is from *Somebody Else Sold the World.* Copyright © 2021 Adrian Matejka. Used by permission of Penguin Books, an imprint of Penguin Publishing Group, a division of Penguin Random House LLC. All rights reserved.

Jill McDonough's "An Hour with an Etruscan Sarcophagus" first appeared in her book *Where You Live*, published by Salt Publishing, 2012.

In Philip Metres's "Disparate Impacts," quotes from the following article appear through the poem: https://www.cleveland.com/court-justice/2019/05/federal-judge-in-cleveland-to-take-senior-status-next-year.html.
    For more information about the case, go to https://www.govinfo.gov/app/details/USCOURTS-ohnd-1_18-cv-02440. For more information about routine housing discrimination for those with criminal records, go to http://www.thehousingcenter.org/wp-content/uploads/2019/12/A-Never-Ending-Sentence-2020.pdf and https://www.cleveland.com/business/2020/01/a-criminal-record-is-a-never-ending-sentence-for-cuyahoga-county-housing-applicants-report-says.html.

In 2015 the US Supreme Court ruled that the Fair Housing Act covers disparate impact claims, which means that it is now against the law to exclude an applicant simply for having a criminal record.

Eden, short for the Emerald Development and Economic Network, Inc. (EDEN), is a 501(c)(3) agency of the Alcohol Drug Addiction and Mental Health Services Board of Cuyahoga County, Ohio, dedicated to "providing housing solutions to people facing housing insecurities and homelessness." See https://www.edeninc.org/about/.

On Judge Boyko's naturalization ceremony, see https://apnews.com/e8faf64afa8 a42f7895b8ed42c24ddbb.

For the full text of Dean Alfange's "My Creed," see https://www.goodreads.com /quotes/82410-my-creed-i-do-not-choose-to-be-a-common.

The poet expresses special thanks to Joseph Gaston for sharing his story. Thanks as well to Maria Smith of the Legal Aid Society of Cleveland for connecting the two and for her insights into collateral sanctions—that is, ongoing punishment for those who have served their time.

Tomás Q. Morín's "Table Talk" appeared in *The Threepenny Review* (Spring 2018).

Melva Sue Priddy's "The Trouble with Young" is from *The Tillable Land*. Copyright © 2022. Used by permission of Shadelandhouse Modern Press. All rights reserved.

Joy Priest's "All My Mothers" appeared in *The Atlantic*, July 19, 2020.

Levi Romero's "Most Skin Hit Road" appeared in *A Poetry of Remembrance: New and Rejected Works*, published by the University of New Mexico Press, 2008.

Patrick Rosal's "Pride Fight" is from *Bonesheperds*. Copyright © 2011 Patrick Rosal. Used by permission of Persea Books, Inc. (New York), perseabooks.com. All rights reserved.

Sonia Sanchez's "Just Don't Never Give up on Love" is from *Homegirls and Handgrenades*. Copyright © 1984, 2007 Sonia Sanchez. Reprinted with the permission of The Permissions Company, LLC, on behalf of White Pine Press, whitepine.org.

Darius Simpson's "We Don't Die" was first published by *New Ohio Review* (Summer 2021).

Jake Skeets's "Let There Be Coal" is from *Eyes Bottle Dark with a Mouthful of Flowers* (Minneapolis: Milkweed Editions, 2019). Copyright © 2019 Jake Skeets. Reprinted with permission from Milkweed Editions, milkweed.org.

Danez Smith's "C.R.E.A.M." is from *Homie*. Copyright © 2020 Danez Smith. Reprinted with the permission of The Permissions Company, LLC, on behalf of Graywolf Press, graywolfpress.org.

M. L. Smoker's "It Comes Down to This" is from the collection *Another Attempt at Rescue* published by Hanging Loose Press in 2005.

Christopher Soto's "Job Opening for Border Patrol Agents" appeared in *PANK*, 2019.

Alina Stefanescu notes that Emma Goldman was deported from the United States in 1919 for advocating higher wages, birth control, eight-hour workdays, and an end to the draft. She was in the USSR to witness the Russian Revolution and escaped to Canada in 1921 to write about it. Stefanescu says, "My parents warned me often that this is what would happen to me if I 'acted free' in Alabama." In "Dialogue in Diptych with Emma Goldman," the left side of the diptych is Stefanescu's, as are the words in italics on the right side. The nonitalicized words on the right have been collaged from the preface and afterword of Emma Goldman's *My Disillusionment in Russia* (August 1925).

Gerald Stern's "May Frick Be Damned" is from *Everything Is Burning*. Copyright © 2005 Gerald Stern. Used by permission of W. W. Norton & Company, Inc.

Rodrigo Toscano's "The Zone" appeared in his collection *The Charm & the Dread* (Fence Books, 2022). Reprinted by permission of Fence Books and Rodrigo Toscano.

Ocean Vuong's "The Gift" is from *Night Sky with Exit Wounds*. Copyright © 2016 Ocean Vuong. Reprinted with the permission of The Permissions Company, LLC, on behalf of Copper Canyon Press, coppercanyonpress.org.

Julie Marie Wade's "Food Giant" appeared in *Shadowbox: A Showcase of Contemporary Nonfiction* (2011).

Afaa Michael Weaver's "American Income" is from *The Plum Flower Dance*. Copyright © 2007 Afaa Michael Weaver. Reprinted by permission of the University of Pittsburgh Press.

Crystal Wilkinson's "O Tobacco" appeared in *Perfect Black,* published by the University Press of Kentucky, 2021.

L. Lamar Wilson's "Burden Hill Apothecary & Babalú-Ayé Prepare Stinging Nettle Tea" was published in *Poetry* magazine July/August 2021.
    Wilson explains: "Before Claude Neal could face trial for the murder of Lola Cannady, a white childhood playmate and presumed lover, a lynch mob killed and dismembered him on October 26, 1934, outside Marianna, Florida, exhibiting and distributing his body parts among the several thousand who had traveled from far and wide to witness the spectacle. On June 16, 1943, after Cellos Harrison won a two-year battle to overturn his murder conviction with a state supreme court ruling, another lynch mob took him outside town and murdered him as well. Burden Hill is

one of this rural North Florida town's oldest Black communities, and the speaker in the poem is the persona of an ancestor who survived these traumas."

Mark Wunderlich's "Shanty" appeared in *God of Nothingness*, published by Graywolf Press, 2021.

Kevin Young's "Ode to the Hotel Near the Children's Hospital" is from *Dear Darkness: Poems*. Copyright © 2008 Kevin Young. Used by permission of Alfred A. Knopf, an imprint of the Knopf Doubleday Publishing Group, a division of Penguin Random House LLC. All rights reserved.

Javier Zamora's "Second Attempt Crossing" is from *Unaccompanied*. Copyright © 2017 by Javier Zamora. Reprinted with the permission of The Permissions Company, LLC, on behalf of Copper Canyon Press, coppercanyonpress.org.

*

The editors would like to thank the following for their indispensable support: all those at Repairers of the Breach, especially Valerie Eguavoen and Tiffany Lytle; all those at the University Press of Kentucky, especially Patrick O'Dowd and Ashley Runyon; United States Artists; University of Arkansas, Fayetteville MFA Program; University of Tennessee–Knoxville's English Department; the *Oxford American* Literary Project; and Berea College's Chris Green, who lent his expertise and grace at a time when this work needed him most. Also, Brandon Anyzeski; Kimberly Burwick; Fred Courtright; Reena Esmail; Kevin Goodan; Chloe Honum; Pauline Howell; Brent Hutchinson; J. Bailey Hutchinson; Elisa and Zuhair Jalloul; Donald Lewis Jones (from the beyond); Jasmine, Julian, Monique, and Jennifer Jones; Rachel Miller; Alicia and Jeremiah P. Ostriker; Brett Ratliff; Robert Shatzkin; Jacob Shores-Argüello; Tejaswini Sudhakar; Beau Sullivan; and all our families and ancestors, to all who have left this earth.

Rebecca Gayle Howell & Ashley M. Jones would like to express their particular gratitude to Emily Jalloul, who acted as associate editor of this book: Emily, *What Things Cost* was made possible by your tireless and expert editorial management. Thank you.

We believe the process of decolonizing our minds is lifelong, and we are grateful to the reader for joining us in that effort and for forgiving us our trespasses.

Most especially, we thank all our contributors and contributing presses, every one of which donated their work to benefit the Poor People's Campaign.

Contributors

Rosa Alcalá is a poet and translator originally from Paterson, New Jersey. Her most recent book of poetry is *MyOTHER TONGUE* (2017). She teaches in the Bilingual MFA Program in Creative Writing at the University of Texas–El Paso. In a past life she shoved baguettes into paper bags, unsuccessfully transferred calls, balanced trays of pigs-in-a-blanket, failed to explain the difference between ser and estar, and sold a baby name book to a famous actor.

Kendra Allen was born and raised in Dallas, Texas, and is the author of the award-winning essay collection *When You Learn the Alphabet* (2019), the poetry collection *The Collection Plate* (2021), and the memoir *Fruit Punch* (2022). Her work has appeared in *The Rumpus, Repellar,* and *Southwest Review*. She currently resides in San Antonio.

A. H. Jerriod Avant is from Longtown, Mississippi. He has MFA degrees from Spalding University and New York University, is the recipient of two winter fellowships from the Fine Arts Work Center in Provincetown, and is currently a PhD student and teaching assistant at the University of Rhode Island.

Ruth Awad is a 2021 National Endowment for the Arts Poetry Fellow and the author of *Set to Music a Wildfire* (2017), winner of the 2016 Michael Waters Poetry Prize and the 2018 Ohioana Book Award for Poetry. She and Rachel Mennies coedited *The Familiar Wild: On Dogs and Poetry* (2020).

Curtis Bauer is the author of three poetry collections, most recently *American Selfie* (2019), which was published in Spanish translation as *Selfi Americano* (2022). He is also a translator of poetry and prose from the Spanish, including *Land of Women* by María Sánchez (2022), *Image of Absence* by Jeannette L. Clariond (2018), *From Behind What Landscape* by Luis Muñoz (2015), and *Eros Is More* by Juan Antonio González Iglesias (2014). He is the publisher and editor of Q Avenue Press Chapbooks and the translations editor for *The Common*. He divides his time between Spain and Texas.

Sandra Beasley is the author of *Made to Explode* (2021); *Count the Waves* (2015); *I Was the Jukebox* (2011), winner of the Barnard Women Poets Prize; *Theories of Falling* (2008); and *Don't Kill the Birthday Girl: Tales from an Allergic Life* (2011), a disability memoir. She also edited *Vinegar and Char: Verse from the Southern Foodways Alliance* (2018). She lives in Washington, DC.

Wendell Berry is a farmer of Lane's Landing and the author of more than eighty books of poetry, fiction, and critical thought. His many awards include the Ivan Sandrof Lifetime Achievement Award from the National Book Critics Circle, Roosevelt Institute's Freedom Medal, Martin E. Marty Award for the Public Understanding of Religion from the American Academy of Religion, and National Humanities Medal. For more than fifty years, he and his wife, the farmer, photographer, and editor Tanya Amyx Berry, have made their home in Henry County, Kentucky, where they and other members of the Berry family collaborate with their neighbors to ensure the area's sustainability through local agrarian economies.

Reginald Dwayne Betts is the author of *A Question of Freedom: A Memoir of Learning, Survival, and Coming of Age in Prison* (2009), which was awarded the 2010 NAACP Image Award for Nonfiction. His three books of poetry are *Shahid Reads His Own Palm* (2010), *Bastards of the Reagan Era* (2015), and *Felon* (2019). Betts is a 2010 Soros Justice Fellow, 2011 Radcliffe Fellow, and 2012 Ruth Lilly and Dorothy Sargent Rosenberg Poetry Fellow. In 2012 President Barack Obama appointed Betts to the Coordinating Council on Juvenile Justice and Delinquency Prevention. He is a graduate of Prince George's Community College, the University of Maryland, and the MFA Program at Warren Wilson College and is currently a PhD student at Yale Law School.

Justin Bigos is a founding editor of the literary journal *Waxwing* and the author of the fiction chapbook *Double Clothesline* (2022) and the poetry book *Mad River* (2017). His writing has appeared in *Ploughshares, Indiana Review, McSweeney's Quarterly,* and *The Best American Short Stories 2015.* After working for a decade in restaurants and thirteen years in higher education, he currently teaches pre-K and is raising his daughter in central Vermont.

Cooper Lee Bombardier is the author of the memoir-in-essays *Pass with Care* (2020), which was a finalist for the 2021 Firecracker Award in Nonfiction. His writing has appeared in *Kenyon Review, Malahat Review, Ninth Letter, CutBank, Nailed Magazine, Longreads, Narratively, BOMB,* and *The Rumpus.* He teaches in the MFA in Creative Nonfiction Program at the University of King's College.

Bryan Borland is founding publisher of Sibling Rivalry Press. His most recent collection, *DIG* (2016), was a finalist for the Lambda Literary Award in Gay Poetry and was selected as a Stonewall Honor Book in Literature by the American Library Association. He lives in Little Rock, Arkansas.

Julia Bouwsma is the sixth Poet Laureate of Maine, serving from 2021 to 2026. She is the author of two poetry collections: *Midden* (2018) and *Work by Bloodlight* (2017). A homesteader, small-town librarian, teacher, and editor, Bouwsma lives off the grid in the mountains of western Maine.

James and Tina Mozelle Braziel are a husband-and-wife writing team. Jim is the author of two novels, *Birmingham: 35 Miles* (2008) and *Snakeskin Road* (2009), and the short story collection *This Ditch-Walking Love* (2021). He teaches in the Creative Writing Program at the University of Alabama at Birmingham. Tina is the author of *Known by Salt* (2019), winner of the Philip Levine Poetry Prize. She directs the Ada Long Creative Writing Workshop at the University of Alabama at Birmingham. Tina and Jim are building their glass cabin by hand.

Jericho Brown is the author of *The Tradition* (2019), for which he won the Pulitzer Prize, the National Book Award, and the National Book Critics Circle Award. He is the recipient of fellowships from the Guggenheim Foundation, Radcliffe Institute for Advanced Study at Harvard, and National Endowment for the Arts, and he is a winner of the Whiting Award. He is also the author of *Please* (2008), which won the American Book Award, and *The New Testament* (2014), which won the Anisfield-Wolf Book Award. He is a professor and the director of the Creative Writing Program at Emory University.

Nickole Brown is the author of *Sister* (2007; new edition issued in 2018). Her second book, *Fanny Says* (2015), won The Weatherford Award for Appalachian Poetry. A chapbook called *To Those Who Were Our First Gods* won the 2018 Rattle Chapbook Prize, and her essay-in-poems entitled *The Donkey Elegies* was published in 2020. Brown comes from a proud family of contractors and housewives, and she was the first from that family to go to college. When she was just thirteen, she lied about her age to bag groceries, and after that she worked gigs that ranged from tending bar to answering phones, from publishing to teaching. She currently lives with her wife in Asheville, North Carolina.

Marci Calabretta Cancio-Bello is the author of *Hour of the Ox* (2016), winner of the Donald Hall Prize, and cotranslator of *The World's Lightest Motorcycle* (2021) by Yi Won. She is a Kundiman Fellow, and her work has appeared in *Catapult, Kenyon Review Online*, and the *New York Times*.

Kayleb Rae Candrilli is the recipient of a Whiting Award and a fellowship from the National Endowment for the Arts. They are the author of *Water I Won't Touch* (2021), *All the Gay Saints* (2020), and *What Runs Over* (2017). Candrilli's work has been published or is forthcoming in *Poetry, American Poetry Review,* and *Ploughshares.* Candrilli also works part time as a fishmonger in Philadelphia.

Marcelo Hernandez Castillo is a poet, essayist, translator, and immigration advocate. He is the author of *Cenzontle* (2018), which was chosen by Brenda Shaughnessy as the winner of the 2017 A. Poulin Jr. Prize. Castillo was born in Zacatecas, Mexico, and immigrated to the California central valley. As an AB540 student, he earned his BA from Sacramento State University and was the first undocumented student to graduate from the Helen Zell Writers Program at the University of Michigan. He is a founding member of the UndocuPoets Campaign, which successfully eliminated citizenship requirements for all major poetry prizes awarded to first books published in the United States. Castillo, along with Christopher Soto and Javier Zamora, were given the Barnes & Noble Writers for Writers Award for their work on behalf of undocumented poets.

Cathleen Chambless is from Miami, Florida. Her debut collection of poetry, *Nec(Romantic)*, was a finalist for the Bisexual Book Awards in 2016. A national activist in Queer literary arts, she currently lives in Boston, Massachusetts.

Victoria Chang is the author of *Obit* (2020), winner of the 2018 Alice Fay Di Castagnola Award from the Poetry Society of America and nominated for a National Book Award; *Barbie Chang* (2017); and *The Boss* (2013), winner of a PEN Center USA Literary Award and a California Book Award. She received degrees from the University of Michigan, Harvard University, and Stanford University as well as an MFA from Warren Wilson College.

Annette Saunooke Clapsaddle is a citizen of the Eastern Band of Cherokee Indians. Her debut novel, *Even As We Breathe*, was a finalist for the Weatherford Award, named one of NPR's Best Books of 2020, and received the Thomas Wolfe Memorial Literary Award. Clapsaddle's work appears in *Yes!* Magazine, *Lit Hub*, *Our State Magazine* and *The Atlantic*. She is an editor for the Appalachian Futures series (University Press of Kentucky) and serves on the board of trustees for the North Carolina Writers Network.

Christian J. Collier is a Black southern writer, arts organizer, and teaching artist who resides in Chattanooga, Tennessee. He is the author of the chapbook *The Gleaming of the Blade* (2021). His works have appeared in *Hayden's Ferry Review, Michigan Quarterly Review, Atlanta Review,* and *Grist Journal*.

Nandi Comer is the author of *American Family: A Syndrome* (2018) and *Tapping Out* (2020), which won the 2020 Society of Midland Authors Award and 2020 Julie Suk Award. She is a Cave Canem Fellow, Callaloo Fellow, and 2019 Kresge Arts in Detroit Fellow. She has worked as a booking manager, waitress, educator, and accountant.

Katie Condon is the author of *Praying Naked* (2020). Her poetry has appeared in *The New Yorker* and *Ploughshares*. She is an assistant professor of English at Southern Methodist University and previously worked as a gardener, waitress at a *Lord of the Rings*–themed restaurant, and basketball camp counselor.

Darius V. Daughtry is a writer, director, educator, and founder of the Art Prevails Project. Daughtry's poetry collection, *And the Walls Came Tumbling*, was published in 2019.

Allison Pitinii Davis is the author of *Line Study of a Motel Clerk* (2017), a finalist for the Ohioana Book Award and the Jewish Book Council's Berru Award in Poetry, and

Poppy Seeds (2013), winner of the Wick Poetry Chapbook Prize. In addition to teaching writing, she has worked behind the counter at a motel, movie theater, and coffee shop.

Geffrey Davis's publications include *Night Angler* (2019), winner of the James Laughlin Award, and *Revising the Storm* (2014), winner of the A. Poulin Prize. A recipient of Bread Loaf, Cave Canem, and National Endowment for the Arts fellowships, Davis teaches at the University of Arkansas and the Rainier Writing Workshop. He has previously worked as a server and dishwasher at an assisted-living community, concessions attendant and box-office cashier at a movie theater, exterior house painter, hotel restaurant prep cook, grocery store manager, and various under-the-table gigs, including apprentice plumber, apprentice roofer, and overnight custodian at furniture factories.

Kwame Dawes is the author of twenty books of poetry and numerous books of fiction, criticism, and essays, including *City of Bones: A Testament* (2017). He is the Glenna Luschei editor of *Prairie Schooner* and teaches at the University of Nebraska, Cave Canem, and Pacific University's MFA Program. He is director of the African Poetry Book Fund, artistic director of the Calabash International Literary Festival, and a Chancellor of the Academy of American Poets. Born in Ghana in 1962, Dawes spent most of his childhood in Jamaica.

Marlanda Dekine is a poet. Their collection of poems, *Thresh & Hold* (2022), won the New Southern Voices Poetry Prize. They are the recipient of many honors, including support from South Carolina Humanities, Emrys, South Carolina Arts Commission, Alternate Roots, Map Fund, The Watering Hole, and *Tin House*. Dekine is a graduate of Furman University (BA in psychology) and the University of South Carolina (MSW).

Natalie Diaz is a Macarthur Foundation Fellow, Lannan Literary Fellow, United States Artists Fellow, Hodder Fellow, and Native Arts Council Foundation Artist Fellow. She is the author of *Postcolonial Love Poem* (2020), winner of the Pulitzer Prize, and *When My Brother Was an Aztec* (2012), which *New York Times* reviewer Eric McHenry described as an "ambitious . . . beautiful book." Diaz teaches at the Arizona State University Creative Writing MFA Program, where she also serves as founding director of the Center for Imagination in the Borderlands.

Alice Driver is a writer based in Arkansas. She is at work on two books: *The Life and Death of the American Worker* and *Turning a Bedroom into a Forest: The Wild Life of Maurice Sendak*. Her writing has been published by *The New Yorker, National Geographic, Oxford American, The New York Review of Books,* and *Time*. Driver has a PhD and MA in Hispanic studies from the University of Kentucky, and she earned her BA from Berea College in Madison County, Kentucky. She also studied Spanish and Portuguese at Middlebury College Language Schools. Driver was born in Oark, Arkansas, a town of 200 residents, in a house built by her potter father and her weaver mother.

Kelly Norman Ellis is the author of *Tougaloo Blues* (2003) and *Offerings of Desire* (2012). She is the recipient of a Kentucky Foundation for Women Writer's grant and is a Cave Canem Fellow and founding member of the Affrilachian Poets. Ellis is an associate professor of English and creative writing and the chair of the Department of English, Foreign Languages, and Literatures at Chicago State University.

Laura Eve Engel is the author of *Things That Go* (2019). She is a recipient of fellowships from the Fine Arts Work Center in Provincetown, Wisconsin Institute for Creative Writing, Helene Wurlitzer Foundation, and Yiddish Book Center. Her work can be found in *The Awl, Best American Poetry, Boston Review, The Nation, PEN America,* and *Tin House.*

Heid E. Erdrich is the author of seven collections of poetry, most recently *Little Big Bully* (2020). She is also the author of a nonfiction indigenous foods memoir and the editor of two anthologies. Erdrich grew up in Wahpeton, North Dakota, and is a member of the Ojibwe, enrolled at Turtle Mountain.

Martín Espada has published more than twenty books as a poet, editor, essayist, and translator. His latest book of poems is called *Floaters* (2021), winner of the National Book Award and a finalist for the *Los Angeles Times* Book Prize. His other poetry collections include *Vivas to Those Who Have Failed* (2016), *The Trouble Ball* (2011), and *Alabanza* (2003). He is the editor of *What Saves Us: Poems of Empathy and Outrage in the Age of Trump* (2019). He has received the Ruth Lilly Poetry Prize, the Shelley Memorial Award, an Academy of American Poets Fellowship, a Letras Boricuas Fellowship, and a Guggenheim Fellowship. A former tenant lawyer, Espada is a professor of English at the University of Massachusetts–Amherst.

Kathy Fagan's fifth poetry collection, *Sycamore* (2017), was a finalist for the 2018 Kingsley Tufts Award. Her latest book, *Bad Hobby,* appeared in 2022. Fagan cofounded the MFA Program at Ohio State University, where she teaches poetry and coedits the Wheeler Poetry Prize Book Series for *The Journal.*

Nikky Finney's poetry collections include *Love Child's Hotbed of Occasional Poetry* (2020) and *Head Off & Split* (2011), winner of the National Book Award. Finney's numerous honors include the Aiken Taylor Award for Modern American Poetry from the University of the South, the Wallace Stevens Award from the Academy of American Poets, and the Art for Change Fellowship from the Ford Foundation. She serves as an ambassador for the University of Arizona Poetry Center's Art for Justice Project and is the John H. Bennett Jr. Chair in Creative Writing and Southern Letters at the University of South Carolina.

Cal Freeman is the author of *Poolside at the Dearborn Inn* (2022), *Brother of Leaving* (2014), and *Fight Songs* (2017). His writing has appeared in *Southword, Passages North, Journal, Commonwealth, Drunken Boat,* and *Poetry Review.* He currently serves as music editor of the *Museum of Americana* and teaches at Oakland University.

Roberto Carlos Garcia is rigorously interrogative of himself and the world around him, conveying "nakedness of emotion, intent, and experience," and he writes extensively about the Afro-Latinx and Afro-diasporic experience. He has published three poetry collections: *Melancolía* (2016), *black/Maybe: An Afro Lyric* (2018), and *[ELEGIES]* (2020).

Ross Gay is the author of four books of poetry: *Against Which* (2006); *Bringing the Shovel Down* (2011); *Catalog of Unabashed Gratitude* (2015), winner of the 2015 National Book Critics Circle Award and the 2016 Kingsley Tufts Poetry Award; and *Be Holding* (2020). His collection of essays, *The Book of Delights*, was published in 2019. He is a founding board member of the Bloomington Community Orchard, a nonprofit, free-fruit-for-all food justice and joy project. He is a professor of English at Indiana University.

Diane Gilliam is the author of three collections of poetry—*One of Everything* (2003), *Kettle Bottom* (2004), and *Dreadful Wind & Rain* (2017)—as well as the chapbook *Recipe for Blackberry Cake* (1999). Gilliam is a recipient of the Chaffin Award for Appalachian Literature, Gift of Freedom Award from A Room of Her Own Foundation for Women, and Pushcart Prize. She lives and writes in Akron, Ohio.

Robert Gipe is the author of three novels and is the founding director of Higher Ground, a community performance project based.at the Southeast Kentucky Community & Technical College in Harlan County, Kentucky. Gipe grew up in Kingsport, Tennessee.

Aracelis Girmay is the author of three books of poems: *the black maria* (2016); *Teeth* (2007), winner of the GLCA New Writers Award; and *Kingdom Animalia* (2011), winner of the 2011 Isabella Gardner Poetry Award and a finalist for the National Book Critics Circle Award and the Hurston/Wright Legacy Award. She is also the author and illustrator of the collage-based picture book *changing, changing.* Girmay was nominated for a Neustadt International Prize for Literature in 2018 and has received support from the National Endowment for the Arts, Whiting Foundation, Civitella Ranieri, Cave Canem Foundation, and Community~Word Project. She is the editor of *How to Carry Water: Selected Poems of Lucille Clifton* (2020) and is on the editorial board of the African Poetry Book Fund.

Kevin Goodan worked for the US Forest Service as a wildland firefighter for ten years, three of those years on the Lolo Interagency Hotshot Crew. His most recent book is *Spot Weather Forecast* (2021). He currently lives in New Hampshire and teaches English at Colby-Sawyer College.

Chris Green has been writing, performing, editing, and publishing poems and scholarship for three decades. His path started in Lexington, Kentucky, and then passed through the mountains of North Carolina, the hills of Indiana, and the valleys of West Virginia before returning to Kentucky. He is currently director of the Loyal Jones

Appalachian Center at Berea College and is working on a nonfiction book about central Kentucky's landscape in terms of its terrain, ecology, economics, power, and race.

Sonia Guiñansaca (Kichwa-Kañari) is a poet, culture strategist, and artist advocate. Born in Ecuador, they migrated to the United States at age five to reunite with their parents in New York. Guiñansaca has helped build some of the largest organizations for undocumented individuals in the United States and cofounded several artistic projects for and by undocumented writers. Guiñansaca has been honored by Voices of Our Nation Arts Foundation, British Council, and Creative Time. They self-published their debut chapbook, *Nostalgia and Borders* (2016), and are coeditor of the anthology *Somewhere We Are Human: Authentic Voices on Migration, Survival, and New Beginnings* (2022).

Richard Hague, a native of Steubenville, Ohio, was nominated for a Pushcart Prize in both poetry and prose in 2019. Winner of a recent contest for creative nonfiction from *Still: The Journal,* he is the author or editor of twenty volumes and the artist-in-residence at Thomas More University.

Pauletta Hansel is the author of nine poetry collections, including *Heartbreak Tree* (2022) and *Palindrome,* winner of the 2017 Weatherford Award. Hansel was Cincinnati's first Poet Laureate. She is the past managing editor of *Pine Mountain Sand & Gravel* and leads community writing workshops and retreats. Her first job was as an assistant in her mother's day-care center.

Joy Harjo is the author of nine books of poetry, including the highly acclaimed *An American Sunrise* (2019); several plays and children's books; and two memoirs, *Crazy Brave* (2012) and *Poet Warrior* (2021). Her many honors include the Ruth Lilly Prize for Lifetime Achievement from the Poetry Foundation, the Academy of American Poets Wallace Stevens Award, two fellowships from the National Endowment for the Arts, and a Guggenheim Fellowship. An internationally renowned performer and writer of the Muscogee (Creek) Nation, Harjo became in 2019 the first indigenous person ever appointed Poet Laureate of the United States.

Allison Adelle Hedge Coke has written many poetry collections, including *The Year of the Rat* (1996), *Dog Road Woman* (1997), *Off-Season City Pipe* (2005), *Blood Run, Burn* (2017), *Streaming* (2014), and *Look at This Blue* (2022), as well as a memoir, *Rock Ghost, Willow, Deer* (2004). She is the editor of ten poetry anthologies, including *Ahani* (2007), *Sing: Poetry of the Indigenous Americas* (2011), *Effigies* (2009), *Effigies II* (2019), and *Effigies III* (2019). Hedge Coke has worked fields, factories, and waters. Today she is a distinguished professor at the University of California–Riverside. A career community advocate and organizer, she most recently directed the Along the Chaparral/Pūowaina project, UCR's Writers Week, and the Sandhill Crane Migration Retreat and Festival.

Marwa Helal is the author of *Ante Body* (2022), *Invasive Species* (2019), and the chapbook *I Am Made to Leave I Am Made to Return* (2017). She won *BOMB Magazine's* Biennial 2016 Poetry Contest and has been awarded fellowships from the Whiting Foundation, Jerome Foundation, NYFA/NYSCA, Poets House, and Cave Canem. Born in Al Mansurah, Egypt, she currently lives in Brooklyn, New York.

Cheryl R. Hopson is an associate professor of English and African American studies at Western Kentucky University in Bowling Green, as well as being a poet and an essayist. Her research interests include twentieth-century African American literature, Black women's fiction and nonfiction, and mothering and motherhood studies. She is currently writing a monograph of twentieth-century novelist, anthropologist, and folklorist Zora Neale Hurston.

Jennifer Horne served as the twelfth Poet Laureate of Alabama (2017–2021). She is the author of three collections of poems and a collection of short stories and has edited four volumes of poetry, essays, and stories. Her latest work is a biography of the writer Sara Mayfield (forthcoming).

Randall Horton is a recipient of the Gwendolyn Brooks Poetry Award, Bea Gonzalez Poetry Award, Great Lakes College Association New Writers Award for Creative Non-fiction, and National Endowment for the Arts Fellowship in Literature. In 2018–2019 he was selected poet-in-residence for the Civil Rights Corps in Washington, DC, which is a nonprofit organization dedicated to challenging systemic injustice in the American legal system. Horton has toured, lectured, and conducted workshops at numerous adult and juvenile detention centers across the nation to provide encouragement and hope to those entangled in the legal system. He is a professor of English at the University of New Haven and is currently the only tenured full professor at a US university or college with seven felony convictions. His latest book is *{#289–128}* (2020).

Ron Houchin lived on the banks of the Ohio River, across from his hometown of Huntington, West Virginia. For thirty years he taught high school in the Appalachian region of southern Ohio. Houchin published nine books of poetry in the United States and Ireland, and his work was honored by the Ohio Arts Council, Dublin Summer Writers' Workshop in Ireland, and Indiana University. In 2013 he received The Weatherford Award for Poetry.

Silas House is the *New York Times* best-selling author of seven novels. His work has recently appeared in *The Atlantic, Time, The Advocate, Oxford American,* and *Garden and Gun.* He is an executive producer and one of the subjects of the Hulu film *Hillbilly,* winner of the Foreign Press Association's Best Documentary Award.

Jason Kyle Howard is the author of *A Few Honest Words* (2012) and coauthor of *Something's Rising* (2009). His work has appeared in the *New York Times, The Atlantic,*

Oxford American, Salon, The Nation, and *The Millions* and on C-SPAN's *Book TV* and NPR. Howard is editor of *Appalachian Review,* a literary quarterly based at Berea College, where he directs the Creative Writing Program. He also serves on the graduate faculty of the Spalding University Naslund-Mann Graduate School of Writing.

Rebecca Gayle Howell's books include *American Purgatory* (2017) and *Render/An Apocalypse* (2013). Among her honors are the United States Artists Fellowship, the Pushcart Prize, Great Britain's Sexton Prize, and two winter fellowships from the Fine Arts Work Center in Provincetown. Howell is an assistant professor of poetry and translation at the University of Arkansas MFA program and the longtime poetry editor for the *Oxford American.* She is coeditor of this book.

Luther Hughes is the author of *A Shiver in the Leaves* (2022) and the chapbook *Touched* (2018). He is the founder of Shade Literary Arts, a literary organization for Queer writers of color, and cohosts *The Poet Salon* podcast with Gabrielle Bates and Dujie Tahat. Recipient of the Ruth Lilly and Dorothy Sargent Rosenberg Fellowship and the 92Y Discovery Poetry Prize, Hughes's work has appeared in *American Poetry Review, Paris Review,* and *Orion Magazine.* He was born and raised in Seattle, where he currently lives. He works at an arts nonprofit.

Su Hwang is a poet, activist, stargazer, and the author of *Bodega* (2019), which received the 2020 Minnesota Book Award in poetry and was a finalist for the 2021 Kate Tufts Discovery Award. Born in Seoul, Korea, she was raised in New York, then called the Bay Area home before transplanting to the Midwest. A recipient of the Jerome Hill Fellowship in Literature, she is a teaching artist with the Minnesota Prison Writing Workshop and the cofounder, with poet Sun Yung Shin, of Poetry Asylum. For most of her life she has worked a constellation of odd jobs, including waiting tables. She currently lives in Minneapolis.

Jessica Jacobs is the author of *Take Me with You, Wherever You're Going* (2019), winner of the Devil's Kitchen and Goldie Awards, and *Pelvis with Distance* (2015), a biography-in-poems of Georgia O'Keeffe that won the New Mexico Book Award and was a finalist for the Lambda Literary Award. An avid long-distance runner, Jacobs has worked as a rock-climbing instructor, bartender, server, and professor and now serves as chapbook editor for *Beloit Poetry Journal.* She lives in Asheville, North Carolina, with her wife, the poet Nickole Brown, with whom she coauthored *Write It! 100 Poetry Prompts to Inspire* (2020). Jacobs's collection of poems in conversation with the Book of Genesis will be out in 2024.

Emily Jalloul is a Lebanese American poet and PhD candidate in English and creative writing at the University of Tennessee, where she is the editor of *Grist: Journal of Literary Arts.* Her previous work has been published or is forthcoming in *Bodega Magazine, Blue Earth Review,* and *Florida Review.* She previously worked in Miami-Dade prisons, where she taught creative writing. She is associate editor of this book.

Ashley M. Jones is the Poet Laureate of Alabama. She is the author of *Reparations Now!* (2021), *Magic City Gospel* (2017), and *dark / / thing* (2019). Among her awards are the Rona Jaffe Foundation Writers Award, a Literature Fellowship from the Alabama State Council on the Arts, and the Lucille Clifton Legacy Award. She teaches at the Alabama School of Fine Arts and Converse College and is the founding director of the Magic City Poetry Festival. She is coeditor of this book.

Bill King grew up outside of Roanoke, Virginia, in the Blue Ridge Mountains. His poetry has appeared in *Kestrel, Appalachian Heritage, Still: The Journal, Southern Poetry Anthology, Naugatuck River Review, Mountains Piled upon Mountains: Appalachian Nature Writing in the Anthropocene,* and many other journals and anthologies. He has an MA in creative writing and a PhD in literature from the University of Georgia and teaches creative writing and literature at Davis & Elkins College in West Virginia. His first chapbook of poetry is *The Letting Go* (2018). His first full-length poetry collection, *Bloodroot,* will be released in 2023. King previously worked as a short-order cook, busboy, landscaper, horticulturist, used book seller, and commercial cleaner.

Yusef Komunyakaa is the author of more than twenty volumes of poetry and essays, most recently *Everyday Mojo Songs of Earth: New and Selected Poems, 2001–2021* (2021). Among his many awards are the Pulitzer Prize for Poetry, the Kingsley Tufts Poetry Award, and the Ruth Lilly Poetry Prize. Raised in Bogalusa, Louisiana, Komunyakaa served in the US Army during the Vietnam War and earned a Bronze Star for his contributions to the military paper *Southern Cross.*

Debora Kuan is the author of two poetry collections, *Lunch Portraits* (2016) and *XING* (2011). She has received residencies at Yaddo, MacDowell, and the Santa Fe Art Institute and is the Poet Laureate of Wallingford, Connecticut.

Edgar Kunz is the author of the poetry collection *Tap Out* (2019), a *New York Times* New & Noteworthy pick. His second book, *Fixer,* is forthcoming in 2023. Kunz has worked various jobs since he was fifteen, including delivering newspapers, tending bar, herding cattle, teaching business ethics in public school, and taste-testing recipes for a multinational food corporation. He lives in Baltimore and teaches at Goucher College.

Dorianne Laux is a Pulitzer Prize finalist whose most recent collection is *Only as the Day Is Long: New and Selected* (2019). She is also the author of *The Book of Men* (2011), winner of the Paterson Poetry Prize, and *Facts about the Moon* (2006), winner of the Oregon Book Award. She recently published a limited-edition chapbook, *SALT* (2020). Laux teaches poetry at North Carolina State and Pacific University. In 2020 she was elected a Chancellor of the Academy of American Poets.

Len Lawson is the author of *Chime* (2019) and the chapbook *Before the Night Wakes You* (2017). He is also editor of *Hand in Hand: Poets Respond to Race* (2017) and *The*

Future of Black: Afrofuturism, Black Comics, and Superhero Poetry (2021). His poetry has been nominated for the Pushcart Prize and Best of the Net. He has earned fellowships from Tin House, Palm Beach Poetry Festival, Callaloo, Vermont Studio Center, Virginia Center for the Creative Arts, Watering Hole, and Obsidian Foundation UK. His poetry has appeared in *African American Review, Callaloo, Mississippi Review, Ninth Letter,* and *Verse Daily* and has been translated internationally. Lawson earned a PhD in English literature and criticism from Indiana University of Pennsylvania and is an assistant professor of English at Newberry College in South Carolina. He has worked as a landscaper, grocery store bagger and comanager, discount variety store manager, convenience store manager, photo lab and shift supervisor at both a pharmacy and a big-box store, manager-in-training at a title loan company, pizza deliverer, city worker, and substitute teacher.

Eugenia Leigh is the author of *Blood, Sparrows and Sparrows* (2014) and *Bianca* (2023). Her poems and essays have appeared in *The Rumpus, Ploughshares, Waxwing,* the Academy of American Poets' *Poem-a-Day,* the *Best New Poets 2010* anthology, and the *2017 Best of the Net* anthology. Leigh has served as a teaching artist with a variety of organizations, including RAISE, the Asian American Legal Defense and Education Fund's undocumented youth group. She also served as poetry editor for *Kartika Review* and *Hyphen,* a news and culture magazine that celebrates the Asian American diaspora. She received her MFA from Sarah Lawrence College.

Keith Leonard is the author of the poetry collection *Ramshackle Ode* (2016). His poems have appeared in *The Believer, New England Review,* and *Ploughshares.* Leonard has received fellowships from the Bread Loaf Writers' Conference, Sustainable Arts Foundation, and Ohio Arts Council.

Layli Long Soldier is the author of *Whereas* (2017), which won the National Book Critics Circle Award and was a finalist for the National Book Award. In 2015 Long Soldier was awarded a National Artist Fellowship from the Native Arts and Cultures Foundation and a Lannan Literary Fellowship for Poetry. She was awarded the Whiting Award in 2016. Long Soldier is a citizen of the Oglala Lakota Nation and lives in Santa Fe, New Mexico.

Nabila Lovelace is a first-generation Queens-born poet; her people hail from Trinidad and Nigeria. *Sons of Achilles* (2018) is her debut book of poems. She currently lives in Tuscaloosa, Alabama.

George Ella Lyon, Kentucky Poet Laureate (2015–2016), has authored poetry, picture books, novels, short stories, and a memoir. Her poem "Where I'm From" is used worldwide as a writing model. Lyon's collections include *She Let Herself Go* (2012), *Many-Storied House* (2013), and *Voices of Justice* (2020). In 2022 Lyon was inducted into the Kentucky Writers Hall of Fame.

Adrian Matejka is the author of four books, most recently *Map the Stars* (2017). He is the recipient of fellowships from the Guggenheim Foundation and the Lannan Foundation. Matejka is editor of *Poetry* magazine.

Jill McDonough's books of poems include *Habeas Corpus* (2008), *Where You Live* (2012), *Reaper* (2017), *Here All Night* (2019), and *American Treasure* (2022). She is the recipient of three Pushcart Prizes and fellowships from the Lannan Foundation, National Endowment for the Arts, Fine Arts Work Center, New York Public Library, Library of Congress, and Stanford's Stegner Program. She taught incarcerated students through Boston University's Prison Education Program for thirteen years. McDonough teaches in the MFA Program at the University of Massachusetts–Boston and offers a course in college reading and writing in Boston jails. She has worked as a chambermaid, waitress, egg poacher, dishwasher, house painter, and English tutor at a Japanese nuclear power plant.

Rose McLarney's collections of poems are *Forage* (2019), *Its Day Being Gone* (2014), and *The Always Broken Plates of Mountains* (2012). She is coeditor of *A Literary Field Guide to Southern Appalachia* and the journal *Southern Humanities Review.* McLarney is associate professor of poetry at Auburn University.

Ray McManus spent half his life working at manual labor jobs in construction, tree removal, farming, and the grocery business until earning his PhD in 2006. Since then, he has authored three books of poetry: *Punch* (2014), *Red Dirt Jesus* (2010), and *Driving through the Country before You Are Born* (2007). He is a professor of English at the University of South Carolina–Sumter and serves as the writer-in-residence at the Columbia Museum of Art.

Erika Meitner is the author of six books of poems, including *Holy Moly Carry Me* (2018)—which won the 2018 National Jewish Book Award and was a finalist for the National Book Critics Circle Award—and *Useful Junk* (2022). She is currently a professor of English at the University of Wisconsin–Madison and has worked as a documentary film production assistant, computer programmer, lifeguard, and a New York City public school teacher.

Philip Metres is the author of ten books, including *Shrapnel Maps* (2020), *The Sound of Listening: Poetry as Refuge and Resistance* (2018), *Pictures at an Exhibition* (2016), *Sand Opera* (2015), and *I Burned at the Feast: Selected Poems of Arseny Tarkovsky* (2015). He is professor of English and director of the Peace, Justice, and Human Rights Program at John Carroll University. He lives with his family in Cleveland, Ohio, and considers his greatest labors being a father and husband.

Joseph Millar has won fellowships from the Guggenheim Foundation and the National Endowment for the Arts. His newest poetry collection is *Dark Harvest* (2021). He has worked as a telephone installation foreman, commercial fisherman, and taxi driver and now teaches at Pacific University's Low-Residency MFA Program.

Faisal Mohyuddin is the author of *The Displaced Children of Displaced Children* (2018) and the chapbook *The Riddle of Longing* (2017). He teaches English at Highland Park High School in Illinois and creative writing at the School of Professional Studies at Northwestern University. He also serves as a master practitioner for the global not-for-profit Narrative 4. He spent a summer during college working alongside his father at the now-shuttered Thompson Steel Company in Franklin Park, Illinois.

Yesenia Montilla is an Afro-Latina poet & a daughter of immigrants. She received her MFA from Drew University in poetry and poetry in translation. She is a Canto Mundo Graduate Fellow and 2020 NYFA Fellow. Her work has been published in the Academy of American Poets' *Poem-a-Day, Prairie Schooner, Gulf Coast,* and *Best of American Poetry 2021.* Her first collection, *The Pink Box* (2015), was long-listed for a PEN Award. Her second collection is *Muse Found in a Colonized Body* (2022). She lives in Harlem, New York.

Tomás Q. Morín is the author of the memoir *Let Me Count the Ways* (2022) and the poetry collection *Machete* (2021). With Mari L'Esperance he coedited *Coming Close: Forty Essays on Philip Levine* (2013). He teaches at Rice University and Vermont College of Fine Arts. Morín has sold shoes, vitamins, and water softener and worked in a cotton field with his mother for one week, which was more than long enough to appreciate the sacrifices his family made to send him to college.

José Olivarez is the son of Mexican immigrants. His debut book of poems, *Citizen Illegal* (2018), was a finalist for the PEN/Jean Stein Award and a winner of the 2018 *Chicago Review of Books* Poetry Prize. It was named a top book of 2018 by *Adroit Journal,* NPR, and the New York Public Library. Along with Felicia Chavez and Willie Perdomo, he coedited the poetry anthology *The BreakBeat Poets Vol. 4: LatiNEXT.*

Alicia Suskin Ostriker is the author of more than twenty books, most recently *The Volcano and After: Selected and New Poems 2002–2019* (2020). In 2015 Ostriker was elected a Chancellor of the Academy of American Poets, and in 2018 she was named New York State Poet Laureate.

Seth Pennington is editor in chief at Sibling Rivalry Press and the author of *Tertulia* (2017). He edited *Assaracus* (2014) and *Stonewall 50* (2019) and coedited *Joy Exhaustible* (2014). He has worked as a paralegal, team leader at an organic grocer, and assistant funeral director. He lives in North Little Rock, Arkansas, with his husband, Bryan Borland.

Craig Santos Perez is the author of two spoken-word poetry albums and five books of poetry. His work has been translated into Chinese, Japanese, and Spanish. Perez is a professor in the English Department at the University of Hawai'i–Mānoa, where he teaches creative writing, ecopoetry, and Pacific literature. He is an affiliate faculty member with the Center for Pacific Islands Studies and the Indigenous Politics Program.

Melva Sue Priddy is the author of *The Tillable Land* (2021), a memoir-in-verse of her childhood, spent laboring on her family's dairy farm in mid-twentieth-century Kentucky.

Joy Priest was born and raised in Louisville, Kentucky. She is the author of *Horsepower* (2020), selected by US Poet Laureate Natasha Trethwey as winner of the Donald Hall Prize for Poetry. She is the recipient of a 2021 National Endowment for the Arts fellowship, a 2019–2020 Fine Arts Work Center fellowship, and the Stanley Kunitz Memorial Prize from the *American Poetry Review.* Her poems have appeared in the Academy of American Poets' *Poem-a-Day* series, *The Atlantic,* and *Virginia Quarterly Review,* and her essays have appeared in *Bitter Southerner, Poets & Writers, ESPN,* and *andscape* (formerly *The Undefeated*). Priest has been a journalist, theater attendant, waitress, and fast-food worker, and she has facilitated writing workshops for adult and juvenile incarcerated women. She is currently a doctoral student in literature and creative writing at the University of Houston.

Ruben Quesada is editor of *Latinx Poetics: Essays on the Art of Poetry* (2022); the author of two poetry collections, *Revelations* (2018) and *Next Extinct Mammal* (2011); and the translator of *Exiled from the Throne of Night: Selected Translations of Luis Cernuda* (2008). His writing has appeared in *Harvard Review, Best American Poetry, American Poetry Review, Ploughshares,* and *Pleiades.* He has been honored by Canto Mundo, Lambda Literary Writers' Retreat, and Vermont Studio Center. Born and raised in Los Angeles to immigrants from Costa Rica, Quesada lives in Chicago

Iliana Rocha was born and raised in Texas. Her newest collection, *The Many Deaths of Inocencio Rodriguez* (2022), won the 2019 Berkshire Prize for a First or Second Book of Poetry. *Karankawa* (2015), her debut, won the 2014 AWP Donald Hall Prize for Poetry. Rocha is poetry coeditor for *Waxwing Literary Journal* and an assistant professor of English at the University of Tennessee–Knoxville.

Levi Romero was selected as the inaugural New Mexico Poet Laureate in 2022 and New Mexico Centennial Poet in 2012. His most recent book is the coedited anthology *Querencia: Reflections on the New Mexico Homeland.* His two collections of poetry are *A Poetry of Remembrance: New and Rejected Works* (2009) and *In the Gathering of Silence* (1996). He is coauthor of *Sagrado: A Photopoetics across the Chicano Homeland* (2013). Romero is an associate professor in the Chicana and Chicano Studies Department at the University of New Mexico and a member of the Macondo Writers Workshop. He is from the Embudo Valley of northern New Mexico.

Patrick Rosal serves as the inaugural codirector of the Mellon-funded Institute for the Study of Global Racial Justice at Rutgers University–Camden, where he is a professor of English. He is the author of five full-length poetry collections, including *The Last Thing: New and Selected Poems* (2021). Among his awards are fellowships from the Guggenheim Foundation, National Endowment for the Arts, and Fulbright Research Scholar Program; Association of Asian American Studies Book Award; Global Filipino Literary Award; and Asian American Writers Workshop Members' Choice Award.

Ciona Rouse is a poet and educator whose work has appeared in *Oxford American, Wildness, Booth,* and *Account.* She is the author of the chapbook *Vantablack* (2017). She has worked in a variety of jobs, including as a belly dancer, executive director of a multimillion-dollar nonprofit, HIV/AIDS counselor, and newspaper carrier, a route she had with her sister when Rouse was five years old.

Yaccaira Salvatierra, a California poet and translator, received the Dorrit Sibley Award for achievement in poetry as well as the Puerto del Sol Poetry Prize. She holds a master's from San José State University and an MFA at Randolph College in Virginia. She is a dedicated educator to resilient, historically marginalized communities. A daughter of immigrants from México and Perú, she lives in Oakland, California.

Sonia Sanchez is a poet, playwright, professor, and activist. She is one of the leaders of the Black studies movement and has authored and edited more than thirty collections, most recently *Collected Poems* (2021).

Janice Lobo Sapigao is a Pinay poet, writer, and educator from San José, California. She is the 2020–2021 Santa Clara County Poet Laureate and a Poet Laureate Fellow with the Academy of American Poets.

Steve Scafidi is the author of *Sparks from a Nine-Pound Hammer* (2001), *For Love of Common Words* (2006), *The Cabinetmaker's Window* (2014), *To the Bramble and the Briar* (2014), and a chapbook *Songs for the Carry-on* (2013). Scafidi is a recipient of the Larry Levis Reading Prize, James Boatwright Prize, and Miller Williams Prize. He works as a cabinetmaker and lives with his family in Summit Point, West Virginia.

Laura Secord is a poet, writer, and teaching artist. She earned her MFA in creative writing from Sierra Nevada University. Her verse novel, *An Art, a Craft, a Mystery,* was published in 2022. She is a Pushcart Prize nominee. Her poems have appeared in *Poetry, Southern Women's Review,* and *The Birmingham Weekly,* as well as the anthology *Voices of Resistance* (2017). She serves on the board of the Magic City Poetry Festival and has a lifetime commitment to women and lost or unvoiced stories. She has worked as a printer, union organizer, health care activist, teacher, sex educator, and nurse practitioner in community health and HIV care.

Jacob Shores-Argüello is a Costa Rican American poet and prose writer. His second book, *Paraíso,* was selected for the inaugural Canto Mundo Poetry Prize judged by Aracelis Girmay. He was a 2018–2019 Hodder Fellow at Princeton University and a Lannan Literary Fellow for Poetry. His work has appeared in *The New Yorker* and *Poetry* magazine.

Carter Sickels is the author of *The Prettiest Star* (2020), winner of the Southern Book Prize, the Ohioana Book Award in Fiction, and The Weatherford Award, and the novel *The Evening Hour* (2012). His writing has appeared in *The Atlantic, Oxford American, Poets & Writers, Guernica,* and *Catapult.* He is an associate professor at Eastern Kentucky University.

Darius Simpson is a writer, educator, and performer from Akron, Ohio. He thinks that, much like the means of production, poetry belongs to and with the masses. Simpson believes in the dissolution of empire and the total liberation of Africans and all oppressed people by any means necessary. All Power to the People. Free the Land. Free All Political Prisoners.

Savannah Sipple is the author of *WWJD & Other Poems* (2019), an American Library Association's Over the Rainbow Recommended LGBTQ+ Reading Selection. She has received awards from the Money for Women/Barbara Deming Memorial Fund and the Kentucky Foundation for Women. Originally from Lee County, Kentucky, Sipple is an associate professor of English at Bluegrass Community and Technical College in Lexington, where she makes her home with her wife, librarian Ashley Sipple-McGraw. Sipple has worked as a gardener, food preserver, camp counselor, receptionist, hospital patient aide, event planner, bookseller, and production manager in televangelism.

Emily Skaja was born and raised in rural Illinois. Her first book, *BRUTE* (2019), won the Walt Whitman Award from the Academy of American Poets. She is the recipient of fellowships from the Civitella Ranieri Foundation and the National Endowment for the Arts. She teaches in the MFA Program at the University of Memphis. She has worked as a kennel attendant, census taker, administrative assistant, teacher, test scorer, fast-food worker, and food delivery driver.

Jake Skeets is the author of *Eyes Bottle Dark with a Mouthful of Flowers* (2019), winner of the National Poetry Series. He is the recipient of a 92Y Discovery Prize, a Mellon Projecting All Voices Fellowship, an American Book Award, and a Whiting Award. He is from the Navajo Nation and is an assistant professor at the University of Oklahoma.

Abraham Smith is the author of six full-length poetry collections—most recently, *Dear Weirdo* (2021). In 2015 he released *Hick Poetics* (2015), a coedited anthology of rural American poetry and related essays. He is an associate professor of English and the codirector of creative writing at Weber State University.

Danez Smith is a Black, Queer, Poz writer & performer from St. Paul, Minnesota. Smith is the author of *Homie* (2020); *Don't Call Us Dead* (2017), winner of the Forward Prize for Best Collection and the Midwest Booksellers Choice Award and a finalist for the National Book Award; and *[insert] boy* (2014), winner of the Kate Tufts Discovery Award and the Lambda Literary Award for Gay Poetry. They are the recipient of fellowships from the Poetry Foundation, McKnight Foundation, Montalvo Arts Center, Cave Canem, and National Endowment for the Arts.

M. L. Smoker is the author of *Another Attempt at Rescue* (2005). With Melissa Kwasny, she coedited *I Go to the Ruined Place: Contemporary Poems in Defense of Global Human Rights* (2009). A member of the Sioux and Assiniboine tribes, Smoker lives in Helena, Montana, where she works in the Indian Education Division of the Office of Public Instruction.

Monica Sok is a Khmer poet and the daughter of refugees. She is the author of *A Nail the Evening Hangs On* (2020). Her work has been recognized with the 92Y's Discovery Poetry Prize. She has received fellowships from the Elizabeth George Foundation, Hedgebrook, Jerome Foundation, Kundiman, MacDowell, National Endowment for the Arts, Poetry Society of America, and Saltonstall Foundation. Sok is a Jones Lecturer at Stanford University and teaches poetry to Southeast Asian youths at the Center for Empowering Refugees and Immigrants in Oakland, California.

Christopher Soto is the author of *Diaries of a Terrorist* (2022) and a chapbook, *Sad Girl Poems* (2016). He is the cofounder of the UndocuPoets Campaign. Soto's writing can be found in *The Nation*, *The Guardian*, *Los Angeles Review of Books*, *American Poetry Review*, and *Tin House*. His work has been translated into Spanish, Portuguese, Japanese, and Thai.

Alina Stefanescu was born in Romania and lives in Birmingham, Alabama, with her partner and several intense mammals. Her books include *dor* (2011) and *Ribald* (2020).

Gerald Stern is the author of more than twenty books of poetry and prose, including *Blessed as We Were: Late Selected and New Poems, 2000-2018* (2020), a finalist for the 2021 PEN/Voelcker Award for Poetry Collection. Among his many awards are the Library of Congress Rebekah Johnson Bobbitt National Award, National Book Award for Poetry, National Jewish Book Award in Poetry, Ruth Lilly Poetry Prize, and Patterson Poetry Prize, as well as fellowships from the Guggenheim Foundation and National Endowment for the Arts. From 2000 to 2002 he served as the first Poet Laureate of New Jersey. Before retiring, Stern taught at such institutions as Temple University, University of Pennsylvania, Raritan Valley Community College, Columbia University, New York University, Sarah Lawrence College, Drew University, and Iowa Writers' Workshop. He also served as president and chief negotiator of a New Jersey teachers' union and led the protests that convinced Iowa state colleges to divest from South Africa during apartheid.

Mikey Swanberg is the author of *On Earth as It Is* (2021), *Good Grief* (2019), and *Zen and the Art of Bicycle Delivery* (2013). He holds an MFA from the University of Wisconsin–Madison and lives in Chicago.

Tony Sweatt, PhD, is managing director of the Appalachian College Initiative at Teach for America Appalachia. Sweatt was born and raised in Harlan County, Kentucky.

Rodrigo Toscano's latest collection is *The Charm & the Dread* (2021). He is the author of ten books of poetry, and his work has appeared in eighteen anthologies, including *Best American Poetry.* He was a National Poetry Series winner and recipient of the Edwin Markham Prize for Poetry. Toscano lives in New Orleans (rodrigotoscano.com).

upfromsumdirt is a poet and visual artist residing in Lexington, Kentucky. He is the author of two poetry collections released in 2020: *Deifying a Total Darkness* and *To Emit Teal.* His afrofuturist collection *The Second Stop Is Jupiter* is nearing completion. He spent fifteen years as an oven operator for an industrial bakery, but for the past fifteen years he has been a bookstore clerk, poetry editor, barista, bookstore owner, visual artist, and graphic designer.

Lyrae Van Clief-Stefanon is the author of *Open Interval* (2009), a National Book Award finalist; *Black Swan,* winner of the 2001 Cave Canem Poetry Prize; and *Poems in Conversation and a Conversation,* a chapbook collaboration with Elizabeth Alexander.

Doug Van Gundy directs the Low-Residency MFA Writing Program at West Virginia Wesleyan College. He is the author of a collection of poems, *A Life above Water* (2007). His poems, essays, and reviews have appeared in many national and international publications, including *Poetry, The Guardian,* and *Oxford American.* With Laura Long, he coedited the anthology *Eyes Glowing at the Edge of the Woods: Contemporary Writing from West Virginia* (2017).

Ocean Vuong is the author of the *New York Times* best-selling novel *On Earth We're Briefly Gorgeous* (2019), forthcoming in thirty languages. A recipient of a 2019 MacArthur "Genius" Grant, he is also the author of the critically acclaimed poetry collection *Night Sky with Exit Wounds,* a *New York Times* Top 10 Book of 2016 and winner of the T. S. Eliot Prize, Whiting Award, Thom Gunn Award, and Forward Prize for Best First Collection. His honors include a Ruth Lilly Fellowship from the Poetry Foundation; fellowships from the Lannan Foundation, Civitella Ranieri Foundation, Elizabeth George Foundation, and Academy of American Poets; and the Pushcart Prize. His second poetry collection, *Time Is a Mother,* was just published.

Julie Marie Wade teaches in the Creative Writing Program at Florida International University. She is the author of fourteen collections of poetry, prose, and hybrid forms, including two collaborative volumes. Her recent books include *Just an Ordinary Woman Breathing* (2020), *Skirted: Poems* (2021), and *Telephone: Essays in Two Voices*

(2021), coauthored with Brenda Miller. Wade makes her home with Angie Griffin and their two cats in Dania Beach.

Afaa Michael Weaver (formerly known as Michael S. Weaver) is primarily a poet, playwright, translator, and editor. His sixteenth collection of poetry, *A Fire in the Hills,* is due out in 2023. He is Professor Emeritus at Simmons University and a member of the MFA faculty at Sarah Lawrence College. He is an alumnus (1987) of Brown University's Graduate Writing Program and a 2017 Guggenheim Fellow.

Lauren Whitehead is a writer and performer. Her poems have been published in several online journals and anthologies, including *The BreakBeat Poets, Vol. 2: Black Girl Magic.* She was featured on *The Slow Down* with former Poet Laureate Tracy K. Smith. Currently, she is a professor of drama at New York University.

Marcus Wicker is the author of *Silencer* (2017) and *Maybe the Saddest Thing* (2012). His poems have appeared in *The Nation, Poetry,* and *The New Republic.* He is an associate professor of English at the University of Memphis, where he teaches in the MFA Program. Wicker has worked as a flooring specialist at a home-improvement store, commercial house painter, and auto parts salesman.

Crystal Wilkinson's books include *Perfect Black* (2021) and *The Birds of Opulence* (2018). Among her many honors are the Ernest J. Gaines Prize for Literary Excellence, NAACP Image Award for Outstanding Literary Work–Poetry, Chaffin Award for Appalachian Literature, and finalist nominations for the John Dos Passos Award, Hurston/Wright Legacy Award, and Orange Prize for Fiction. She is a professor of English in the MFA in Creative Writing Program at the University of Kentucky.

Phillip B. Williams is a Chicago native and author of *Mutiny* (2021) and *Thief in the Interior* (2016), winner of the 2017 Kate Tufts Discovery Award and a 2017 Lambda Literary Award. He received a 2017 Whiting Award and fellowship from the Radcliffe Institute for Advanced Study. He previously worked as an HIV tester and counselor and a high school English tutor.

Tyrone Williams was born in Detroit, Michigan, and earned his BA, MA, and PhD at Wayne State University. His work includes *c.c.* (2002), *On Spec* (2008), *The Hero Project of the Century* (2009), *Adventures of Pi* (2011), *Howell* (2011), *As Iz* (2018), and, with Pat Clifford, *washpark* (2021). Williams teaches literature and theory at Xavier University in Cincinnati, Ohio.

Keith S. Wilson is an Affrilachian Poet and Cave Canem Fellow. He is the recipient of a National Endowment for the Arts fellowship and serves as assistant poetry editor at *Four Way Review* and digital media editor at *Obsidian Journal.* His first book, *Fieldnotes on Ordinary Love,* was published in 2019.

L. Lamar Wilson is the author of *Sacrilegion* (2013), a Thom Gunn Award finalist; coauthor of *Prime: Poetry and Conversation* (2014); and associate producer of *The Changing Same* (2019), which streams at American Documentary and airs on PBS. Wilson's poems and essays have been widely anthologized and have appeared in *Poetry, Poem-a-Day, New York Times, Interim, TriQuarterly, Oxford American, The Root, South,* and *Washington Post* and on NPR. After spending nearly two decades in the nation's top newsrooms, including at the *Times* and the *Post,* Wilson has received fellowships from the Cave Canem, Civitella Ranieri, Ragdale, and Hurston-Wright Foundations; is an Affrilachian Poet; and teaches creative writing, African American poetics, and film studies at Florida State University and the Mississippi University for Women.

Jane Wong is the author of *Meet Me Tonight in Atlantic City* (2023), *How to Not Be Afraid of Everything* (2021), and *Overpour* (2016). A Kundiman Fellow, she is the recipient of a Pushcart Prize and fellowships and residencies from the US Fulbright Program, Harvard's Woodberry Poetry Room, Artist Trust, 4Culture, Fine Arts Work Center, Bread Loaf, Hedgebrook, Willapa Bay, Jentel Foundation, SAFTA, and Mineral School. She has an MFA in poetry from the University of Iowa and a PhD in English from the University of Washington and is an associate professor of creative writing at Western Washington University. She grew up in a Chinese American take-out restaurant and previously worked as a department store sales associate, public library aide, orchestra usher, museum attendant, copywriter, and writing tutor.

Mark Wunderlich was born in Winona, Minnesota, and grew up in rural Fountain City, Wisconsin. He is the recipient of numerous awards, including a Wallace Stegner Fellowship from Stanford University, two fellowships from the Fine Arts Work Center in Provincetown, and fellowships from the National Endowment for the Arts, Massachusetts Cultural Council, and Amy Lowell Trust. He is a member of the literature faculty at Bennington College in Vermont and makes his home in a 300-year-old stone house in New York's Hudson Valley near the village of Catskill. His latest book, *God of Nothingness,* was published in 2021.

Justin Wymer is a first-generation Appalachian writer and educator who holds degrees from Harvard University, the Iowa Writers' Workshop, and the University of Denver. His first poetry collection, *DEED* (2019), won the Antivenom Poetry Award. His work has appeared in *Boston Review, Conjunctions, Kenyon Review, Lana Turner, Manchester (UK) Review,* and *West Branch.* Wymer has worked as a fry cook, lawn mower, dog sitter, peer counselor, and professor.

Vicente Yépez is a writer, educator, and graduate of the University of Arkansas' Creative Writing MFA Program. Raised along the Mexico-Texas border, Yépez is also the founder and host of *Fútbol for the People,* a bilingual podcast and media channel that discusses the intersection of soccer, ethics, and working-class politics.

Kevin Young is the author of fifteen books of poetry and prose, including *Stones* (2021), short-listed for the T. S. Eliot Prize; *Blue Laws: Selected & Uncollected Poems 1995–2015* (2016), long-listed for the National Book Award; *Book of Hours* (2015), winner of the Lenore Marshall Prize from the Academy of American Poets; and *Jelly Roll: A Blues* (2003), a finalist for both the National Book Award and the *Los Angeles Times* Book Prize for Poetry. Young, the poetry editor of *The New Yorker,* is a member of the American Academy of Arts and Sciences, American Academy of Arts and Letters, and Society of American Historians. In 2020 Young was named a Chancellor of the Academy of American Poets and the Andrew W. Mellon Director of the Smithsonian's National Museum of African American History and Culture.

Javier Zamora was born in La Herradura, El Salvador, in 1990. His father fled El Salvador a year later, and his mother fled when Javier was about to turn five. Both parents' migrations were caused by the US-funded Salvadoran Civil War (1980–1992). In 1999 Zamora migrated through Guatemala and Mexico to Arizona with the aid of other migrants. He is the author of *Unaccompanied* (2017). His honors include the Radcliffe Fellowship from Harvard University, Stegner Fellowship from Stanford, and Lannan Literary Fellowship. In 2016 Zamora, alongside Marcelo Hernandez Castillo and Christopher Soto, received the Barnes & Noble Writers for Writers Award for their founding of the UndocuPoets Campaign.

Index of Author Names